Puritan Papers

A Symposium of Papers Read at Two Annual
Puritan and Reformed Studies Conferences,
Westminster Chapel, London

PURITAN PAPERS

Volume 3
1963–1964

EDITED BY

J. I. Packer

FOREWORD BY

W. Robert Godfrey

P&R PUBLISHING
P.O. BOX 817 • PHILLIPSBURG • NEW JERSEY 08865-0817

Previously published as separate annual volumes by Tentmaker Publications. Compiled and reformatted by the den Dulk Christian Foundation.

Published by the den Dulk Christian Foundation, Kingsbury, California, and by P&R Publishing Company, Phillipsburg, New Jersey, on behalf of the Committee of the Westminster Conference.

Page design by Tobias Design
Typesetting by Carol Shaffer, Dan Malda

Printed in the United States of America

Library of Congress Cataloging-in-Publication Data

Puritan papers / edited by D. Martyn Lloyd-Jones ; foreword by
W. Robert Godfrey.
     p. cm.
Vols. 2 & 3 edited by J. I. Packer.
Includes bibliographical references.
Contents: v. 1. 1956–1959—v. 2. 1960–1962—v. 3. 1963–1964.
ISBN 0-87552-468-0 (pbk.)
1. Puritans. I. Lloyd-Jones, David Martyn. II. Packer, J. I. (James Innell)

BX9327.P87 2001
285'.9—dc21

                     2001032900

CONTENTS

CONTRIBUTORS

G. E. Duffield is a historian and publisher.

R. A. Finlayson was professor of systematic theology at Free Church College, Edinburgh, prior to his retirement and death.

W. Robert Godfrey is president and professor of church history at Westminster Theological Seminary in California.

W. J. Grier was the founder-manager of the Evangelical Book Shop in Belfast, Ireland.

O. R. Johnston was, at the time of his death, national director of C.A.R.E., an evangelical body committed to Christian social development.

D. Martyn Lloyd-Jones (1899–1981) was first co-pastor and then pastor of Westminster Chapel in London from 1939 to his retirement in 1968.

Iain Murray, a founding trustee of the Banner of Truth Trust, has written more than ten books, including *The Puritan Hope, Jonathan Edwards,* and *D. Martyn Lloyd-Jones.*

J. I. Packer is Board of Governors Professor of Theology at Regent College in Vancouver and executive editor of *Christianity Today.*

D. M. Whyte was head of the London City Mission prior to his retirement.

Foreword

W. Robert Godfrey

Puritanism has been controversial from its beginning. The principles and passions of the Puritans, along with the powerful attraction of their movement in the seventeenth century, made them profoundly influential in church and society. Their convictions and impact also made them very unpopular with many in their own day and ever since. The Puritans have had severe critics from the beginning. William Shakespeare, for example, disparaged them in *Twelfth Night:*

> Maria: Marry, sir, sometimes he is a kind of puritan.
> Sir Andrew: O, if I thought that, I'd beat him like a dog.

A popular song of the early seventeenth century accused them of hypocrisy:

> Pure in show, an upright holy man,
> Corrupt within—and called a Puritan.

Lord Macaulay, in a famous statement, caricatured them as killjoys: "The Puritan hated bear-baiting, not because it gave pain to the bear, but because it gave pleasure to the spectators."

Yet even Macaulay had grudgingly to recognize the fortitude and commitment of the Puritan: "The Puritan was made up of two different men, the one all self-abasement, penitence, gratitude, passion, the other proud, calm, inflexible, sagacious. He prostrated himself in the dust before his Maker; but he set his foot on the neck of the king."

Scholarship in recent decades has recognized the vitality and power of the Puritan movement for its lasting impact not only in religion, but also in politics, education, economics, and science. The great increase in knowledge about the Puritans and the recognition of their influence has done little, however, to change the widespread perception of the Puritans as busybodies who sought to eliminate pleasure from life, by force if necessary, in the service of their arbitrary and unattractive God.

In the light of these attitudes it is truly remarkable that about fifty years ago two young scholars conceived the idea of holding a conference on Puritanism as a practical help for pastors and Christians generally. Surely a modern conference largely devoted to the study of Puritan thought as a vital resource for the contemporary church would not commend itself to many. But O. Raymond Johnston and James I. Packer had an advantage over many: they had actually read the Puritans. They had so profited spiritually from their own study of the Puritans that they wanted others to share in the rich spiritual blessing that had been theirs. In the late 1940s they consulted with D. Martyn Lloyd-Jones, minister at Westminster Chapel, London, who enthusiastically embraced the idea and offered the chapel as a meeting place for what became known as "The Puritan Conference."

The first conference took place in December 1950. Six papers, each about an hour in length, were read over the course of two days, one in the morning and two in the afternoon. After each paper a discussion followed of about one hour, often a very vigorous exchange of ideas. The basic form of the conference has remained the same over the years. For nearly thirty years Dr. Lloyd-Jones chaired the sessions of the conference and from 1959 contributed an annual paper and led the discussions. His commitment to the conference reflected his conviction: "As I see things, it is of supreme importance for the future of the Christian faith in this country that we should experience a revival of interest in the literature of the great Puritans of the seventeenth century."[1]

James I. Packer organized the conference for many years and contributed regularly for the first twenty years. His keen study and analysis helped set a very high standard for the papers. His presentations, along with those of Dr. Lloyd-Jones, ensure that the volumes of the conference papers from those years are of great value.

No conference was held in 1970. Dr. Lloyd-Jones objected strongly to some of the ecumenical positions taken by Dr. Packer. Dr. Lloyd-Jones was approached by several men who asked him to chair a reconvened conference of the same character as the earlier ones. He agreed to do this, and so the Westminster Conference was held in 1971 and has continued to operate under that name.

The basic purpose of the conference has remained the same for the fifty years of its existence. As Dr. Packer wrote in a foreword to the 1958 conference papers,

> [the conference] exists because its organisers believe that historic Reformed theology in general, and the teaching of the great Puritans in particular, does justice to certain neglected Biblical truths and emphases which the church today urgently needs to re-learn. This is not, of course, to imply that Puritan expositions of Scripture are infallible and final, or that the Puritans always succeeded in balancing truth in exactly the right proportions; nor is it suggested (forsooth!) that the way to solve problems which face Christians of the twentieth century is to teach them to walk and talk as if they were living in the seventeenth. What is meant is simply that the Puritans were strongest just where Protestants today are weakest, and their writings can give us more real help than those of any other body of Christian teachers, past or present, since the days of the apostles.

The pursuit of that "real help" from the Puritans was very much the purpose of the conference. Again, Dr. Packer: "The interests of the Conference, therefore, are practical and constructive, not merely academic. . . . the aim of the Conference is to make a constructive application of what is learned to our own situation."

The conference played a vital role in reinvigorating evangelicalism with a strong Reformed influence in Great Britain and beyond. The decision to publish the conference papers annually in 1956 further extended its influence. God used this conference—along with the work of great preachers and scholars, the Evangelical Library, the Banner of Truth Trust, and other agencies—to renew British evangelicalism.

The historical importance of the Puritan Conference and its papers is clear. For that reason alone the decision of the den Dulk Christian Foundation to reprint these papers is sound and proper. But these papers are much more than historical documents, and the foundation—dedicated primarily to the publication and dissemination of Reformed literature—has seen that. The republication of these studies will continue their original purpose: to furnish Christians today with insight into the rich heritage of Puritan thought. In the shallowness, pragmatism, and confusion of much current evangelicalism, the depth, conviction, and steadiness of the Puritans can again help renew the churches.

Part 1

Diversity in Unity

1963

1

THE PURITAN APPROACH TO WORSHIP

J. I. Packer

I formulated this title with some care, because I did not want to have to handle my subject controversially. Indeed, I looked forward to preparing this paper as a welcome relief from controversy, of which I have had my fair share during the past few months. It is sometimes said that Evangelicals are not interested in worship. If by worship one means the technicalities of liturgical study, this may be true. But I do not suppose that I am the only Evangelical who finds that the actual exercise of worship, the deliberate lifting of one's eyes from man and his mistakes to contemplate God and His glory, grows increasingly precious as the years go by, and brings solace and refreshment to the spirit in a way that nothing else can do.

Certainly, this was the experience of the great Puritans; and what I want to do now is to allow them to share it with us, and lead us deeper into the enjoyment of it for ourselves. Hence my choice of the word "approach" in my title. We are to follow the Puritans in their *approach* to worship, which was, as we shall see, itself an *approach* to God. My main concern is thus not with the controversies about worship which divided the Puritans both from Anglican officialdom and from each other, but rather with the view of the nature of worship, and of the principles for practicing it, on which in fact they were all agreed.

The Externals of Worship

But their controversies about the formal and external aspects of worship were real and sustained, religiously motivated and passionately pursued, and to establish my right to pass them by in the body of my paper I must first deal briefly with them now. I shall not trace their historical details, nor take sides (for I do not want to start them all over again!), but I shall try to bring into focus the problems which occasioned them, so that we see just how much—and at some points, how little—divided the conflicting parties. The problems themselves, as we shall see, remain living issues for us today.

Three main questions lay at the root of all the arguing. They were as follows:

1. *In what sense are the Scriptures authoritative for Christian worship?*

It is usually said, that, whereas Luther's rule in ordering public worship was to allow traditional things that were not contrary to Scripture and seemed helpful, it was Calvin's rule to admit nothing that the Bible did not directly prescribe; and that the Church of England officially followed Luther's principle, whereas the Puritans within its ranks espoused that of Calvin. This way of putting it gives the impression that Luther and the reformed Church of England did not regard Holy Scripture as constituting an authoritative rule for worship at all—which was, of course, the constant Puritan accusation right up to the Civil War. It also gives the impression that the Puritan critique of Anglican public worship represented a reversion to the principles and practice of

Calvin at Geneva—which, to be sure, the Puritans themselves thought it was. But both impressions are misleading.

A truer way of stating the issue would be to say that the authority and sufficiency of Scripture in all matters of Christian and church life was common ground to both sides, but that they were not agreed as to how this principle should be applied. In other words, their disagreement related to the interpretation and contents of Holy Scripture, rather than to the formal principle of the nature and extent of its authority. This is how it was that all parties to the debate could believe that their own position was a biblically proper one.

German, Swiss, and English Reformers held common basic principles about worship. They agreed that Christian worship must express man's reception of, and response to, evangelical truth, and they were substantially in agreement as to what that truth was. They agreed in analyzing worship as an exercise of mind and heart in praise, thanksgiving, prayer, confession of sin, trust in God's promises, and the hearing of God's Word, read and preached. They were in agreement also as to the nature and number of the gospel sacraments, and their place in the Church's worship. They took the same view of the office of the Christian minister in leading the worship of the congregation. They agreed also that each church, or federation of churches ("every particular or national Church," as Article 34 puts it) is responsible for settling the details of its own worship in accordance with the apostolic principle that all must be done "unto edifying" (1 Cor. 14:26), and that as a means to that end everything must be done "decently and in order" (14:40). Finally, they were all agreed that each church has liberty (the presupposition of its responsibility) to arrange its worship in the way best adapted to edify its own worshippers, in the light of their state, background, and needs; so that they all took it for granted that the worship of varied churches in varying pastoral situations would vary in detail.

The only real differences regarding worship between any of the first generation of Reformers were differences of personal judgment as to what would edify and what would not—differences of the kind reflected in Calvin's judgment that the second (Edwardian) Prayer Book of 1552 contained *multas tolerabiles ineptias* ("many bearable pieces of foolishness"), or in the troubles at Frankfort in 1554, when the "Coxian" group of exiles adhered to the 1552 Prayer Book as being sufficiently sound and edifying, while the "Knoxians" felt obliged to abandon it in favor of an alternative order drawn up on the Geneva pattern.

The idea that direct biblical warrant, in the form of precept or precedent, is required to sanction every item included in the public worship of God was in fact a Puritan innovation, which crystallized out in the course of the prolonged debates that followed the Elizabethan settlement. It is an idea distinct from the principle that tainted ceremonies, which hide the truth from worshippers and buttress superstitious error, should be dropped, as both dishonoring God and impeding edification. On this latter principle all the English Reformers were agreed from the start, as the 1549 Prayer Book, Preface "Of Ceremonies" shows; though they did not succeed in agreeing as to its application, which was why in 1550 Hooper clashed with the authorities over episcopal vesture, and why in the 1560s those who were first called Puritans felt obliged to campaign against the Prayer Book requirement of surplices, wedding rings, baptizing with the sign of the cross, and kneeling at Holy Communion. But this new principle went further, declaring that no justification of nonbiblical rites and ceremonies in worship as convenient means to biblically prescribed ends could in the nature of the case be valid (in other words, that the line taken in the Preface "Of Ceremonies" was wrong); all ceremonies must have direct biblical warrant, or they were impious intrusions. The same principle was applied to church government.

The attempt to put the Puritan ideal of church life and worship onto this footing led to some curiosities of argument, such as the "proof" that two services a Sunday were obligatory, from Numbers 28:9–10, which prescribes two burnt offerings each Sabbath; or the "proof" that catechizing was a duty, from "hold fast the form of sound words" (2 Tim. 1:13); or the "proof" that liturgical forms were unlawful, from Romans 8:26, or the "proof" that the minister should stand in one place throughout the service from "Peter stood up in the midst of the disciples" (Acts 1:15); or the "proof" of the necessity of the controversial "prophesyings" (area preaching meetings, at which several ministers spoke successively on the same passage of Scripture), from 1 Corinthians 14:31 ("ye may all prophesy one by one, that all may learn and all may be comforted"). Much of this can be cogently defended, in terms of the principle that all things must be done unto edifying, but it is hard to regard these biblical arguments as anything like conclusive.

It should also be noticed that when the Puritans singled out some of the *ineptiae* of the Prayer Book as intolerable; when they challenged the principle that each church has liberty to ordain nonbiblical ceremonies in worship where these seem conducive to edification and reverence; when they repudiated all set prayers; when they rejected kneeling in public worship, the Christian year, weekly Communion, and the practice of confirmation; they were not in fact reverting to Calvin, but departing from him, though, as Horton Davies says,[1] it is doubtful whether they realized this.

Even if they had realized it, however, it would not have affected their position; for their basic concern was not to secure Reformed solidarity, as such (much though they made of this idea in controversy), but simply to obey God's authoritative Word. But the question at issue was: How should the sufficiency of Scripture be understood in connection with worship? The Puritans thought the official Anglican view on this point lax and wrong-headed; Anglican spokesmen like Hooker criticized the developed Puritan view as legalistic and irrational. Which was right? The question still presses today. Do we agree with John Owen that "God's worship hath no accidentals . . . all that is in it and belonging to it, and the manner of it, is false worship, if it have not a divine institution in particular?" The problem is not simple, and much can still be said on both sides.

2. *What regulations are proper for Christian worship?*

There were, and are, three possible ways of ordering public worship: to have a set liturgy like the Book of Common Prayer, or a manual of general guidance like the Westminster Directory, or to leave it entirely to the individual minister or congregation to regulate its own worship at will. These alternatives are historically associated with Anglicans, Presbyterians, and Independents and Quakers respectively. Which now is preferable? How strong are the objections to each? Does liturgical worship necessarily breed formality and deadness? Is extempore prayer necessarily uneven in quality? Does it really make it harder for worship to be congregational than it is if a known form is being used? Does a regular order followed Sunday by Sunday quench the Spirit? Is it necessary, if a congregation would honor the Holy Spirit, for it to refuse to tie itself to an established pattern of worship, and simply at each meeting to wait on the Spirit for a fresh leading? On these issues, Evangelicals would differ now, as the Puritans differed in their day. Baxter, for instance, like Calvin and Knox, approved of a liturgy with room for extempore prayer at the minister's discretion; but Owen maintained that "all liturgies, as such, are . . . false worship . . . used to defeat Christ's promise of gifts and God's Spirit." Which was right? Here again, is an issue which is not simple, and cannot be regarded as dead.

3. *What discipline is proper in connection with worship?*

No doubt there would be general agreement that the attempts made under Elizabeth and the Stuarts to enforce strict national uniformity to the Book of Common Prayer were regrettable, and did more harm than good. Nobody, one hopes, would wish to defend the kind of discipline administered upon nonconformists by the Courts of High Commission and Star Chamber before the Civil War, and the judges and J.P.s of England during the years of the Clarendon Code. Yet a problem remains. Granted that the discipline we have mentioned was ungodly in its rigidity and disregard for tender consciences, is there to be no discipline in connection with public worship at all? Today, in some Protestant churches where set prayers are the rule, rituals and prayers from the Roman mass are introduced, and in others where extempore prayer is practiced, ministers are heard basing their public intercessions on the heresy that all men are God's children. In both these instances worship is spoiled through the doctrinal aberration of the minister. Is there not need for discipline in such cases? But of what sort? What steps are appropriate today in face of such disfigurements as these? The problem exercised the Puritans in their day, and it will be well if it continues to exercise us in ours.

The Inner Reality of Worship

But these problems concerned the forms and externals of worship only, and our present interest is rather in the inner reality of worship, as the Puritans understood it. Here, wherever else they differed, they were at one, and the written material they have left us is completely homogeneous, as we shall hope to show by a fairly wide range of quotations. What is worship? It is, says John Owen, an activity designed to "raise unto God a revenue of glory out of the creation." In the broadest sense of the word, all true piety is worship. "Godliness is a worship," wrote Swinnock. "Worship comprehends all that respect which man oweth and giveth to his Maker. . . . It is the tribute which we pay to the King of Kings, whereby we acknowledge his sovereignty over us, and our dependence on him. . . . All that inward reverence and respect, and all that outward obedience and service to God, which the word (sc., godliness) enjoineth, is included in this one word worship."[2] Usually, however, the Puritans used the word in its narrower and more common sense, to signify all our communion with God: invocation, adoration, meditation, praise, prayer, and the receiving of instruction from His word, both in public and in private.

Worship must be, as our Lord said, "in spirit and in truth" (John 4:24). The Puritans understood this as meaning that, on the one hand, worship must be inward, a matter of "heart-work," and, on the other, worship must be a response to the revealed reality of God's will and work, applied to the heart by the Holy Spirit. Therefore they insisted that worship must be simple and scriptural. Simplicity was to them the safeguard of inwardness, just as Scripture was the fountainhead of truth. The austere simplicity of Puritan worship has often been criticized as uncouth, but to the Puritans it was an essential part of the beauty of Christian worship. This comes out in a pair of sermons by Owen on Ephesians 2:18, entitled "The nature and beauty of gospel worship," in which the weightiest of all the Puritan theologians formulates to perfection the Puritan ideal of worship in scarcely veiled antithesis to the Prayer-book formalism of Laud. ("The beauty of holiness" as Laud was pleased to call it.) It is worth quoting at some length.

Owen begins by making the point that the true "decency," "order," and "beauty," of Christian worship lies in its Trinitarian and evangelical character, as an exercise of faith on the worshippers' part: "It is a principle deeply fixed in the minds of men that the worship of God ought to be orderly, comely, beautiful and glorious. . . . And indeed that worship may be well suspected not to be according to the mind of God which comes short in these properties. . . . I shall add unto this, only this reasonable assertion, . . . viz. That what is so in his worship and service, God himself is the most proper judge. If then we evince not that spiritual gospel worship, in its own naked simplicity, without any other external, adventitious helper or countenance, is most orderly, comely, beautiful, and glorious, the Holy Ghost in the Scripture being judge, we shall be content to seek for these things where else, as it is pretended, they may be found. . . . In the spiritual worship of the gospel, the whole blessed Trinity, and each person therein distinctly, do in that economy and dispensation, wherein they act severally and peculiarly in the work of our redemption, afford distinct communion with themselves unto the souls of the worshippers." (Owen shows how this is set forth in his text, which speaks of access to the Father through the Son by the Spirit.) "This" (he continues) "is the general *order* of gospel worship, the great *rubric* of our service. Here in general lieth its *decency*. . . . If either we come not unto it by Jesus Christ, or perform it not in the strength of the Holy Ghost, or in it go not unto God as a Father, we transgress all the rules of this worship. This is the great *canon,* which if it be neglected, there is no *decency* in whatever else is done in this way. And this in general is the *glory* of it. . . . Acting faith on Christ for admission, and on the Holy Ghost for his assistance, so going on in his strength; and on God, even the Father, for acceptance, is the work of the soul in this worship. That it hath anything more glorious to be conversant about, I am yet to learn. . . ."[3]

In similar terms, Owen from his text gives theological substance to the idea of uniformity in worship: "The saints . . . have all their access 'in one Spirit': and this is the spring of all the *uniformity* that God requires. So the apostle tells us, that as to the gifts themselves (sc. abilities for leading the church in corporate worship) there are diversities of them, and difference in them; 1 Corinthians 12:4–6. But where then is uniformity? . . . The apostle answereth, verse 11. ('All these worketh that one and self-same Spirit'). Here lies the uniformity of gospel worship, that though the gifts bestowed on men for the public performance of it be various, . . . yet it is one Spirit, that bestows them all among them . . . , one and the same Spirit discovers the will and worship of God to them all; one and the same Spirit works the same graces for their kind in the hearts of them all; one and the same Spirit bestows the gifts that are necessary for the carrying on of gospel worship in the public assemblies. . . . And what if he be pleased to give out his gifts . . . variously . . . , 'dividing to every one severally, as he will'? yet this hindereth not, but that as to the saints mentioned, they all approach unto God by the one Spirit, and so have uniformity in their worship throughout the world. This is a catholic uniformity. . . ."[4]

Finally, Owen scouts the idea that ornate buildings and rituals have, or can have, anything to do with the "beauty" that God seeks and finds in the worship of His faithful people. He reminds us that Christians are themselves the temple and dwelling place of God, and that true worship, though done on earth in the body, is actually "performed in heaven," inasmuch as "those who have an access unto the immediate presence of God, and to the throne of grace, enter into heaven itself." (Owen appeals for proof to Heb. 6:20; 9:24; 10:19, 21; Rev. 4). The idea that ritual pageantry in services and decoration of church buildings, is of itself an enriching of worship thus appears as a ludicrous irreverence. "What poor low thoughts have men of God and his ways, who think there lies an acceptable glory and beauty in a little paint and varnish!"[5]

Complementary to Owen's analysis is Charnock's anatomizing of worship in his sermon entitled "Spiritual Worship," on John 4:24: "Worship is an act of the understanding, applying itself to the knowledge of the excellency of God, and actual thoughts of his majesty. . . . It is also an act of the will, whereby the soul adores and reverenceth his majesty, is ravished with his amiableness, embraceth his goodness, enters itself into an intimate communion with this most lovely object, and pitcheth all his affections upon him."[6] Only the regenerate can worship God acceptably, says Charnock, for only they have hearts that truly go out to Him in adoration and self-subjection. Therefore "we must find healing in Christ's wings, before God can find spirituality in our services. All worship issuing from a dead nature, is but a dead service."[7]

Charnock goes on to show that spiritual worship is performed only by the Spirit's active help, since it requires sincerity and singleness of heart ("unitedness" Charnock calls it; "concentration" would express his meaning). It involves acts of faith, love, humbling, and self-distrust, and must be an expression of the heart's desire for God. A spiritual worshipper actually aspires in every duty to know God. . . . To desire worship as an end, is carnal; to desire it as a means, and act desires in it for communion with God in it, is spiritual and the fruit of a spiritual life. . . ."[8] Also, spiritual worship will be joyful: "The evangelical worship is a spiritual worship, and praise, joy, and delight are prophesied of as great ingredients in attendance on gospel ordinances, Isaiah 12:3–5. . . . The approach is to God as gracious, not to God as unpacified, as a son to a father, not as a criminal to a judge. . . . Delight in God is a gospel frame, therefore the more joyful, the more spiritual. . . ."[9] In worship we must seek to reflect back to God by our response the knowledge that we have received of Him through His revelation.

God is a Spirit infinitely happy, therefore we must approach him with cheerfulness; he is a Spirit of infinite majesty, therefore we must come before him with reverence; he is a Spirit infinitely high, therefore we must offer up our sacrifices with deepest humility; he is a Spirit infinitely holy, therefore we must address him with purity; he is a Spirit infinitely glorious, we therefore must acknowledge his excellency . . . he is a Spirit infinitely provoked by us, therefore we must offer up our worship in the name of a pacifying mediator and intercessor.[10]

"That all true believers whose minds are spiritually renewed have a singular delight in all the institutions and ordinances of divine worship is fully evident," writes Owen, and quotes Psalms 42:1–4; 63:1–5; 84:1–4, to prove his point.[11] That the saints love public worship is a constant Puritan theme. Why their delight in it? Because in worship the saints not merely seek God; they also find Him. Worship is not only an expression of gratitude, but also a means of grace, whereby the hungry are fed, so that the empty are sent away rich. For "there is in worship an approach of God to man."[12] "God's presence in his ordinances" is a reality; "God is essentially present in the world, graciously present in his Church." "God delights to approach to men, and converse with them in the worship instituted in the gospel."[13] And men honor God most when they come to worship hungry and expectant, conscious of need and looking to God to meet them and supply it.

The ordinances of Christian worship, declares Owen, are "means of the communication of a sense of divine love, and supplies of divine grace unto the souls of them that do believe. They are "ways of our approaching unto God," and "we are always to come unto God, as unto an eternal spring of goodness, grace, and mercy, of all that our souls do stand in need of." "To make a pretence of coming unto God, and not with expectation of receiving good and great things from him, is to despise God." An aimless, careless, casual, routine habit of churchgoing is neither rational nor reverent. Asks Owen, with piercing rhetoric:

What do men come to hear the Word of God for? What do they pray for? What do they expect to receive from him? Do they come unto God as the eternal fountain of living waters? As the God of all grace, peace and consolation? Or do they come unto his worship without any design as unto a dry and empty show? . . . Or do they think they bring something unto God, but receive nothing from him? . . .

> To receive anything from him they expect not, nor do ever
> examine themselves whether they have done so or no? . . .
> It is not for persons who walk in such ways, ever to attain
> a due delight in the ordinances of divine worship.[14]

Owen's application of this is uncomfortably searching: "Many of the better sort of professors are too negligent in this matter. They do not long and pant in the inward man after renewed pledges of the love of God; they do not consider how much they have need of them . . . ; they do not prepare their minds for their reception of them, nor come with the expectation of their communication unto them; they do not rightly fix their faith on this truth, namely that these holy administrations and duties are appointed of God in the first place, as the way and means of conveying his love and a sense of it unto our souls. From hence springs all that luke-warmness, coldness, and indifferency unto the duties of holy worship, that are growing among us."[15]

This, surely, is a word for our times.

Activities of Worship

The Puritan lists of the parts and constituent activities of worship normally include the following: praise (especially the singing of psalms), prayer (confession, adoration, intercession), preaching, the sacraments ("ordinances"), and also catechizing and the exercise of church discipline. In all these activities, the Puritans maintained, God comes to meet His people met together in His Son's name, but most of all in preaching. Preaching is the most solemn and exalted action, and therefore the supreme test, of a man's ministry: "they (Puritans) hold that the highest and supreme office and authority of the Pastor is to preach the gospel solemnly and publicly to the Congregation by interpreting the written Word of God, and applying the same by exhortation and reproof unto them."[16] For preaching in the church is supremely the ministration of the Spirit, in a way that (pace Richard Hooker) the mere reading of the Word to the Puritans' minds never could be; therefore it is the supreme means of grace. So Thomas Goodwin writes:

> It is not the letter of the Word that ordinarily doth convert, but the spiritual meaning of it, as revealed and expounded. . . . There is the letter, the husk; and there is the spirit, the kernel, and when we by expounding the Word do open the husk, out drops the kernel. It is the meaning of the word which is the word indeed, it is the sense of it which is the soul. . . . Now, preaching in a more special manner reveals God's word. When an ointment box is once opened, then it casts its savour about; and when the juice of a medicinal herb is once strained out and applied, then it heals. And so it is the spiritual meaning of the Word let into the heart which converts it and turns it to God.[17]

For congregations, therefore, the hearing of sermons is the most momentous event of their lives, and the Puritans pleaded with worshippers to appreciate this fact, and listen to the Word preached with awe, attention, and expectancy. Baxter put the point thus, in the course of his "Directions for Profitable Hearing the Word Preached" in the *Christian Directory:*

> Come not to hear with a careless heart, as if you were to hear a matter that little concerned you, but come with a sense of the unspeakable weight, necessity, and consequence of the holy word which you are to hear; and when you understand how much you are concerned in it, it will greatly help your understanding of every particular truth. . . .
>
> Make it your work with diligence to apply the word as you are hearing it. . . . Cast not all upon the minister, as those that will go no further than they are carried as by force. . . . You have work to do as well as the preacher, and should all the time be as busy as he . . . you must open your mouths, and digest it, for another cannot digest it for you . . . therefore be all the while at work, and abhor an idle heart in hearing, as well as an idle minister.

> Chew the end, and call up all when you come home in secret, and by meditation preach it over to yourselves. If it were coldly delivered by the preacher, do you . . . preach it more earnestly over to your own hearts. . . .

We complain today that ministers do not know how to preach; but is it not equally true that our congregations do not know how to hear? And instruction to remedy the first deficiency will surely be labor lost unless the second is remedied too.

Not, however, that the hearing of sermons is an end in itself, or that ardent sermon-tasting and preacher-hunting is the height of Christian devotion. Thomas Adams speaks sternly against the assumption that listening to sermons is all that matters, reminding us that preaching must lead on to prayer and praise:

> Many come to these holy places, and are so transported with a desire of hearing, that they forget the fervency of praying and praising God . . . all our preaching is but to beget your praying; to instruct you to praise and worship God. . . . I complain not that our churches are auditories, but that they are not oratories; not that you come to sermons (for God's sake, come faster), but that you neglect public prayer: as if it were only God's part to bless you, not yours to bless God. . . . Beloved, mistake not. It is not the only exercise of a Christian to hear a sermon; nor is that Sabbath well spent that despatcheth no other business for heaven. . . . God's service is not to be narrowed up in hearing, it hath greater latitude; there must be prayer, praise, adoration. . . .[18]

Here too, surely is a word for Christian people today.

Spheres of Worship

There are, said the Puritans, three spheres of Christian worship: public, in the local church; domestic, in the family circle; private, in the closet. Of these three, public worship is the most important. David Clarkson was entirely typical when, preaching on Psalm 87:2 under the title "Public Worship to be preferred before Private," he argued from Scripture that "the Lord is more glorified by public worship," "there is more of the Lord's presence in public worship," "here are the clearest manifestations of God," "there is more spiritual advantage to be got in the use of public ordinances," and "public worship is more edifying."[19] Strikingly, yet characteristically (for many others made the same point), he reminds us that public worship is "the nearest resemblance of heaven" that earth knows: for "in heaven, so far as the Scripture describes it to us, . . . all the worship of that glorious company is public. . . . They make one glorious congregation and so jointly together sing the praises of him that sits on the throne, and the praises of the Lamb, and continue employed in this public worship to eternity."[20] Similarly, Swinnock insists that on the Lord's Day church must come first, and everything else be built around it. "Esteem the public ordinances the chief work of the day, and let thy secret and private duties be so managed that thy soul may be prepared for them, and profited by them."[21]

But family worship was also, to the Puritans, vitally important. Every home should be a church, with the head of the house as its minister. Daily and twice daily, the Puritans recommended—the family as a family should hear the Word read, and pray to God. Sunday by Sunday, the family should seek to pool the profiting of its members from the public ordinances; day by day, its members should seek to encourage each other in the way of God. Parents must teach their children the Scriptures; all members of the household must be given time and a place to pray. Thus, informally, but conscientiously the worship and service of God in the home must be carried on.

Conclusion

Incomplete though this survey has necessarily been (we have said nothing, for instance, of the sacraments), it has at least sketched in the main outline of Puritan ideals for worshippers—reverence, faith, boldness, eagerness, expectancy, delight, whole-heartedness, concentration, self-abasement, and above all a passion to meet and know God Himself as a loving Father through the mediation of His Son. This ideal was common to them all—to those like Sibbes and Archbishop Usher, who conformed to the Prayer Book liturgy; to those like Owen, who thought all liturgies unlawful; and to those like Baxter, who were happy to alternate between "free" and "set" prayers, and were equally at home in either. Here, in their conception of what the worshipper's spirit and goal should be, the Puritans were at one; and perhaps we may venture the judgment that their agreements here were more significant than their differences, and that it is within the area of their agreements that their teaching can help us most today.

But still one question remains. How do we begin to get from where we are to where the Puritans show us that we ought to be in our own practice of worship? How can we, cold-hearted and formal as we so often are—to our shame—in church services, advance closer to the Puritan ideal? The Puritans would have met our question by asking us another. How do we *prepare* for worship? What do we do to rouse ourselves to seek God?

Here, perhaps, is our own chief weakness. The Puritans inculcated specific preparation for worship—not merely for Holy Communion, but for all services—as a regular part of the Christian's inner discipline of prayer and communion with God. Says the Westminster Directory: "When the congregation is to meet for public worship, the people *(having before prepared their hearts thereunto)* ought all to come. . . ." But we neglect to prepare our hearts; for, as the Puritans would have been the first to tell us, thirty seconds of private prayer upon taking our seat in the church building is not time enough in which to do it. It is here that we need to take ourselves in hand. What we need at the present time to deepen our worship is not new liturgical forms or formulae, but more preparatory "heart-work" before we use the old ones. So I close with an admonition from George Swinnock on preparation for the service of the Lord's Day, which for all its seeming quaintness, is, I think, a word in season for very many of us:

Prepare to meet thy God, O Christian! betake thyself to thy chamber on the Saturday night, confess and bewail thine unfaithfulness under the ordinances of God; shame and condemn thyself for thy sins, entreat God to prepare thy heart for, and assist it in, thy religious performances; spend some time in consideration of the infinite majesty, holiness, jealousy, and goodness, of that God, with whom thou art to have to do in sacred duties; ponder the weight and importance of his holy ordinances . . . ; meditate on the shortness of the time thou hast to enjoy Sabbaths in; and continue musing . . . till the fire burneth; thou canst not think the good thou mayest gain by such forethoughts, how pleasant and profitable a Lord's day would be to thee after such a preparation. The oven of thine heart thus baked in, as it were, overnight, would be easily heated the next morning; the fire so well raked up when thou wentest to bed, would be the sooner kindled when thou shouldst rise. If thou wouldst thus leave thy heart with God on the Saturday night, thou shouldst find it with him in the Lord's Day morning.[22]

2

SCRIPTURE AND "THINGS INDIFFERENT"

Iain Murray

In 1522 at the Manor House at Sodbury, in Gloucestershire, William Tyndale laid the foundation principle of English Protestantism when he confronted the ecclesiastics who gathered around the dinner table of Sir John Walsh with what John Foxe calls "open and manifest Scripture." Four years later the same principle began to be applied to leaven the whole nation with the secret arrival from Flanders of the first printed New Testaments in English and Tyndale, the translator, now a hunted exile, justified his illegal action in these terms: "I perceived by experience how that it was impossible to establish the lay people in any truth, except the Scripture were plainly laid before their eyes. . . . God hath put a rule in the Scripture, without which thou canst not move an hair of thine head, but that it is damnable in the sight of God."[1]

At the price of great suffering Protestantism won its way in this country, not because of the superior numbers or learning of its adherents, but because through the Scriptures rivers of spiritual life had been opened up, so that instead of the teaching and traditions of a corrupt Church, men and women were hearing the words of the living God. When Tyndale's friend, John Rogers, was tried before his martyrdom, one of his Catholic judges declared: "Thou canst prove nothing by the Scripture: the Scripture is dead and must have a lively exposition." At which Rogers exclaimed, *"No, no, the Scripture is alive."*

It is this conviction which explains why Christians endured so much at the beginning of the Reformation to translate and spread the Bible: they knew that here alone are the words of eternal life and that man can only live as he receives every word which proceeds out of the mouth of God. Scripture is the voice of God, and whether or not we are the subjects of God's blessing or wrath may be experimentally determined by whether or not we reverence and obey what is written in Scripture. To be without Scripture is to be without God and without hope in the world. Moreover, Scripture is the only infallible record we have of the will of Christ. Prior to the Reformation, Englishmen had no means of telling what had the approbation of Christ, because, as John Hooper wrote in 1547, "he that had sought all the churches in England before the sixteen years, should not have found one Bible." It was only when Scripture was reopened that Anti-Christ, who previously had been disguised as "the best Christian man," was found to be in possession of the professing Church. And when this apostate Church turned in wrath upon its would-be reformers, those who suffered for their faith in Scripture had no doubt that they were dying in the cause of the Lord Jesus Christ.

Questions at Issue

The question of the authority of the Bible, raised at the outset of the English Reformation, was not, however, immediately settled. It was not settled when there was an official acceptance of Protestantism in the reign of Edward VI (1547–1553), nor was it settled after the Marian terror by Elizabeth's Act of Uniformity in 1559; rather the reign of Elizabeth witnessed the emergence of a Puritan movement within professing Protestantism and the whole driving force of this movement was the conviction that the full authority of the Word of God had not yet been accepted by the English Church. The struggle which ensued in the following hundred years was not merely a Puritan attempt to secure alterations in clerical dress, or religious ceremonies, or externals of church order as such: it lay deeper than all these particular issues.

The Puritans claimed that the Scriptures are not only a full revelation of the Gospel of Christ but also that they contain all things necessary for the government and worship of His Church. They believed it to be a fundamental principle that just as no spiritual teaching is to be accepted which is not found in Scripture, so nothing of spiritual significance is to be added to the Church beyond what is warranted by the written Word. This principle— *the regulative principle of Scripture,* as it was later called—they held to be bound up with the Bible's own teaching about its authority and upon the basis of this principle they laid down their whole policy for the reformation of the Church in two major propositions:

> 1. Everything introduced into the Church without scriptural sanction is unlawful.

> 2. The form of the visible Church in the New Testament is permanently binding upon all generations of Christians.

Against these propositions the defenders of the Elizabethan Church settlement, notably John Whitgift (c. 1530–1604) and Richard Hooker (c. 1554–1600), formulated two counter-propositions:

> 1. They alleged that the Puritans had misconceived the intention of Scripture: while the Bible is binding in all matters relating to salvation, it did allow liberty to the Church to introduce "things indifferent" (*adiaphora* was

the technical term), that is to say, things which were not forbidden by Scripture and things which Christian prudence might suggest to be beneficial to the government or worship of the Church in certain circumstances.

2. They denied that the pattern of the New Testament Church was permanently obligatory on the grounds that the information which the Scriptures give us on this subject is *not* sufficient, as the Puritans claimed, but incomplete and indecisive, suggesting that Christ did not intend any one form of Church government to be of Divine authority.

Preliminary Observations

Before we turn our attention to what is involved in these conflicting statements, let me make a few preliminary comments:

1. The Puritan teaching on the regulative principle of Scripture is almost as obsolete in England as the teaching that the earth is flat. Since the last forty years of the seventeenth century when the idea of any Church government by "divine right" was scouted and laughed out of court, evangelicals and nonevangelicals alike have generally concurred in regarding the Puritan position as naive and untenable. The only persons whom the recent Methodist-Anglican Report could muster to support the idea that "the Church may only do what is explicitly affirmed and commanded in Holy Scripture" are Reformation radicals, Anabaptists, and Puritans of the seventeenth century.[2] All that we need here say of this attitude is to observe that it is not based upon any refutation of the Puritan position. What John Owen wrote to Samuel Parker in 1669 is still true. Parker, a staunch upholder of the Act of Uniformity of 1662, attacked the regulative principle as "the foundation of all Puritanism," but in reply to his arguments Owen declared that Parker had used "no engines but what have been discovered to be insufficient to that purpose a hundred times." Owen quotes Parker's chief argument in these words, "What the Scrip-

ture forbids not, it allows; and what it allows is not unlawful; and what is not unlawful may lawfully be done." "This tale, I confess, we have been told many and many a time," says Owen, "but it hath been as often answered that the whole of it, as to anything of reasoning, is captious and sophistical."[3] Despite three centuries of declamation, if the Puritans' works on Church polity were reopened, justification would be found for Owen's assertion.

2. At first sight it might appear that Puritan teaching on this issue has no urgent relevance to our contemporary situation. Someone might say, "What is the use of our discussing the *extent* of the authority of Scripture when what is really challenged today is whether the Bible has any final authority at all?" The Puritan answer to such a question would be that it suggests a man-centered assessment of the situation: the rejection of the inerrancy of the Bible by the modern world is a problem to evangelicals, but there is a more fundamental problem, and that is, "Why are we not enjoying more of the manifest favor of God upon our churches?" In the light of that question it is by no means irrelevant to ask, "To what extent does God intend His Word to be our sole guide and rule? Is Scripture regulating our Church life today to the extent which Christ wills that it should?"

It is not impossible that we have been so preoccupied with defending the Scripture that we have not been sufficiently fearful lest we should fail to obey the Word ourselves. The Puritan's first deduction from his belief that Scripture is the voice of God was that he would be personally accountable to the Lord with regard to all that His Word contains. "While we have Christ's Word for the things we do or refuse to do," says Henry Barrow, "we need not fear the threats of any vain men; neither be amazed at any vain titles of church, sacraments, etc. For this we know, that there is no church can excuse us for the breach of God's law before that great Judge."[4]

We shall not recapture the spirit of this quotation until we reexamine our whole view of Scripture. A renewed study of the regulative principle at the present time would not be a musty theological excursion into the problems of some bygone era; rather, it would confront us with the very test which our modern Christianity needs, and it would throw our minds forward to that Day when all our deeds done in the body will be judged by the rule of Scripture: "Our whole preaching must be Scripture proof," says Thomas Brooks, "or we and our works must burn together." The Puritans show us how personal responsibility must at once follow a belief in Scripture infallibility.

3. Another reason why this subject is relevant to us is that it forces us to consider where the boundary lies between a lawful practice of expediency and a sinful compromise: in other words, what is the point at which Scripture ceases to be our only guide and leaves us to devise new forms and methods according to the circumstances in which we are placed? We are entering an era when church traditions of all kinds are breaking down, and experiments are increasingly being called for in evangelism, worship, and church government. New departures in music, religious drama, and visual aids are all being made and some churches have already gone so far as to substitute a film for a sermon on Sunday evenings. The fundamental question surely is, *How far does the Scripture allow all this?* There is no disagreement about the fact that the exercise of prudence, wisdom, and common sense are Christian duties; the disagreement between ourselves and the Puritans is that we have acted as though there is a wide area of church practice which lies outside the scope of the New Testament. They drew the line between legitimate expediency and disobedience at a different point from that at which we draw it. As evangelicals we have been inclined to believe that wherever our failure lies, it does not lie in our disobedience to Scripture. But if the Puritan teaching on the regulative principle is true, it places our conduct in a different light.

Essentials and Nonessentials

Before we leave these observations one further question must be raised. It will be seen that if the Puritan teaching on the regulative principle is given prominence, then inevitably the question of our practice in church order, government, and worship assumes an importance which it has not been customary for evangelicals to give to it. We may therefore be predisposed to conclude, with Whitgift, that the Puritans, by calling attention to external matters and to issues not "essential to salvation," were not rightly distinguishing between fundamentals (the Gospel and the doctrines of the faith) and secondary issues. Whitgift told Cartwright that the tendency of the Puritan policy was to bring about "the overthrow of the gospel through contention about external things. . . . Surely, if they be matters 'necessary to salvation,' then is there some just cause of breaking the peace of the church for them; but, if they be matters of no such weight, then can you not excuse either yourself or them."[5] In similar vein Bishop Hall declared that it was "a thousand times better to swallow a ceremony than to rend a church."

Richard Hooker used this same distinction between essentials and nonessentials in replying to the Puritan charge that the Elizabethan Church settlement did not accept the authority of Scripture in its entirety. He claimed that to reject the Puritan view of biblical authority in no way denied "the absolute perfection of Scripture," because God designed Scripture to be "a full instruction in all things unto salvation necessary . . . so the Scripture, yea, every sentence thereof, is perfect, and wanteth nothing requisite unto that purpose for which God delivered the same."[6] Such things as ceremonies, order, discipline, and government, Whitgift and Hooker asserted, are distinct from the Gospel and matters of faith, and by alleging the need of scriptural authority on issues not necessary for salvation the Puritans were guilty of "racking and stretching" the Bible to cover areas over which God never intended it to give definite instruction.

We can only briefly indicate the nature of the Puritan reply to this charge. They held that the one foundation upon which a sinner's salvation depends is the truth concerning the Person and Work of Jesus Christ (1 Cor. 3:11). Yet there are also a number of other truths plainly revealed in Scripture which cannot strictly be said to be "necessary for salvation," for a man may misapprehend them or be misled over them and yet be saved. "I doubt not but divers of the fathers of the Greek church," says Cartwright, "which were great patrons of free-will (at least as their words pretend) are saved, holding the foundation of the faith, which is Christ."[7] Whitgift struggles to avoid this (chiding Cartwright for "speaking so dangerously") because the argument breaks down his premise that the Scriptures only speak clearly on what is "necessary for salvation." As an orthodox Elizabethan Protestant he has to agree that the Scripture is decisive against free-will. And so, if Cartwright is correct, the Bible speaks authoritatively on what is a "nonessential"—nonessential, that is according to Whitgift's definition, namely, not necessary for salvation. Whitgift cannot accept this conclusion and instead replies that if a person dies in the opinion of free-will he cannot be saved.

To the Puritans, Whitgift was trying to maintain a distinction which could not be maintained. And they regarded their opponents' habit of discriminating between essentials and nonessentials as a dangerous procedure. Dangerous, not because it claimed to exalt Christ and the Gospel to the supreme place, but because it failed to emphasize that the New Testament offers no safety to those who knowingly neglect the least of Christ's commandments. Samuel Rutherford says:

> We urge the immutability of Christ's laws, as well in the smallest as greatest things, though the commandments of Christ be greater or less in regard to the intrinsical matter, as to use water in baptism, or to baptise is less than to preach Christ, and believe in him, 1 Cor. 1:17. Yet they are both alike great, in regard of the authority of Christ the Commander, Matt. 28:18–19. And it's too great boldness to alter any commandment of Christ for the smallness of the matter, for it lieth upon our conscience not because it is a greater or a lesser thing . . . but it tieth us for the authority of the law-giver: Now God's authority is the same when he saith, *You shall not worship false gods,* and when he saith, *You shall not add of your own one ring or*

pin to the Ark, Tabernacle, Temple, yea, either to break or teach others to break one of the least of the commandments of God, maketh men the least in the Kingdom of God, Matt. 5:18.[8]

It is true that a person may be saved by grace who through the influence of circumstances and wrong teaching has not been able to see all that Scripture requires concerning the Church; the Puritans never made correct views on Church polity the test of saving grace. But their recognition that not all revealed truths are foundation-truths without which none is saved, does not mean, as Henry Barrow points out, that we may make "some doctrines and some part of Christ's Testament fundamental and substantial, others accidental and such as may be altered and violate without any prejudice or danger to the soul."[9] The fact that a man may be defective in knowledge and practice, and yet be saved through being on the foundation which is Christ, provides no warrant for dividing up Scripture into essentials and nonessentials—placing rules concerning the visible church in the second category, as though they could be safely left unkept.

John Robinson, the pastor of the Pilgrim Fathers, makes the following observations on this distinction about essential truths:

> Howsoever, I do acknowledge a difference of truths, and that some are more, and some less principal, yet do I wish more conscience in the application of this distinction. For although the ministers and people in the English Church are limited in their obedience to the New Testament by civil and ecclesiastical laws, this is made a salve for every sore, that they have the substance of the gospel, the doctrine of faith, all fundamental truths and whatsoever is necessary to salvation. In which defence (as it is made) there are these evils.
>
> 1. In it men not only endeavour, which is too much, the curing of Babel [i.e., the established Church], but indeed to make Babel believe she stands in no great need

of curing: and that her wounds are neither deadly, nor dangerous.

2. It tends to vilify and make of small moment many of the Lord's truths, and ordinances. . . .

3. This pleading by the ministers that they hold and enjoy every fundamental truth, and whatsoever is of necessity to salvation, considering the end of it, which is, the stopping of the people from pressing unto further obedience and profession of the will of God and ordinances of Christ, is injurious both to the growth and sincerity of the obedience of God's people . . . it insinuates that it is sufficient if men so serve God as they can obtain salvation, though with disobedience of a great part of the revealed will of God: occasioning them thereby to serve him only, or chiefly for wages as hypocrites do. As if a child should be taught so far to honour and please his father as he might get his inheritance, but not much to trouble himself about giving or doing any further honour or service.[10]

It was a travesty of the Puritans' position for Whitgift to say that Cartwright counted "external government more precious than the doctrine of faith."[11] The history of Elizabethan Puritan evangelism makes such a charge ludicrous. What the Puritans did say was that the right ordering of the Church cannot be disconnected from the Gospel: "God hath not only ordained that the word should be preached, but hath ordained also in what order and by whom it should be preached."[12] They were convinced that when God's order is violated the Gospel itself will soon be perverted. Thus Tyndale asserts that it was when bishops and hierarchy arose in the Church that "the plough went awry; the Scripture waxed dark; Christ was no more seen."[13] On the other hand, it is when the Church keeps close to the Word that the Gospel shines forth in its purity and power. Rutherford, looking back on seventy years of struggle in England to secure a better ordering of the visible Church, did not scruple to write in 1646, "Consider if thousands more would not have been converted if Christ's government had been set up for which Mr. Cartwright, Mr. Udal, Mr. Deering, and the godliest did supplicate the Parliament."[14]

The Controversy over the Regulative Principle

The study of Puritan teaching has generally begun with the first usage of the actual term "Puritan" in the 1560's after Queen Elizabeth had come to the throne. Nevertheless there is good reason to believe that if we take this date as the starting point of the Puritan movement we adopt a view which the Puritans themselves would not have accepted. From the time when in the 1570s John Whitgift accused Thomas Cartwright, the Elizabethan Puritan leader, of starting a "fire of discord," the standard official line against the Puritans was that they were innovators guilty of disturbing the Church with novel opinions. This propaganda came to its climax in the words of the Act of Uniformity of 1662: "Whereas in the first year of the late Queen Elizabeth there was one uniform order of common service and prayer, and of the administration of sacraments, rites and ceremonies, in the Church of England . . . yet . . . by the great and scandalous neglect of ministers in using the said order of liturgy, great mischiefs and inconveniences have arisen and grown."[15]

In contrast to this propaganda it can be held that the essential teaching of the Elizabethan Puritans goes back to the beginning of the English Reformation—thirty years before Elizabeth came to the throne in 1558. There appear to be at least two reasons why this has frequently not been recognized.

1. Attention has not been given to the clash in policy between William Tyndale (c. 1494–1536) and Thomas Cranmer (1489–1556). These two men were more or less contemporaries in age, though when Cranmer became Archbishop of Canterbury in 1533, Tyndale, a hidden fugitive in Flanders, had only three years to live. Tyndale was not only a translator, he was a natural leader and an exceptionally stirring writer with a policy in his mind which he was able to impress upon others. It was not without reason that Sir Thomas More called him "the captain of the English heretics."

Cranmer, as we know, was also a policy maker, guiding the Reformation to the official position which it was given in the reign of King Edward, but these two policies, while both pursuing Protestant interests, were not compatible with one another. And the essential difference between the two comes out in regard to the regulative principle of Scripture.

Cranmer gradually came to accept the Scripture as the sole authority in matters of faith, but he did not accept that the Church is limited in her ceremonies, practices, and government only to the New Testament. An example of this is the fact that in 1539 he held that the use of confession was "very requisite and expedient" though agreeing that it was not expressly enjoined in Scripture.[16] Similarly, in Edward's reign, while he accepted "that Bishops and Priests were not two things, but both one office in the beginning of Christ's religion"[17] he saw no need to return to the New Testament order in this respect.

In contrast to this, Tyndale demanded that not only the creed of the Church but also her organization and services should have scriptural sanction. "We bring God's testament," he says, "for all we do." One of the articles charged against the writings of Tyndale's friend, John Frith, by his Catholic persecutors was that he held the following "heresy": "The Spirit would that nothing should be done, but that which is expressly rehearsed in the Scripture."[18]

Likewise this "heretical" statement was attributed to Tyndale: "Ceremonies of the Church have brought the world from God." In support of this assertion, John Foxe quotes the following words of Tyndale: "Seek the Word of God in all things, and without the Word of God do nothing though it appear ever so glorious."[19] Tyndale's position was that anything introduced into the Church without a precept or promise of Scripture is mere superstition. Listen to him applying this to the Confirmation service: "If Confirmation have a promise, then it justifieth as far as the promise extendeth. If it have no promise, then is it not of God, as the bishops be not. . . . After that the bishops had left preaching, then feigned they this dumb ceremony of confirmation, to have somewhat at leastway whereby they might reign over their dioceses. . . . They will say that the Holy Ghost is given through such ceremonies. If

God had so promised, so should it be; but Paul saith (Gal. 3), that the Spirit is received through preaching of the faith."[20]

Tyndale's words, of course, are describing the practice as it was under Popery, but in demanding a Scripture promise, or warrant, he was using a principle which was not to lose its relevance after Acts of Uniformity had made the nation "Protestant."

An examination of Tyndale shows that there is little in the teaching of the Elizabethan Puritans which was not a continuity of what may be found in embryo in the martyr's writings. Tyndale held the equality of the ministerial office over against Episcopacy; he denounced the presence of bishops in Parliament: he sought that the diaconate should be restored to its proper New Testament function; he wanted benefices restored to the people, not disposed of by lords, spiritual or secular: he held that the authority of the Church is derived solely from Christ and that in the spiritual realm "the king is as deep under the spiritual officer, to hear out of God's Word what he ought to believe, and how to live, and how to rule, as is the poorest beggar in the realm." He also taught that ministers should be called to their work by the congregation of believers, otherwise men would be appointed in churches "not whom virtue and learning, but whom the favour of great men commended."

2. A second reason why Puritanism has so frequently been regarded as originating in Elizabethan times is because it was in the interests of Protestant solidarity not to disclose the seriousness of the differences which existed between the Reformers in England in the reign of King Edward. Some of the most important documents relating to this have yet to be printed in English. The major differences center around the controversy between John Hooper and Nicholas Ridley, in 1550, and between John Knox and Thomas Cranmer in 1552–53. These two controversies were both vitally concerned with the regulative principle, and they marked the beginning of an official Protestant opposition to this principle—an opposition which was based on the accusation that Hooper and Knox, along with others, were causing needless disputes by failing to practice things which were not contrary to

Scripture but merely indifferent. The two particular things in question were the wearing of vestments and the rubric in the Second Book of Common Prayer requiring a kneeling posture at the communion table.

Hooper and Knox opposed these two things on the grounds that the Church had no authority to impose rites possessing religious significance[21] which were not prescribed in Scripture: "There is nothing to be done in the Church," says Hooper, "but it is commanded by the Word of God, either expressly or by necessary collection."[22] Nicholas Ridley, Bishop of London, and Archbishop Cranmer regarded this statement as so obviously impossible and disruptive that it scarcely required any scriptural refutation. They put the emphasis in their rejoinders on what they conceived would be the evil consequences if this teaching was accepted. Ridley replying to Hooper says:

> If this reason should take place, "the Apostles used it not, therefore it is not lawful for us to use it"—or this either, "They did it, therefore we must needs do it"—then all Christians may have no abiding place, all must, under pain of damnation, depart from their possessions, as Peter said they did, *Behold, we have left all things,* etc.; we may have no ministration of Christ's sacraments in Churches, for they had no Churches, but were fain to do all in their own houses; we must baptize abroad in the fields as the Apostles did; we may not receive the holy communion but at supper, and with the table furnished with other meats, as the Anabaptists do now stiffly and obstinately affirm that it should be; our naming of the child in baptism, our prayer upon him, our crossing, and threefold abrenunciation, and our white chrisom, all must be left, for these we cannot prove by God's Word, that the Apostles did them.[23]

Cranmer writes in the same vein to the Lords of the young King's Privy Council who held the reins of authority in the Church:

I know your Lordships' wisdom to be such that I trust ye will not be moved by these glorious and unquiet spirits, which can like nothing but that is after their own fancy, and cease not to make trouble and disquietness when things be most quiet and in good order. If such men should be heard, although the Book were made every year anew, yet should it not lack faults in their opinion.

But, say they, it is not commanded in the Scripture to kneel, and whatsoever is not commanded in the Scripture is against the Scripture, and utterly unlawful and ungodly. But this saying is the chief foundation of the error of the Anabaptists and of divers other sects. This saying is a subversion of all order as well in religion as in common policy. If this saying be true, take away the whole Book of Service. For what should men travail to set an order in the form of service, if no order can be set but that (which) is already prescribed by the Scripture. And because I will not trouble your Lordships with reciting of many Scriptures of proofs in this matter, whosoever teacheth any such doctrine (if your Lordships will give me leave) I will set my foot by his to be tried by fire, that his doctrine is untrue, and not only untrue, but also seditious, and perilous to be heard of any subjects, as a thing breaking the bridle of obedience and loosing them from the bond of all princes' laws.[24]

Twenty years later John Whitgift was to develop the same line of reasoning against Cartwright. "If all ought of necessity to be reduced to the form of government used in the Apostles' time," he writes, "then Christian princes must forego their authority in the Church."[25] Such a conclusion was monstrous to Whitgift. Similarly he claimed there could be no sound logic in Cartwright's argument that "the Church in St. Paul's time was a perfect body without archbishops and archdeacons; therefore, they are not necessary in the Church of Christ," because if this reasoning was sound you could also argue, "It was then perfect without Christian magistrates: therefore, Christian magistrates are to be removed from the Church." "This kind of reasoning," he concludes, "is most perilous, and openeth a door to anabaptism and confusion."[26]

The Puritan Exposition of "Adiaphora"

The main strength of Ridley's and Cranmer's case against the regulative principle lies in their claim that such things as vestments and the posture at communion are neither good nor bad in themselves, but indifferent, and therefore if the Church should determine that vestments and kneeling are prudent and useful then individual Christians should submit. They reasoned that there are many things which cannot be resolved from Scripture, e.g. what places Christians should meet, at what times, how often the Lord's supper should be observed and so on, and therefore it must be lawful for the Church to determine what cannot be determined by Scripture.

The Puritan answer to this position was this: they did not assert that the Church could do *nothing* except what was prescribed in Scripture. It was a caricature of Puritanism which affirmed that they looked for every detail in the New Testament. What they did hold was that nothing was to be made a part (as distinguished from a circumstance)[27] of worship and nothing of *spiritual* significance was to be added to the government of the Church except what Scripture prescribed or warranted by just inference.

The area within which we are to determine things for ourselves is the area of *natural* circumstances. Indifferent things, they held, are not in themselves *moral* or *spiritual things,* but they are such natural things as are physical or belonging to ordinary human life. For example, it is not a part of worship where the worship takes place, or how long it lasts, or of what material the pulpit or the communion cup is made. Or in the realm of Church government, it is not a moral thing what the nationality of the Church officer is, but it is a moral thing that he be such an officer as Christ has appointed in His Church. In one area we need the warrant of Scripture; in the other we do not.

So in 1547, when John Winram, Sub-prior of St. Andrew's, exclaimed to John Knox, "Will ye bind us so straight, that we may do nothing without the express Word of God? What and if I ask a drink? Think ye that I sin? And yet I have not God's Word for me," the Scottish Reformer replied: "I wonder that ye compare things profane and holy things so indiscreetly together. . . . One meat I may eat, another I may refuse, and that without scruple of conscience. I may change one with another, even as oft as I please. Whether may we do the same in matters of religion? May we cast away what we please, and retain what we please? If I be well remembered, Moses, in the name of God, says to the people of Israel, 'All that the Lord thy God commands thee to do, that do thou to the Lord thy God: add nothing to it; diminish nothing from it.' By this rule think I that the Kirk of Christ will measure God's religion, and not by that which seems good in their own eyes."[28]

Yet the Puritans' opponents were continually taking up Winram's argument— "the Scriptures are too general to regulate everything, therefore the demand for a Scripture warrant is absurd"—and in 1646 Rutherford was still having to repeat that they had always recognized an area of common things, not belonging to the spiritual sphere but to ordinary natural life (eating, sleeping, etc.) which require no Scriptural precept for their practice: "Time, and place, name, country, form, figure, habit or garments to hold off injuries of sun and heaven, as such are never commanded, never forbidden of God, and therefore the change of these circumstances can be no change of a commandment of God. We never advanced circumstances, as such to the orbe and sphere of morals."[29] These are all things which are genuinely indifferent and which are therefore to be determined by wisdom and common sense.

This leads us to the heart of the controversy over things indifferent. Based upon the distinction made above, the Puritans went on to show that any practice in the Church purporting to be indifferent (and therefore not needing scriptural warrant) is only to be recognized as such if it fulfils certain conditions. George Gillespie gives the following:[30]

1. *"It must be only a circumstance of divine worship: no substantial part of it: no sacred, significant and efficacious ceremony."*

In other words if a minister, like Hooper, preached in an ordinary merchant's cloak, that was a natural, indifferent thing, but if the minister's dress was intended to convey a spiritual meaning (like the white surplice as a symbol of purity) it ceased to be indifferent. This explains why the controversy over vestments and other ceremonies in Edward's reign was so closely connected with the regulative principle. The Book of Common Prayer claimed a religious value and significance for such ceremonies which, though not contained in Scripture, "be apt to stir up the dull mind of man to the remembrance of his duty to God, by some notable and special signification whereby he might be edified." To the Puritans this addition of things of supposed spiritual value in the Church could not be justified under the plea that they were things indifferent.

In the same way (they held) while the Church may lawfully determine the most expedient times for worship and the most suitable places for meeting, she has no authority to invest particular days or seasons with religious importance, nor to attach any spiritual blessing to buildings or church-yards.

2. *"That which the Church may lawfully prescribe by her laws and ordinances, as a thing left to her determination, must be one of such things as were not determinable by Scripture."*

Whatever is appointed or prohibited in Scripture, either by precept or example, or whatever may justly be inferred from the same, cannot be indifferent.

3. *"If the Church prescribe anything lawfully . . . her ordinance must be accompanied with some good reason and warrant given for the satisfaction of tender consciences."*

Because a thing is itself indifferent it does not mean that the Church can appoint it apart from any consideration of Scripture. "As we may not use any indifferent thing at our pleasure," says Gillespie, referring to the individual Christian, "so neither may the Church, at her will and pleasure, command the use of it; but as our practice, so the Church's injunction must be determined and squared" according to the rules given in God's Word; "for those things which are in their nature indifferent are never indifferent in their use, and that because the use of them is either according to the rules of the Word, and then it is expedient, or not, and then it is unlawful."[31]

These general rules governing actions and things not so specifically prescribed by Scripture, are stated by the same writer as follows:

1. All particular actions should have reference to God's glory (1 Cor. 10:31; Rom. 14:7–8).

2. No action, though legitimate in itself, should be done if it might be a stumbling block or a possible occasion of spiritual harm to others (Rom. 14:21; 1 Cor. 10:23); rather, "as in the whole course of our life, so especially in the policy of the Church, we may do nothing (be it never so indifferent in itself) which is not profitable for edification, 1 Cor. 13:26, "Let all things be done to edifying." From which precept Pareus inferreth that nothing ought to be done in the Church which doth not manifestly make for the utility of all and every one."

3. We must never act contrary to the peace and purity of our conscience, for although a thing may be indifferent yet if our conscience judges it to be unlawful we may not lawfully do it (Rom. 14:14).

The Puritans wrote a great deal on the definition of things indifferent[32] and the scriptural rules governing their use, and the bulkiness of the material they have left on the subject certainly suggests that they did not oversimplify the issue or by-pass its difficulties. *Adiaphora* became a storm center of controversy because the whole strength of the case against the Puritan position rested on the contention that, provided the Church did not appoint what was forbidden by Scripture, she might regulate her worship and government by such general rules as 1 Corinthians 14:40, "Let all things be done decently and in order." Thus, it was claimed that vestments and episcopacy are indifferent things (not being expressly prohibited by the Word) and therefore warranted if they forwarded the general rule of promoting "order." The Puritans were consequently forced to show in detail from Scripture that the New Testament writers never class anything of spiritual significance as *adiaphora* and that the "general rules" contained in the texts referred to above do not mean that in the whole sphere of her life the Church has only general principles to follow, the "spirit" of which she is free to implement by the addition or alteration of such particular spiritual matters as she deems fit. Ridley and Whitgift supposed that this must be the meaning of the Scripture because otherwise Church life would be an impossibility—various things being necessary for its continuity which Scripture does not specify, e.g. the provision of suitable buildings.

The Puritan reply, as we have seen, was that the general rules in Scripture give ample guidance over circumstantial matters and indifferent things which we are free to order, but that this is quite different from providing a general sanction for the preservation of such things as Whitgift was pleading for. "We deny not but certain things are left to the order of the Church," says Cartwright, "because they are of the nature of those which are varied by times, places, persons, and other circumstances, and so could not at once be set down and established for ever; and yet so left to the the order of the Church, as that it do nothing against the rules aforesaid.[33] But how doth this follow, that certain things are left to the order of the church, therefore to make a new ministry by making an archbishop, to alter the ministry that is appointed by making a bishop or pastor without a church or flock, to make a deacon without appointing him his church whereof he is deacon and where he might exercise his charge of providing for the poor, to abrogate clean both the name and office of the elder, with other more—how, I say, do these follow that, because the church hath power to ordain certain things, therefore it hath power to do so of these which God hath ordained and established?"[34]

Evidence for the Regulative Principle

Though we have seen the Puritan defence against the charge that they ignored the province of legitimate *adiaphora,* we cannot leave the matter here. The whole spirit of the Puritan position was far from defensive and the charge in fact had arisen as a counter to their positive assertion of the regulative principle. It is on our assessment of this principle that our final verdict on the Puritans must depend, for while we may admire their piety and their preaching, the movement itself would never have swept this country and across the Atlantic to New England as it did apart from their conviction that the regulative principle is inseparable from New Testament Christianity. It remains for us, therefore, to outline the evidence which had led them to this conclusion. Their case rested on the considerations which may be set out as follows.

1. *Scripture is a complete guide for the Church's faith and practice.*

> *The holy Scriptures are now completely and unalterably perfect,* containing such exact rules for the Churches of God in all states and ages, both under the Old and New Testament, that not only the people of God of all sorts and degrees, but also the men of God, and officers of the Church, of all sorts and ages, may thereby be made perfect, thoroughly furnished unto all good works. "All Scripture is given by inspiration of God . . . that the man of Cod may be perfect, thoroughly furnished to every good work," 2 Tim. 3:16–17. And in his first Epistle to Timothy (which is the Church's Directory for divine worship, discipline, and government) he saith, "These things write I unto thee—that thou mightest know how thou oughtest to behave thyself in the House of God, which is the Church of the living God." (This is spoken in reference to matters of Church-government peculiarly), 1 Tim. 3:14–15.

So wrote some of the leaders of the London presbytery of ministers in 1646 in their work, *The Divine Right of Church-Government.*[35]

Likewise Rutherford writes, "Whatever makes us perfect, thoroughly furnished unto all good works, and is written for this end that any Timothy, or faithful pastor might know how he ought to behave himself in the House of God . . . must hold forth a perfect platform of Discipline,[36] which doth not vary, ebb and flow, and alter according to the civil government, laws, manner and customs of men: But the Scriptures of God doth so instruct all members of the visible Church, both governors and governed, 2 Tim. 3:16–17; 1 Tim. 3:14–15. *Therefore,* the Scripture must hold forth a perfect form of Discipline."[37] He also proceeds to show that the Scripture does not restrict its authority to matters of faith, for Paul "speaketh of many special positive precepts and rules of policy, as of poor widows, the alms to be given to them; the not rebuking of an elder, the office of elders governing, and of elders labouring in the Word and Doctrine, the not receiving an accusation against an elder, but under two or three witnesses, the public rebuking of those who offend publicly, the not admitting to the ministry raw and green soldiers not tried, and many other particulars of policy, of all which he saith gravely, 1 Tim. 5:21, 'I charge thee before God and the Lord Jesus Christ, and the elect angels, that thou observe these things,' these things was not one commandment, but all the precepts of faith and of Church-government spoken of in this epistle."

This claim for the completeness of the instruction which the Scripture supplies for the Church was also borne out, the Puritans held, by those texts which expressly exclude human additions or subtractions from the Divine Word (Deut. 4:2). (Rutherford spends four pages on this verse alone, Deut. 12:32; Rev. 22:18–19.) John Owen applies what he believes to be the significance of these and other verses to the question of liturgies imposed by human authority in worship, when he writes:

> Whereas God himself having instituted his own worship and all the concernments of it, doth also assert his own authority and will as the sole cause and rule of all the worship that he will accept, no instance being left on record of any one that ever made additions to what he had appointed, on any pretence whatever, or by virtue of any authority whatever, that was accepted with him; and whereas the most eminent of those who have assumed that power to themselves, as also the judgment of the reasons necessary for the exerting of it, as to matter and manner, have

been given up, in the righteous judgment of God, to do things not convenient, yea, abominable unto him (as in the papal church),—it is not unlikely to be the wisdom of men to be very cautious of intruding themselves into this thankless office.[38]

2. Christ has been given exclusive authority for settling the laws and government of His Church and He has made His will known only in Scripture.

Says Rutherford:

If the Church be a visible politic kingdom as it is, Matt. 13:45–48; 16:19; 8:12, and if the Word be the Word, scepter and law of the kingdom as it is, Matt. 6:10; 13:11; Luke 4:43; Matt. 4:23; Mark 13:8; Luke 21:10, 14; 13:10, yea the sword and royal power of the King, Rev. 1:16; 19:15, by which He ruleth and reigneth in His church, Isa. 11:4; Ps. 110:2; Heb. 1:8–9; Ps. 45:3–7; Isa. 61:1–2; 2 Cor. 10:4–6; 1 Peter 2:4–7, and if by this Word the King reigneth, bindeth, looseth, and conquereth souls and subdueth His enemies, Matt. 18:18–20; 16:19; Rev. 6:2, then certainly Christ must reign politically, and externally in His Church and walk in the midst of the golden candlesticks, Rev. 2:1. And if Christ ascending to heaven as a victorious King leading captivity captive, gave gifts to men, and appointed an external policy for the gathering of the saints by the ministry of certain officers of His kingdom, as it is, Ps. 68:18, "that the Lord God might dwell among them," and Eph. 4:11–16, then He must reign in the external policy of pastors, teachers, elders, by Word, sacraments and discipline. Now the King Himself, the Lord who reigneth in His external policy must be the only lawgiver, James 4:12; Isa. 33:22. There can be no Rabbis or Doctors on earth who, as little kings, can make laws under Him, Matt. 23:8–10, yea, nor Apostles who can teach how the worship should externally be ordered, but what they receive of the King of the Church, 1 Cor. 11:23; Acts

15:13–18, how the house should be governed, Heb. 3:1–5: yea, nothing more reasonable, than that whatsoever is commanded by the God of heaven should be done in and for the house of the God of heaven, under the pain of His wrath, Ezra 7:23.[39]

The crucial text is probably Matthew 28:20, *"Teaching them to observe all things whatsoever I have commanded you. . . ."* Commenting on this and kindred texts where the Lord requires precise obedience to His appointments, Owen asks whether the sense of such verses is only "to prevent the addition of what is *contrary* to what God hath appointed," leaving us liberty to add such things as "may tend to the furtherance and better discharge of his appointments" (as the Puritans' opponents urged) or whether the Puritan interpretation is not the one which has the fairest evidence of expressing the intention of Scripture. He writes:

Our Lord Jesus Christ directs his apostles to teach his disciples "to do and observe whatever he commanded them." Those who contend for the latter [i.e., Puritan] interpretation of those and the like precepts before mentioned, affirm that there is in these words a restriction of the matter of their commission to the express commands of Christ. What he commands, they say, they were to teach men to observe, and nothing else; nor will he require the observance of aught else at our hands. The others would have his intention to be, whatever he commanded, and whatever seemeth good to them to command, so it be not contrary unto what was by him commanded; as if he had said, "Teach men to observe whatever I command them; and command you them to observe whatever you think meet, so it be not contrary to my commands." Certainly this gloss at first view seems to defeat the main intendment of Christ, in that express limitation of their commission unto his own commands. So also under the Old Testament: giving order about his worship, the Lord lets

Moses know that he must do all things according to what he should show and reveal unto him. In the close of the work committed unto him, to show what he had done was acceptable to God, it is eight or ten times repeated that he did all as the Lord commanded him; nothing was omitted, nothing added by him. That the same course might be observed in the following practice which was taken in the first institution [i.e., of the New Testament Church] the Lord commands that nothing be added to what was so appointed by him, nothing diminished from it.[40]

According to the Puritans, the New Testament makes all spiritual obedience and spiritual duties derive their obligation from the fact that they are sanctioned by the authority of Christ. The Church can only be a steward of His laws; her duty is to carry out His appointments. Therefore to invest requirements *of her own* with a religious importance or to give authority to *her own* institutions, is to offend against the authority of Christ in His Word and comes under the same rebuke with which He condemned the Pharisees for their self-appointed religious ceremonies of washings, their broad phylacteries, wide hemmed garments (Matt. 23:5), and the rest: "In vain do they worship me, teaching for doctrines the commandments of men" (Matt. 15:9). The Lord Jesus Christ is the only source of authority in the Church, and He has delegated no authority to man in matters of faith, Church government, or worship. "The single fact that the rule of Church power in the worship of God is the rule of Scripture, is decisive of the whole controversy in regard to rites and ceremonies, and ties up the Church to the ministerial office of administering a directory made for it, instead of presumptuously attempting to make a new directory for itself."[41]

Once we see the relationship of the regulative principle to the Lordship of Christ it is no longer a mystery how such a Christ-centered man as Samuel Rutherford could engage so earnestly in Church polemics.

3. *If human additions are allowed in the Church they will subvert and undermine what the Scripture does teach.*

Once the regulative principle is departed from there is an inevitable tendency that additions will alter and take away from Scripture. This may be denied by those who reject the principle, they may say that their additions are not contrary to Scripture, only "beside" it, but to the Puritans the testimony of Church history, both in the Bible and since, was unmistakable. They saw the tendency at work in the early Fathers, they saw it full blown in the Papacy, and they had grappled with its Catholic champions in the Reformation battle. In 1519 Eck, the Pope's defender, had declared that it is "sufficient that the Church say such a thing is truth and to be done and the scripture does not gain-say it."[42] The argument was that it is no denial of Scripture to say that its testimony is not complete, for the New Testament was never intended to give the total or final form of the Church's faith or order. Foxe records the following incident in the trial of the Marian martyr, Laurence Saunders, before Bishop Bonner: "A heretic he would now prove him, and all those," said Bonner, "who did teach and believe that the administration of the sacraments and all orders of the Church are most pure which do come most nigh to the order of the primitive Church. For the Church was then in her infancy, and could not abide that perfection which was afterward to be furnished with ceremonies. And for this cause Christ Himself, and after him the apostles, did in many things bear with the rudeness of that Church."[43]

Yet while the Marian burnings were still a vivid memory, Whitgift's only answer to Cartwright's query why the New Testament office of elders ("seniors") was not recognized in the English Church was that the presence of "the Christian magistrate" now made the disciplinary work of elders unnecessary, and therefore the New Testament practice could not be our guide in this matter as God had not then made the improvement in His Church such as England experienced under Queen Elizabeth: "We ask not what the church was able to do then, or what it is able to do now; but whether the same government ought to be now that was then; and whether a Christian magistrate have no more authority in the government of the church now, than the heathenish and persecuting magistrate had then . . . God hath much better provided for his church by placing in it civil and Christian magistrates, whose authority is so ample and large, than by placing seniors; wherefore, where Christian magistrates be, the government of seniors is superfluous."[44]

In the same manner Richard Hooker argues that even though Episcopacy was not the Church order appointed in the New Testament, that is no reason why it may not now be regarded as the best form of Church government:

> Albeit the Scriptures did no way insinuate the same (i.e. Episcopacy) to be God's ordinances, and the Apostles to have brought it in, Albeit the Church were acknowledged by all men to have been the first beginner thereof a long time after the Apostles were gone; yet is not the authority of the bishops hereby disannulled, it is not hereby proved unfit or unprofitable for the Church. . . . All things we grant which are in the Church ought to be of God. But forasmuch as they may be two ways accounted such, one if they be of his own institution and not of ours, another if they be of ours, and yet with his approbation: this latter way there is no impediment but that the same thing which is of men may be also justly and truly said to be of God, the same thing from heaven which is from earth. Of all good things God himself is author, and consequently an approver of them. The rule to discern when the actions of men are good, when they are such as they ought to be, is more ample and large than the law which God hath set particular down in his holy word; the Scripture is but a part of that rule, as hath been heretofore at large declared. If therefore all things be of God which are well done, and if all things be well done which are according to the rule of well-doing, and if the rule of well-doing be more ample than the Scripture; what necessity is there, that every thing which is of God should be set down in holy Scripture?[45]

To the Puritans this kind of reasoning undermined Scripture. Just as the Papists effectively brought in another Gospel by arguing that the Scriptures are not complete in the particulars of doctrine and that what they are silent upon, e.g., purgatory, we may teach if the Church thinks fit, so also the rejection of the regulative principle with regard to the Church meant that human institutions replaced the New Testament practice: Church discipline by the eldership was replaced by Elizabeth's civil authority (who "disciplined" many Gospel ministers out of their pulpits), parity of ministers was replaced by hierarchy, the election of ministers by congregations and their ordination by presbyters was replaced by episcopal authority, and so on.

Conclusions

1. Once the regulative principle is discarded there is no other principle which can keep the Church true to the simplicity of the New Testament: "When this general truth is denied, there is no limit that can be put to the introduction of the inventions of men into the government and worship of Christ's house."[46] If it is once conceded that Scripture is not sufficient for the ordering of the Church, then there is no way of preventing the corruption of her government and worship as under Popery.

This was what Knox and others saw in 1552 when they argued that if such ceremonies as kneeling were retained there could be no consistent stand against Popery, for Catholics could say, "The profit that cometh of your kneeling is nowhere in God's Word expressed, but only in the imagination of your own brains . . . wherefore our ceremonies ought equally to remain with your kneeling."[47]

2. Christian liberty cannot be preserved without the maintenance of the regulative principle, "seeing Christian liberty expressly exempteth us altogether from obedience to men's laws not warranted by Christ's Word, Gal. 5:1; Col. 2:20."[48]

3. The opposition expressed against the regulative principle is not without significance. For while some good men were found in opposition to the Puritan position, the generality of those who

contended against the principle in the Elizabethan period and later too, often showed a desire to restrict Scripture rather than be restricted by it. John à Lasco, the Polish Reformer who was in England in Edward's reign, wrote a lengthy letter to Cranmer on the regulative principle in which he says near the close: "Now indeed for a long time I have hoped, and now ardently hope, to see the reasons and testimonies out of the Scriptures by which you think your opinion can be defeated. For who would not willingly embrace those views which carry less reproach rather than those which we see obviously load a man with hatreds and malice and suspicions of various kinds."[49]

In later years men who held the regulative principle were frequently to be harried and persecuted by the less spiritual successors of Cranmer and Ridley, while Catholics and godless parsons were left in peace.

4. The regulative principle is essentially a uniting principle amongst Christians, for as far as it is truly applied, it puts away all man-appointed practice and promotes a common concern to give allegiance to Scripture alone. Far from being a divisive principle, says Owen, "it is easily demonstrable that without the admittance of it, as to its substance and principal end, all peace and agreement among churches are utterly impossible."[50]

While it was not given to Christians of the Presbyterial and Independent persuasions in the seventeenth century to conclude all the difficulties connected with a scriptural Church polity, their common acceptance of the regulative principle led them to a wide measure of agreement on many issues which would otherwise have been impossible, and there is good reason to believe that with an adherence to the same principle Christians may yet be given further light on Scripture to bring us through the hazards which troubled the Puritan movement in the 1640s.

5. While the regulative principle will always arouse controversy in this world, its main force is not to make men controversialists but God-fearing. Man's life is not, says Cartwright, "as the days of an oak," it is but a mere mortal span shut in by the narrow boundaries of birth and death. We are not here then to spend

our brief lives in a strife of words; but if we profess this principle, we must look to God alone, stand in awe at His Word, serve Him in obedience to His statutes, and pray that as His "commandment is exceeding broad" so may we by Christ's Word dwelling richly in us, be taught an increasing conformity to all His revealed will. For *"Then shall I not be ashamed, when I have respect unto all thy commandments"* (Ps. 119:6). This was the essential spirit of Puritanism: may God restore such grace to His Church today!

3

CHARLES HADDON SPURGEON: PREACHER

D. M. Whyte

The *Times* reviewer, in a sympathetic assessment of C. H. Spurgeon's republished autobiography *The Early Years,* began his review with this paragraph:

"It is odd that when lists of eminent Victorians are drawn up the name of Spurgeon rarely figures in the first six. Yet he was Victorian if ever there was one, not merely in his life span (1834–92) but also in his outlook and gifts. He was one of the most dramatic and voluble figures of that dramatic and voluble age. He could more consistently command a great audience than Mr. Gladstone. He became a butt for the smart humorists; his fame lingered long after his death. Yet to describe his impact at this remove of time and to discern its effect would defeat any but a most meticulous social historian."

Spurgeon's Career

Charles H. Spurgeon was born at Kelvedon, Essex, on June 19, 1834, and died at Mentone in southern France on January 31, 1892. Though but fifty-eight when he died, he had preached for forty years to immense audiences. His sermons were printed from the beginning and read all over the world.

Spurgeon was brought up in Calvinistic circles and from his early years was accustomed to read the Puritans. At Newmarket in a school where he was an usher, Spurgeon declares: "I had the first lessons in theology from an old cook. . . . There are some Christian people who taste, and see, and enjoy religion in their own souls, and who get at a deeper knowledge of it than books can ever give them, though they should search all their days." He preached his first sermon in a cottage at Teversham, near Cambridge, when a boy of sixteen, and a tutor in the school of his former master, Mr. Leeding. Speaking about this period Spurgeon writes, "I was for three years a Cambridge man, though I never entered the University. I could not have obtained a degree, because I was a Nonconformist." (The Act of Uniformity of 1662 had excluded Nonconformists from the Universities, and this prohibition was not repealed until 1871). He went on—"Moreover, it was a better thing for me to pursue my studies under an admirable scholar and tender friend, and to preach at the same time. I was, by my tutors' own expressed verdict, considered to be sufficiently proficient in my studies to have taken a good place on the list had the way been open. 'You could win in a canter' said he to me."

He was from 1852 to 1854 pastor of the Baptist congregation at Waterbeach, near Cambridge. From there, to the sorrow of his greatly increased country flock, he was called to the pastorate of the Baptist congregation at New Park Street, Southwark, London. His two years in Waterbeach were amongst the happiest and most fruitful of his ministry. Looking back from the eminence of his latter years he could write: "There are times without number in which I have wished that I could become the pastor of some little country church, with two or three hundred hearers, over whose souls I could watch with incessant care."

His success at New Park Street was immediate and phenomenal. The place was crowded and an extension to the old building became necessary. While it was being enlarged, he preached in Exeter Hall in the Strand, to vast and overflowing congregations. When this enlargement failed to provide the accommodation necessary—it was in Spurgeon's own words "attempting to put the sea into a teapot"—the decision was taken to build a new and larger church. The congregation returned to Exeter Hall on Sunday evenings. But when the proprietors of Exeter Hall intimated that they were unable to let that building to one congregation continuously, Spurgeon chose to take the Surrey Music Hall—"a place the Lord prepared for us." Here he ministered for three years, his congregation numbering at times ten thousand.

Disaster marked the beginning of his ministry in the Surrey Music Hall: a disaster sufficient to have destroyed a lesser man, certainly one who relied upon "the arm of flesh alone." An unscrupulous group (eyewitnesses indicate that it was a concerted effort) raised the cry of fire during the prayer. In the panic that ensued, which however was kept to the minimum by the masterfulness of Spurgeon, seven people lost their lives, and Spurgeon was led from the pulpit "as one dead."

For a fortnight he was beside himself with grief and despair, until suddenly while walking in the garden of the house of one of his deacons with his wife Susannah, she tells us, "he turned to me, and with the old sweet light in his eyes said, 'Dearest, how foolish I have been! Why! what does it matter what becomes of me, if the Lord shall be glorified?' and he repeated with eagerness and intense earnestness Philippians 2:9–11, 'Wherefore God has highly exalted Him, and given him a name which is above every name: That at the name of Jesus every knee should bow, of things in heaven, and things in earth, and things under the earth; And that every tongue should confess that Jesus Christ is Lord, to the glory of God the Father.' 'If Christ be exalted,' he said, and his face glowed with Holy fervour, 'let Him do as He pleases with me.' "

While Spurgeon and his officers were exonerated from blame by the Coroner's Court, the attacks of the popular press increased, and his wife averred that "he carried the scars of that conflict to his dying day," and one of his biographers writes: "A depression complex deepened upon him, from which he never recovered."

In 1861 the Metropolitan Tabernacle in Newington Butts, a site chosen by Spurgeon because of its association with the martyrs of the Reformation, was opened. Here Spurgeon ministered until his death. From the first it was attended by crowds. No fewer than seven thousand persons constituted the normal congregation. A church of more than five thousand members, an orphanage, almshouses, a theological college, and a colportage association were built up, and all the institutions were maintained with full and growing efficiency till the great preacher's death. Indeed, they exist to this day, and if not to the same extent, still notably contribute to the life and witness of the Church. William Robertson Nicoll, an erudite admirer of Spurgeon, has said of his labors: "There is no doubt that his life was shortened by the tremendous weight of his labors and responsibilities. There have been few men whose death moved so profoundly all sections of the British people."

In the light of this brief resumé of Spurgeon's life we may well share the reviewer's puzzlement at the neglect of Spurgeon, and the apparent eclipse of his influence for the twentieth century.

The Preacher's Influence

The reviewer himself offers one explanation for this: "Spurgeon was so much the apotheosis of his age that he has failed to retain any significance." In other words, the *Zeitgeist* has so changed that Spurgeon can mean nothing to this generation. The reviewer concludes: "The whole of this volume, with its unabating concern for the Bible, for salvation, for Divine judgment in matters great and small, will strike oddly on most minds today."

Another suggestion offers itself for consideration, all the more forcefully because both in reading Spurgeon's story and assenting to his theological understanding one must conclude with Scripture that "the natural man," whether of the nineteenth, first, or twentieth centuries, "receiveth not the things of the Spirit of God."

What was Spurgeon? He was first and foremost a preacher of the Gospel. In a letter written in September 1853 to his uncle, who had invited him to preach at Stambourne, he writes "I am yours to serve to the utmost; not on the Sabbath, but all the week. I have a good sphere of labour here, but I want to do more, if possible. There is a great field, and the labourers must work with all their might. I often wish I were in China, India or Africa, so that I might preach, preach, preach all day long. It would be sweet to die preaching." In a sermon delivered in New Park Street Chapel in August 1855, on the text "For though I preach the gospel, I have nothing to glory of, for necessity is laid upon me; yea, woe is unto me, if I preach not the gospel!" (1 Cor. 9:16), he was clearly voicing a conviction about his own ministry when he declared: "If a man be truly called of God to the ministry, I will defy him to withhold himself from it. A man who has really within him the inspiration of the Holy Ghost calling him to preach cannot help it. He must preach. . . . He will feel that he must preach among the nations the unsearchable riches of Christ."

More than one preacher has been denominated "the Prince of Preachers," but none with more justice than Spurgeon. J. C. Carlile, the biographer of Spurgeon, having listed a number of outstanding preachers of Spurgeon's day, including Joseph Parker of the City Temple and Liddon of St. Paul's, concludes: "But there, like a lonely Alpine peak, was Spurgeon, with a glory all his own."

Herein lies the explanation of the Spurgeon enigma. The preacher's effect is immediate. To exert an influence upon succeeding generations the preacher must be a theologian as well as a preacher, as was John Calvin; or an ecclesiastical statesman as well as a preacher, as was John Knox. Significantly, we may note that while George Whitefield was immeasurably the greatest *preacher* of the Evangelical Revival in the eighteenth century, John Wesley, the teacher and organizer, has left more of a mark upon succeeding generations. Equally significantly for our study is the fact that Spurgeon himself declared: "My own model, if I may have such a thing in due subordination to my Lord, is George Whitefield."

The preaching office is not belittled by this understanding.

The Church of God is given, in the Divine Providence, but few formative theologians and ecclesiastical statesmen. She is, however, given an apostolic succession of preachers of the Gospel. The greatest of them, "in due subordination to the Lord," may be succeeding preachers' models.

Spurgeon ideally serves the present generation of preachers as a model. The principles of preaching remain unchanged; only the application differs. Spurgeon exemplifies the principles. The Evangelical preacher finds in him one who in the rising flood of liberal theology, in the words of J. C. Carlile, "stood unflinching as a rock against the incoming tide," and "served the new generation by keeping his feet upon solid foundations."

Spurgeon's Conversion

Our profitable task, is, therefore, to consider Charles Haddon Spurgeon the Preacher. The old adage, "preachers are not made but born," finds support in Spurgeon's case. His case argues well the fruitfulness of the godly home, and the reality of the covenant assurance that "the promise is to you and to your children." His father, John, and grandfather, James, with whom he spent his earliest years, were Independent ministers. But he could trace his ancestry back to the beginnings of Dissent, and he writes of one in 1677, "a namesake, and perhaps an ancestor, Job Spurgeon, of Dedborn," who "had to suffer both in purse and person for the testimony of a good conscience," and concludes: "There is a sweet fitness in the passing of a holy loyalty from grandsire to father, and from father to son. I like to feel I serve God 'from my fathers.' "

Birth in a godly home was no substitute for the new birth into the Heavenly Father's kingdom. It is one of the unexplained mysteries of Spurgeon that while he was from birth surrounded by the spiritual care and devotion of godly parents and grandparents, to which he bears glowing testimony in his autobiography, where he writes, "I was privileged with godly parents, watched with jealous eyes, scarcely ever permitted to mingle with questionable associates, warned not to listen to anything profane or licentious, and taught the way of God from my youth up," it was in a Primitive Methodist Chapel, under the ministry of "a very thin looking man, a shoemaker, or tailor, or something of that sort, who went up into the pulpit to preach because the minister did not come that morning," that he was converted. The text of life was Isaiah 45:22, "Look unto me, and be ye saved, all the ends of the earth." The decisive challenge was conveyed in the shouted words, "Young man, look to Jesus Christ. Look! look! look! You have nothing to do but to look and live." Upon which Spurgeon says, "I saw at once the way of salvation." The date of this life-changing experience was January 6, 1850.

That he was more than the child of a godly home, and one singularly marked out by temperament and Divine providence for the Lord's service, is evidenced by the surprising independence and conviction of the young convert. It should be remembered that at this time he was not above sixteen years old, yet he manifests a maturity of spiritual judgment equal to that of men twice his years. His parents and grandparents were Independents. He became a Baptist. He wrote to his father only a matter of weeks after his conversion, "I firmly believe and consider that baptism is a command of Christ, and shall not feel quite comfortable if I do not receive it"; and to his mother a few weeks later: "Conscience has convinced me that it is a duty to be buried with Christ in baptism, although I am sure it constitutes no part of salvation." To his father again he writes, "I have humbly to beg your consent, as I will not act against your will. . . . I have no doubt of your permission. We are all one in Christ Jesus; forms and ceremonies I trust, will not make us divided." In the same convinced but tolerant manner he tells his mother, "Grandfather has written to me; he does not blame me for being a baptist, but hopes I shall not be one of the tight-laced, strict communion sort. In that, we are agreed . . . I can, and hope I shall, be charitable to unbaptized Christians, though I think they are mistaken." In a more humorous vein in reply to his mother's quip, "Charles, I have often prayed the Lord that you might be converted, but never asked him that you might be a Baptist," he replied that the Lord had answered her with His usual bounty and had given her more than she asked.

So early Spurgeon displayed that independence of judgment and integrity of spirit which was to be remarked through his long years as a preacher of the Gospel.

There is something more than sentiment in the adage "preachers are born and not made." Of them it can be said, as Scripture says of Jeremiah, "Before I formed thee in the belly, I knew thee; and before thou camest forth out of the womb I sanctified thee, and ordained thee a prophet unto the nations" (Jer. 1:5), and as Paul the Apostle testifies, the preacher may say, "God separated me from my mother's womb, and called me by his grace, to reveal his Son in me, that I might preach him among the Gentiles" (Gal. 1:15).

Spurgeon's Gifts

This providential preparing of the preacher's life is nowhere better seen than in the physical and mental equipment that God provided for his servant Charles Haddon Spurgeon. He was pre-eminently equipped to be a minister of the Gospel of divine grace. In physical appearance, Principal Tulloch tells us, "he is certainly not interesting in face or figure—very fat and podgy; but there is no doubt about the fellow, look as he may." Another writer says of him, "his figure is awkward, his manners plain, and his face except when illumined by a smile, admittedly heavy." His biographer J. C. Carlile, describing the appearance of Spurgeon in the pulpit, tells us that "the countenance heavy and uninteresting, became changed, and the dull sleepy eyes lit up until they glowed and burned." Adding to these accounts the almost constant physical pain he suffered from headaches and rheumatic gout, we see in him a preacher who proved, with the Apostle he so admired, that God's "grace is sufficient," and His strength is made perfect in weakness, and that "God has chosen the base things of the world, and things that are despised, to bring to nought things that are: that no flesh should glory in his presence."

If there was nothing in the appearance of Spurgeon to draw an audience, there was everything in his voice. It is a unanimous testimony that his voice was both compelling and winsome. One has called it "probably the most wonderful voice God ever made." In Robertson Nicoll's judgment, it was "as clear as a silverbell, and as winning as a woman's. It filled without the slightest effort the largest building in which he preached." A remarkable story is told of its compelling power by Augustine Birrell, politician, educationalist, and author who, attending the Tabernacle, could find a seat only in the top gallery, between a woman eating an orange and a man sucking a peppermint. Finding the combined odors unbearable, he was about to leave when, he tells us, "I heard a voice, and I forgot all else." It was Spurgeon giving out the first hymn!

Spurgeon looked upon himself as a steward of God's gifts, and while endowed with so splendid an instrument for speaking forth the Savior's glory, he did not neglect the proper cultivation of the gift. All through his life he was learning to preach and thought it essential to practice such little things as emphasis, sibilants, aspirants, and final "g's." Lesser men might regard this work as unnecessary or beneath their attention, but not Spurgeon. He testified to the service rendered during the early days of his preaching at the Music Hall by an anonymous correspondent, "who used to send me," he writes, "a weekly list of my mispronunciations and other slips of speech." Showing a more than human good grace and wisdom he declares: "Possibly some young men might have been discouraged, if not irritated by such severe criticisms; but they would have been very foolish, for, in resenting such correction, they would have been throwing away a valuable aid to progress."

Mentally, Spurgeon was well endowed. He had a copious and accurate memory, "which furnished him on the instant, with the comparisons, facts and images, best calculated to throw light upon his ideas"; so wrote Dr. Grandpierre of Paris. But this gift too had been trained, and continued to be trained throughout the preacher's life. He records the early but costly efforts of his grandmother to train his memory. "My grandfather," he tells us, "was very fond of Dr. Watts' hymns, and my grandmother, wishing to get me to learn them, promised me a penny for each one that I could say to her perfectly. I found it an easy and pleasant method of earning money, and learned them so fast that grandmother said she must reduce the price to a halfpenny each and afterwards to a farthing, if she did not mean to be quite ruined by her extravagance." The profit of such an early encouragement he admits when he adds: "No matter on what topic I am preaching, I can even now, in the middle of any sermon, quote some verse of a hymn in harmony with the subject."

The notebooks to which his wife refers as the constant companions of his expeditions in later years, served to stimulate and stock his memory.

James Douglas, writing about Spurgeon's intellect, could say: "He did with ease and spontaneously, mental feats which men of name strive in vain to accomplish. He could grasp all the bearings of his subject, hold his theme in hand, and display his thoughts like troops, at the tactical moment." T. R. Glover, a critical commentator, in a series of articles in *The Times* in 1932, wrote that Spurgeon's was an "untrained mind, without discipline of ordered study." But, as we have seen, it was far from untrained, although denied the formal education of the Universities. We shall have further opportunity in a moment of assessing the range and penetration of his mental powers.

As a young man he had resolved: "I am bound to give myself to reading, and study and prayer, and not to grieve the Spirit by unthought-of effusions." "He would sit down to five or six large books, and master them at one sitting, and his memory did not fail him on what he read." In a lecture given to his students he professed his conviction about study. "Unstudied thoughts coming from the mind without previous research, without the subjects in hand having been investigated at all, must be of a very inferior quality, even from the most superior men."

Dinsdale T. Young's opinion of Spurgeon's mental power and profundity is to be preferred to Dr. Glover's. In a centenary tribute of Spurgeon he said, "I venture to cite his Down-Grade controversy in evidence of his intellectual greatness . . . Charles Haddon Spurgeon showed an intellectual power, a grasp of theology, a reasoning faculty and a luminous insight, in that controversy, which ought not to be overlooked."

The gifts God gave him were singular, but his success owes as much to his determination to be "a workman that needeth not to be ashamed" as to his gifts. He is a standing evidence of the truth of the proverb, "practice makes perfect." Men of lesser gifts will have less success than a Spurgeon, or any other equally gifted servant of God, but they need make no less use of the gifts God has given them. This is the practical conclusion to draw from his prodigious ministry.

Spurgeon's Preparation

Let us turn now to consider the use of these gifts in his preaching ministry. He was a master craftsman. A cursory study of his preparation for the pulpit might suggest that he was of the Psalmist's conviction, "My tongue is the pen of a ready writer." Nothing could be further from the truth. He saw no greater danger attending the young preacher than an indolent reliance upon verbal fluency. 'If you seek these gifts as pillows for an idle head, you will be much mistaken, for the possession of this noble power will involve you in a vast amount of labour in order to increase and retain it."

His diligence and speed in reading have already been alluded to, but a word must be said here about the range of his reading. His brother remarked, "I kept rabbits, chickens and pigs, and a horse; he kept to books." At quite an early age he became acquainted with the Puritan divines which constituted a major part of the parental library, and which were so profoundly to influence his life.

His reading, however, was catholic. His sermons and writings abound with evidence of its eclectic range. Devotional classics well known to all, such as Bunyan's *Pilgrim's Progress, The Holy War,* and Baxter's *Reformed Pastor,* shared place with lesser known works such as Edward Young's *Night Thoughts,* and the better known but unexpected devotional food of George Herbert's *The Temple.*

Ancient philosophy from the works of Plato and other Greek

philosophers had not only been read but sufficiently mastered to become part of the mental outlook of Spurgeon, and to appear allusively in the earliest of his preaching: never, perhaps, more clearly than in a youthful and immature, yet great, sermon entitled "The Immutability of God," preached from Malachi 3:6, "I am the Lord, I change not; therefore ye sons of Jacob are not consumed."

Acquaintance with the English School of skeptical philosophers is also evidenced by his references to Bacon and Hume.

The greatest of the poets also served to inform this insatiable reader. Shakespeare's plays had been thoroughly and many times read: a rather strange fact considering his marked disapproval of the theater! Milton, Tennyson, and a host of other poets were read, mastered, enjoyed, and put to divine service.

Perhaps the best evidence of the range of his theological reading is to be found in his book published for the students of the Pastor's College, entitled *Commenting and Commentaries*. He writes in the Preface: "I have toiled, and read much, and passed under review some three or four thousand volumes. From these I have compiled my catalogue, rejecting many yet making a very varied selection." It is a measure of the care and discriminating judgment of Spurgeon that the catalogue will still serve the student.

His reading was generally innocent of any special objective, homiletical or otherwise. His aim was simply to "fill the cask and keep it full" (so comments Richard Ellsworth Day). It was this, no doubt, which enabled him to preach extemporaneously, as he declares he did regularly at his Monday evening prayer meetings; and with such apparent ease at all times. "When standing up, on such occasions, my mind makes a review, and enquires, 'What subject has already occupied my thought during the day? What have I met in my reading during the past week? What is most laid upon my heart at this hour?'" But he adds, "It is no use to rise before an assembly and hope to be inspired upon subjects of which one knows nothing. . . . " However, "the thought of a man who finds himself upon his legs dilating upon a theme with which he is familiar may be very far from his first thoughts; it may be the cream of his meditations warmed by the glow of his heart."

To the extensive reading of Spurgeon must be added this

habit already alluded to, of keeping a record, in notebooks, of interesting sights and experiences which would serve him in his preaching ministry. He read widely in the books of life, as well as in the books of paper and print. Numberless sermons display the fruit of this harvest, perhaps none more notably than one entitled "There Go the Ships," preached in the Metropolitan Tabernacle in 1875 from Psalm 104:26. It begins: "I was walking the other day by the side of the sea, looking out upon the English Channel." He goes on to describe the becalmed ships, being sent on their way by a change in the wind. " 'There go the ships,' " he said, "was the exclamation that naturally rose to one's lips." He makes this a starting point for a sermon on the Christian's voyage through life, "to the port of peace." "The voyage of a ship," he writes in the course of the sermon, "on the main ocean seems to me to be an admirable picture of the life of faith."

When he was composing his written work he made great use of research. He occupied his secretaries' time with numerous visits to libraries and museums, notably the British Museum, in order to bring all into the garner house. Writing in the preface to volume 3 of *The Treasury of David,* his commentary on the Psalms, a very thesaurus of spiritual quotations, he can say: "I have never flinched from a difficulty, or spared exertion in order to make the work as complete as it lay in my power to render it, either by my own endeavors or the help of others."

What can only be called, in view of these facts, the final preparation of his pulpit work took place in the early evening of each Saturday. Having entertained friends in the afternoon, he would retire to his study at six to prepare the sermon for Sunday morning. The sermon for Sunday evening would be prepared on Sunday afternoon.

There he would sit. "I confess that I frequently sit hour after hour praying and waiting for a subject, and that this is the main part of any study; much hard labour have I spent in manipulating topics, . . . making skeletons out of verses . . . almost every Saturday of my life I prepare enough outlines of sermons to last me for a month, but I no more dare use them than an honest mariner would run ashore a cargo of contraband goods."

He writes: "My habit is to look to the Lord for guidance, and when my text comes with power to my soul I take it without hesitation; but I dare not select my own themes."

The reality and conviction of Spurgeon's preaching may be traced to this source. He says: "I am always sure to have the most happy day when I get a good text in the morning from my Master . . . ;" for so receiving it (and here surely is the secret) he delivered it, "after meditating on it for my own soul's comfort—not in the professional style of a regular sermon-maker, but feasting upon it for myself." It was then "well spoken, because well-known, well-tasted and well felt."

His wife records a remarkable instance of the preacher's preparation. Having labored all evening with a text, consulted the commentaries and the authors, he retired to bed, planning to arise early in order to complete his preparations. To his despair he awoke in the morning later than usual and remonstrating with his wife was presented with an outline of the sermon he had been seeking to prepare, which he had delivered in his sleep, and his wife had taken down. The indebtedness of preachers to their wives seems to be without end!

The fruit of this preparation was set out in note form on half a sheet of ordinary note paper, possibly overflowing to the other side of the sheet. An example may be seen in *The Early Years*.[1] "Then," says Fullerton, "he went to the pulpit with the assurance that he would be able to clothe his ideas appropriately at the moment, many of his illustrations coming to him during the delivery of the sermon."

That the preparation and preaching of his sermons demanded sweat, blood, and tears is sufficiently illustrated from what has preceded. Preaching was a dual office, one of labor and one of joy. This duality is noted in a comment on the inside back cover of the second volume of his manuscript, sermon outlines, given in facsimile in *The Early Years*—"Better is the end of life than the beginning. Better the end of labour than the starting. These sketches are so many proofs of the power of faith. By faith I got them. They are evidences of God's love—for oft have they come just at the moment when had they tarried, I had been undone.

Blessed be God—for making men so much his darlings as to let them speak His Word."

Spurgeon in Action

We must now follow Spurgeon into the pulpit and seek to see the master craftsman, his preparatory labors behind him, present the message he believes the Lord has given him to the assembled thousands. Prayer has not been mentioned as part of that preparation, not because it was neglected but rather because his preparation was the preparation of himself. This was prayer. W. Fullerton tells us that "if we look into the inner life of this man of God, we shall not find Spurgeon often on his knees; and that not because he did not pray, but because he prayed incessantly." For most men, we imagine, it is in private prayer that they draw nearest to God. Not so Spurgeon, if the testimony of Fullerton is to be believed, for he writes again: "He told me himself that he never got so near to God as on the Tabernacle platform when he prayed." Perhaps it was because, as his wife tells us, he greatly valued the season of devotion in the half-hour before commencing the service that he stood so close to the throne of God on the Tabernacle platform.

Prayer sustained his ministry and whatever success attended it Spurgeon ascribed to prayer. When asked for an explanation of his phenomenal success, he would frequently reply: "My people pray for me." He bore testimony to the power of united prayer when he asked, looking back on the days of revival, "Shall we ever forget Park Street, those prayer meetings when I felt compelled to let you go without a word from my lips because the Spirit of God was so awfully present that we felt bowed to the dust?"

So Spurgeon would stand to lead the worship of God's people, and to set before them the Word of God: a man ready for the task because prepared by labor and prayer for this divinely appointed service.

Reading the varied accounts of his preaching, we may remark upon its outward form and its inner impulse: the former being always kept to the command of the latter.

A report from the *Evening Star* describes his manner thus: "There never was a popular orator who did not talk more and better with his arms than with his tongue. Mr. Spurgeon knows this instinctively. When he has read his text, he does not fasten his eye on the manuscript, and his hands on a cushion. As soon as he begins to speak, he begins to act."[2] Another report balances that description, when it tells us: "His manner was perfectly unrestrained but not irreverent."

All, even his detractors, unite in describing his language as simple, plain, and Anglo-Saxon. A scathing critic, J. Ewing Ritchie, at the end of a tirade of denunciation is obliged to confess: "He preaches to the people in a homely style and they like it, for he is always plain and never dull."

The editor of the sermons, F. W. Robertson, of Brighton, commends the pulpit language of Spurgeon by quoting the letter of a friend who wrote to him: "Mr. Spurgeon and his vulgar slang(!) is a violent reaction from the cold, unfelt conventionalities with which men have grown so familiar, . . . he recognizes the men and women before him as flesh and blood."

If the preacher's language was plain and simple, it was not that he was dealing with trivial subjects. He served no slops to his hearers, but good, strong, red meat. But he endeavored to make the message clear in both language and structure. One never goes very far in a Spurgeon sermon without coming to his plan of campaign. The main divisions, very often three, as with Simeon, but not exclusively or even mostly so, were set before his audience, crystallized into a single phrase or sentence. They then knew what he intended, by God's grace, to teach them in that sermon. This homiletic lesson he learned, he tells us, from a youthful experience of following a fox-hunt with a shopping-basket. When upon reaching home, he found "all the goods amalgamated—tea, mustard and rice in one sorry mess, I understood the necessity of packing my subject in good stout parcels, bound round with the thread of my discourse; and this makes me keep to firstly, secondly, and thirdly, however unfashionable the method may now be."

The humorous side of Spurgeon, a matter of some comment both from his admirers and detractors, served the same homiletic purpose. His aim was always to hold the attention of his hearers in order that they might pay attention to the Word of God. Thus in the course of a series of lectures, published under the title *Eccentric Preachers,* he declared: "All these eccentric preachers"—he had discussed Latimer, Hill, John Berridge, and Billy Bray, amongst others—"were in downright earnest, and because they were so their humour sometimes comes to the front." Humor, like any other manner of speech, was not to be used as an end in itself, but as a means of serving truth. He goes on: "Had these men been triflers with holy things, or jesters upon sacred topics, they would have been worthy of all the censure which has been poured upon them"; but this was not their spirit at all, any more than it was Spurgeon's own. And when men are in earnest, natural and unforced touches of humor will help to make their words stick in the mind and the conscience. All attractive and memorable forms of speech are in fact grist to the preacher's mill. For "men are so careless about all matters of their souls that we have not only to preach to them, but to induce them to hear us. A great part of our labour lies in seeking out attractive illustrations, parables, and choice sayings, by which we may coax men to attend to their own interests; and even then we fail unless a higher power intervenes."

We may not pass from a consideration of Spurgeon's oratorical techniques without noting his dramatic power. Passages abound in his sermons which display his mastery of living description. It was as if he saw before him the very scene he describes. One passage of Scripture that lends itself to high dramatic presentation, yet is most susceptible to pathos, is the story of Noah and the Flood. But listen, or rather see, in this passage from his sermon "The Sin of Unbelief," how Spurgeon, trembling on the brink of the ludicrous and melodramatic, still leaves one haunted by a vision of the majesty and the terror of judgment. "Hark, unbeliever, dost thou not hear that rumbling noise? Earth's bowels have begun to move, her rocking ribs are strained by dire convulsions from within; lo! they break with the enormous strain, and forth from between them torrents rush, unknown since God concealed them in the bosom of our world. Heaven is split in sunder! It rains. Not drops, but clouds descend. A cataract like that of old Niagara, rolls from Heaven with mighty noise. Both firmaments, both deeps—the deep below and the deep above—do clasp their hands. Now unbelievers, where are you now? There is your last remnant. A man—his wife clasping him round the waist—stands on the last summit that is above the water. See him there? The water is up to his loins even now. Hear his last shriek! He is floating—he is drowned. And as Noah looks from the ark he sees nothing. Nothing! It is a void of profound. Sea monsters whelp and stable in the palaces of kings. All is over-thrown, covered, drowned. What hath done it? What brought the flood upon the earth? Unbelief. By faith Noah escaped from the flood. By unbelief the rest were drowned."

Conviction and Compassion

There were other men in Spurgeon's day as bountifully provided with oratorical gifts. He had, however, "a glory all his own," seen not in the form but in the spirit of his preaching. He was a *convinced* man. He wrote: "Some people have received twenty different 'gospels' in as many years, . . . I thank God that he early taught me the Gospel, and I have been so perfectly satisfied with it, that I do not want to know another."

This conviction breathed in the words he preached. An anonymous writer, in a pamphlet entitled *Why So Popular? An Hour with Rev. C. H. Spurgeon,* wrote: "If I cannot discover the secret of your popularity in what you preach, can I find it in any peculiarity in your mode of preaching? That is in my judgment, the explanation of the secret. You have strong faith, and, as a result, *intense earnestness.*"

Bound by his conviction of the truth of his message, he was moved by the compassion he felt for sinners. The two sentiments are found together in these words, taken from a sermon: "It will be the height of my ambition to be clear of the blood of all men. If, like George Fox, I can say in dying, 'I am clear, I am clear,' that would be all the heaven I could wish for."

For Spurgeon, the passion for souls was a mark of a man's call to preach the Gospel. "Two things are absolutely requisite to make a man a preacher: 1. special gifts; 2. a special call," he wrote. But we may well ask, how may a man know he is called? His next words answer the implied question. "No college, no bishop, no human ordination, can make a man a minister; but he who can feel as did Bunyan, Whitefield, Berridge, or Rowland Hill, the strugglings of an impassioned longing to win the souls of men, may hear in the air the voice of God saying, 'Son of Man, I have made thee a watchman.'"

Hear him now pleading and persuading his congregation in a sermon entitled "Return, Return":

> O dear hearts, what can be your hindrance in trusting the Saviour? What is it that keeps some of you away from Christ? I do try to put the Gospel so plainly and simply that all may understand it. I have had it said to me, lately, I dare say a dozen times, by persons in spiritual trouble who have come many a mile to see me. . . . "Nobody has encouraged and helped us as you have by your sermons; you seemed as if you did not want to put any of us back, but as if you longed to bring us all to the Saviour; and that is why we have come to see you." Well, now I think they would not have said that so often if it had not been true. I do not frighten you away from Christ, at least I do not mean to do so, I would much rather beckon you to come to Him."

In his autobiography he frankly discloses his passion for souls. "When I first began to preach at Waterbeach my first concern was, Would God save any souls through me? . . . How my heart leaped for joy when I heard tidings of my first convert! . . . A poor labouring man's wife . . . she was the first seal upon my ministry, and a very precious one." In the same passage of the autobiography he extols the preacher's office and the eternal consequences of his work. "I would rather be the means of saving a soul from death than the greatest orator in the world. I would rather bring the poorest woman in the world to the feet of Jesus than I would be made Archbishop of Canterbury. I would sooner pluck one single brand from the burning than explain all mysteries. . . . Oh what bliss it will be to fly to heaven, and to have a multitude of converts before and behind, and, on entering the glory to be able to say, 'Here am I, Father, and the children thou has given me.'"

The source of this compassion was his deep communion with Christ. Robertson Nicoll says of him: "He is one of the very few English preachers who have been at once popular and at the same time imbued with the very spirit of the mystics." We would concur with that judgment to the extent that Spurgeon was aware, with the mystics, of a living, all-embracing Deity. But it was "the God and Father of our Lord Jesus Christ" in whose presence he lived, and mysticism, either as a world-renouncing system of discipline and devotion which seeks on earth the beatific vision, or as a unifying concept held to underlie the many religions of the world, was completely foreign to Spurgeon's mind.

Writing in an apologetic work of very great value, Spurgeon dwells on the immanence of God's transcendence. (Incidentally, how unenlightened, one is almost tempted to use the word illiterate, are those modern theologians who find obstacles to faith in the metaphors of transcendence!) For Spurgeon "God was out there" but was also "a God down here." He writes: "Trusting in God, we are not exercising a dreamy dependence upon a far away and inactive power." Later he adds: "The line between things secular and sacred is imaginary and mischievous. We believe God for time as well as for eternity, for earth as well as for heaven, for the body as well as for the soul." And again: "At home in our Father's house everything communes with us of his Glory. . . . It was no wonder that a great saint called the birds his "sisters," for we seem akin to all that comes of our Maker's hand." "Nature to him (the Christian) is but a name for an effect whose cause is God. He perceives God everywhere, even the God of Gethsemane and the Cross.

> One Spirit—His
> Who wore the plaited thorns with bleeding brows
> Rules universal nature.
> Faith floods the universe with Deity by revealing that
> unbounded Presence which is evermore its life, its bliss.

This was to Spurgeon a deeply personalized experience, beginning with the knowledge of Jesus Christ received in conversion and growing in ever increasing reality throughout his Christian life. Hear him again: "I bear witness that never servant had such a Master as I have, never brother had kinsman such as He has been to me; never spouse had such a husband as Christ has been to my soul; never sinner a better Saviour, never Soldier a better Captain; never mourner a better Comforter than Christ hath been to my spirit. I want none beside Him. In life He is my life, and in death He shall be the death of death; in poverty Christ is my riches, in sickness he makes my bed; in darkness He is my star, and in brightness He is my Sun. By faith I understand that the blessed Son of God redeemed my soul by His own heart's blood, and by sweet experience I know that He raised me up from the pit of dark despair and set my feet on the rock. He died for me. This is the root of every satisfaction I have. He put all my transgressions away."

We have seen something of Spurgeon the Preacher. In order not to distort the picture it is necessary at least to mention his pastoral concern. He was never content merely to preach. His youthful concern about tract distribution to cottagers in Cambridges; his division of the city into districts each with an elder in charge of its pastoral administration; the provision of the Almshouses, the Orphanage, and the Pastors' College, each give evidence of his pastoral concern.

His wife tells us that Tuesday evenings were set aside by him for attending the Tabernacle, in order to deal with the numbers of people needing his pastoral counsel and prayer.

A Servant of the Word

It is impossible in a paper of this nature and length to do more than indicate the outstanding features of Spurgeon's life and ministry. As he aimed at an "All Round Ministry," even this is an exacting task, and one in which we shall inevitably fail to say all that should be said. We must, however, endeavor in this concluding portion of the paper to say something about the subject-matter of Spurgeon's preaching.

Spurgeon was a man of many books but a preacher of one book, the Bible. "To find a sure foothold somewhere," he wrote, "men have tried to rest in an infallible Church, or in their own supposed infallible reason . . . we prefer to cast our anchor once and for all in an infallible revelation." He is not obscurantist, for he writes, "Between the revelation of God in His Word and that in His works, there can be no actual discrepancy. Between the interpretation of the works and the interpretation of the Word, there may be great differences. We have never held the doctrine of the Infallibility of Scripturists." But men need knowledge in order to have faith. "However willing a man may be to put his trust in God, his faith must largely depend upon his knowledge. How can knowledge be gained? Can we go from Nature's God? Perhaps. But it would be a far more effective business if Nature's God would come down to us and be His own Expositor." Spurgeon believed that God had done this. In an early sermon he declared: "This volume is the writing of the living God: each letter was penned with an Almighty finger; each word dropped from the everlasting lips, each sentence was dictated by the Holy Spirit."

It was the preacher's responsibility, therefore, as Spurgeon advised his students, to ensure that his "sermons should have real teaching in them, and their doctrine should be solid, substantial and abundant."

This necessarily involves the preacher in expository preaching. In his work *Commenting and Commentaries,* Spurgeon sanctions other forms of preaching but extols expository preaching and commenting above all. "Since topical preaching, hortatory preaching, experimental preaching, and so on—all exceedingly useful in their way—have almost pushed proper expository preaching out of place, there is more need that we should, when we read passages of Holy Writ, habitually give running comment upon them."

Spurgeon practiced what he preached. His sermons abound with teaching. He stresses the necessity of presenting the whole counsel of God—but insists that "those truths which are not vital to the soul's salvation, nor even essential to practical Christianity, are not to be considered upon every occasion of worship. . . . "

"One great master theme is the good news from heaven, tidings of mercy through the atoning death of Jesus, mercy to the chief of sinners upon their believing in Jesus."

In the later volumes of *The Metropolitan Tabernacle Pulpit,* a textual index is given. Humility and conviction overcomes any preacher reading it; he discovers that while the published sermons of Spurgeon account for only one third of his output, the *Index* for 1888, for example, reveals that at that time the only book that had not been preached upon, and presumably expounded, was 2 John. Almost every chapter of the Bible had been the subject of a sermon by the time Spurgeon's ministry ended. The Psalms in the Old Testament, and John's Gospel in the New Testament, supplied most sermon matter. Isaiah was apparently his favorite prophet, Romans his favorite Epistle, with the Song of Solomon and Hebrews minor favorites.

Eulogy may have appeared to be the purpose of this paper. Such was not our intention; we have simply attempted to recount the facts of Spurgeon's faith and preaching, and let them speak for themselves. But in any case, let us now redress the balance a little.

Spurgeon often sinned against his own canons of preaching The published sermons manifest a very varied quality and value. In some he has clearly attempted too much, and has had to neglect part of his message. Some, and those among the most favored, may be judged to transgress the rules of homiletics which he himself laid down.

Is the text in John 20:15 which furnished the title of his famous discourse, "Supposing him to be the gardener," anything more than a pretext in the way in which Spurgeon uses it? He tells us the aim of his sermon thus: "We shall not make a mistake if we now indulge ourselves in a quiet meditation upon our ever-blessed Lord, supposing him to be the gardener.

> We are a garden walled around,
> Chosen and made peculiar ground."

The same judgment might be passed on the sermon already alluded to, "There Go the Ships," preached from Psalm 104:26. All that Spurgeon teaches in the sermon is scriptural, no doubt, but it certainly did not come out of that text. It is interesting to note that these two sermons are among those chosen by Spurgeon and revised by him for inclusion in the series, "Preachers of the Age," under the title *Messages for the Multitudes.* To commit the very error we have been censuring in Spurgeon, however, we may say of these blemishes, "What are they among so many?", compared with the great mass of pure and profitable expositions of God's Word which the published volumes of sermons contain.

Spurgeon's Puritanism

Now we turn to matters which could, and properly should, serve as single Spurgeon studies in their own right—his Puritanism, controversialism, and Calvinism.

As we saw, Spurgeon grew up in Puritanism. It gave him his first theological reading. Puritan divinity was a life-long love, and source of inspiration. His library, full of Puritan divines, twelve thousand volumes in all, amongst them many first editions, was tragically allowed to be bought and transported to America to the William Jewell College, in Liberty, Missouri, in 1905.

The following opinion of Spurgeon's Puritanism is given in Fullerton's biography: "He was the one teacher of the century whose mind was steeped in Puritan ideas, theology and literature. In fact this remarkable man knew more about Puritanism than any of the Puritans themselves. . . . His mind was early surrendered to the Puritan hermeneutics, and all his homiletic power was modified by the impress of the medieval mould." The writer concludes critically, "He never emancipated his intellect from the fascination exercised over him by Charnock, and Owen, and Coles."

This is saying more than Spurgeon would allow. He writes, "Believing that the Puritan school embodied more of Gospel truth in it than any other since the days of the Apostles, we continue in the same line of things." It was to him the Gospel, not the Puritan tradition as such that was authoritative.

He was not a party man. He would as well disagree with Puritan writers as any others if they appeared to be at variance with Scripture. Listen to his judgment on certain Puritans whom he took to be insisting on a title to Faith in Christ, other than the simple command of God to believe, and thereby to be establishing works-righteousness. "Some preachers in the Puritan times, whose shoe latchets I am not worthy to unloose, erred much in this matter. I refer not merely to Alleyne and Baxter, who are far better preachers of the Law than of the Gospel, but I include men far sounder in the faith than they, such as Roger of Dedham, Shepherd, the author of *The Sound Believer* and especially the American, Thomas Hooker, who has written a book upon qualifications for coming to Christ." The whole sermon, "The Warrant of Faith," an early one preached in 1863, shows his independence of mind and integrity of spirit.

Next to the theological content of Spurgeon's Puritanism, which will be considered when we deal with his Calvinism, we see Puritan influence most markedly in his moral concern. He was a preacher of righteousness. His moral concern shows itself in many sermons. Let us take one at random, "All or Nothing," or "Compromises Refused," preached in 1886, from five texts. Here are typical quotations. "Do not imagine the work is accomplished" (he is talking about the relation of conversion to final salvation). "Our blessed Master has to fight for every inch of ground which he wins in the human heart." Again—"Yes, says the Devil, you must be a Christian, that is evident. . . . But, says he, stop in the world and be a Christian. . . . Trust yourself with Christ and then indulge yourself in whatsoever your heart desires. Do you not know he is a Saviour of Sinners? . . . Oh I charge you, by the living God, never be duped by such a treacherous lie as this, for it is not possible that you can find any rest or salvation while you live in sin."

Spurgeon opposes antinomianism and perfectionism, preaching progressive sanctification. Without this, he says, one must question the reality of faith. He writes: "While I am fully persuaded that perfection is utterly impossible to any man beneath the sky, I feel equally sure that, to every believer, future perfection is certain beyond a doubt. . . . 'The Lord will perfect that which concerneth me.'"

Spurgeon the Controversialist

Controversy played a great part in Spurgeon's ministry. To it he attributed, under the providence of God, the popularity of his early days. It would however be false to suggest that he used controversy for this end. But because he was made the object of bitter attack, the crowds went to hear him, and once hearing him, many returned to hear him again.

Our concern must be with the major controversial issue rather than Spurgeon's smaller battles such as that over baptismal regeneration. "By the time Spurgeon had reached his early fifties the threat to Evangelicalism could no longer be ignored. He sounded a vigorous alarm; and his so doing marked his entry upon the last and not least important stage of his great career": so writes E. J. Poole-Connor. Mrs. Spurgeon was of the opinion that this final controversy cost him his life, for he was a sick man when he engaged in it.

Shortly, the story of the controversy begins in 1887, when Dr. Booth, Secretary of the Baptist Union, wrote to Spurgeon to ask his advice about the heterodox preaching and publications of men who belonged to the Union. Then, in Spurgeon's monthly magazine, *The Sword and Trowel,* a series of articles appeared lamenting the declension from the faith. The Rev. R. Shindler, of the Pastors' College, was the author. Next, Spurgeon defended the position taken up, in four articles on "The Down Grade" in August, September, October, and November 1887. The title is taken from a phrase in one of the articles. The "Down Grade" was only the end of a long series of disturbing incidents. The editors of *The Early Years* can entitle a chapter—"The Down-grade Foreshadowed."

Spurgeon desired the Union to make a clear-cut statement of faith, in which it would endorse the fundamentals of thc Reformed position. He suggested the statement of faith of the Evangelical Alliance might well serve.

But satisfaction could not be gained. Booth refused Spurgeon permission to publish his correspondence in which evidence was given of heterodox opinions. The Council of the Union refused to face the issues raised, burking—as seems to be endemic in decent Protestantism—the question of discipline.

In October 1887 Spurgeon resigned from the Union, writing to Booth, "I do this with the utmost regret but I have no choice. The reasons are set forth in the Sword and Trowel for November and I trust you will excuse me repeating them here. I beg you not to send anyone to me to ask for reconsideration. I fear I have considered too long already."

From the controversy, when all the facts are known, Spurgeon emerges with his character enhanced. It cannot, however, be said that his reputation as a controversialist was increased. The four articles referred to rather reveal his weakness in this role.

The strength of the heterodox position was its reliance upon a "scientific" literary approach to the Bible. Now Spurgeon refused to meet the challenge on this ground. As early as 1855 he had indicated his position on this matter when preaching on "The Bible." He asks the unbeliever's question, "How do you know that God wrote the book?" and says, "That is just what I shall not try to prove to you." Later in the same paragraph, he says: "there is never any necessity for Christian ministers to make a point of bringing forth infidel arguments in order to answer them. It is the greatest folly in the world."

Spurgeon no doubt has much on his side in taking the higher ground of the inspiration of Scripture, endorsed by the authority of Christ as his strongest argument. At least it should have carried weight with those who professed to be Christians. But it is surely necessary, even from within the walls of the strong fortress, to be ready to throw down the siege ladders with which the enemy seeks to scale the walls. Such a task was not beyond Spurgeon's powers, and perhaps if he had been a younger and healthier man he would have undertaken it. In particular instances of biblical interpretation he shows a fine insight which convincingly removes difficulties. But it was only in general apologetic, that he displayed his best controversial powers. Perhaps after all there is something in T. R. Glovers' opinion that his was "an untrained mind without the discipline of ordered study," if what is meant is that he lacked that thorough grounding in linguistic and literary studies that Glover himself had, and which is the necessary prerequisite of effective biblical apologetic.

Before leaving our consideration of this matter we should perhaps ask what Spurgeon thought was the right course of action for a Church or Union of Churches to take in the face of heresy.

It seems clear, to start with, that he considered a Confession of Faith to be necessary. He spoke most enthusiastically about the Westminster Confession. He caused the Baptist Confession of Faith of 1689 to be re-issued in the second year of his ministry at New Park Street, although he safeguarded the well-loved Reformation principle of private judgment in the prefatory words, "This little volume is not issued as an authoritative rule or code of faith, whereby you are to be fettered, but as an assistance to you in controversy, a confirmation in faith, and a means of edification in righteousness."

He saw strength in independency, in churches withdrawing from fellowship with Unions which, to quote his own words, "begin to look like confederacies of evil." But this was not to be taken as an occasion for founding new denominations, for, he wrote, "there are denominations enough," and "thieves and robbers would climb in."

He confidently hoped for a renaissance of Reformed teaching. "The cause of God goes on in spite of foes, and His truth is sure to conquer in the long run, however influential its opposers." He prayed for, and seemed to foresee, "a day . . . when in a larger communion than any sect all those who are one in Christ Jesus may be able to blend in manifest unity." What were the means to this happy end? "This can only come," he wrote in the last article of the four on the Down-grade, "by the way of growing spiritual life, clearer light upon the one eternal truth and a closer cleaving in all things to Him who is the Head even Christ Jesus." Can more be said or done?

Spurgeon the Calvinist

The Calvinism of Spurgeon was not book Calvinism, but experimental Calvinism. Reading the Puritans, as he had done from childhood, he was well acquainted with the theology of Calvin, but the decisive experimentally came, he tells us, "one weeknight, when I was sitting in the house of God, not thinking much about the preacher's sermon, for I did not believe it. The thought struck me, how did you become a Christian? I sought the Lord. But how did you come to seek the Lord? The truth flashed across my mind in a moment—I should not have sought Him unless there had been some previous influence in my mind to make me seek Him. I prayed, thought I, but then I asked myself how came I to pray? I was induced to pray by reading the Scriptures. How came I to read the Scriptures? I did read them, but what led me to do so? Then, in a moment, I saw that God was at the bottom of it all, and that He was the author of my faith, and so the whole doctrine of grace opened up to me, and from that doctrine I have not departed to this day, and I desire to make this my constant confession, 'I ascribe my change wholly to God.'"

From that moment Calvin cast his spell upon Spurgeon. His boast was, "I am a true Calvinist after the order of John Calvin himself, and probably I have read more of his work than any of my accusers ever did."

He admired Calvin because he believed that Calvin interpreted aright "the old Gospel." He urges his students to read Calvin; but note why: "Of all commentators I believe John Calvin to be the most candid. In his expositions he is not always what moderns would call 'Calvinistic.' That is to say, where Scripture maintains the doctrine of Predestination and Grace he flinches in no degree, but inasmuch as some Scriptures bear the impress of human free action and responsibility, he does not shun to expound their meaning in all fairness and integrity."

In two well-documented articles in *The Banner of Truth* entitled "The Forgotten Spurgeon," Iain Murray observes that while "his success as an evangelist is remembered, the theology which lay behind it is forgotten." Murray contends that it was because Arminianism was the prevalent religious outlook "and because Spurgeon stood against this that his arrival in London was looked upon with such disfavour in the religious world." Murray suggests that there was another major controversy in Spurgeon's ministry, especially at the beginning, over this matter.

I cannot concur. Not that I deny the opposition of Arminians or the prevalence of an Arminian religious outlook, although Spurgeon's own testimony was that Calvinism was very prevalent in London. Writing to his father in 1853 he affirmed: "It is Calvinism they want in London, and any Arminian preaching will not be endured." Again in 1855 he wrote, "the people are Calvinistic, and they could not get on with anything else." But in fact most of the open opposition to Spurgeon, as Murray admits, came from those most devoted to Calvinism as a system, the Hyper-Calvinists, of whom James Wells was the acknowledged leader; and Spurgeon's early battles were as much against those who made too much of Calvinism as those who denied it outright. It appears to me that the explanation of the opposition to Spurgeon in the early years is to be found not in the theological field, but rather in the moral field. It sprang chiefly from a ministerial sin which is as old as the New Testament, the tragic fault characterized by Shakespeare as "the green-eyed monster, jealousy."

If Spurgeon's Calvinism was experimental, bound up with his vision "that God was at the bottom of it all," he also held it as an intellectual system. In his sermon on "The Bible" in 1855 he points to the fundamental and vital truths of the Gospel epitomized in the well-known five points of Calvinism. "Election, according to the foreknowledge of God, the natural depravity and sinfulness of man, particular redemption by the blood of Christ, effectual calling by the power of the Spirit, and ultimate perseverance by the efforts of God's might."

Calvinism has two major difficulties for most people: one, the apparent denial of human free-will, and the other, the arbitrary choice of the elect. How does Spurgeon deal with these issues? He does not deny the doctrines, but he does not go beyond them and say more than the Scripture reveals. He denies human free-will but he asserts human responsibility. He writes, "I see, in one place, God in Providence presiding over all, and yet I see, and I cannot help seeing, that man acts as he pleases, and that God has left his actions in a great measure, to his own free-will. Now, if I were to declare that man was so free to act that there was no control of God over his actions, I would be driven very near to atheism; and if, on the other hand, I should declare that God so overrules all things that man is not free enough to be responsible I should be driven at once into Antinominism or Fatalism. That God predestines, and yet that man is responsible, are two facts that few can see clearly. They are believed to be inconsistent and contradictory, but they are not; the fault is in our weak judgement."

He preaches the sovereignty of God in the election of His Saints, but in almost every sermon appeals to all who hear him to come to the Savior. The story is surely apocryphal, but it seems to accord with Spurgeon's attitude that, as Fullerton affirms, he should on one occasion have prayed, "Lord, hasten to bring in all thine elect—and then elect some more."

Hear him again in the sermon entitled, "The Old Gospel for the New Age," marrying together the two facts of particular election and a universal invitation, as he preaches on the text, "Come unto me all ye that labour and are heavy laden, and I will give you rest." "Be it also remembered that when Christ gave this promise, he knew the number of those who were comprehended in that word 'All.' Though to us that 'All' included the multitude that no man can number, yet. 'The Lord knoweth them that are his'; and when he said, 'Come unto me, all ye that labour and are heavy laden and I will give you rest,' he did not speak without knowing that there are tens of thousands, and millions, and hundreds of millions, that labour and are heavy laden, and he meant to speak to all that vast throng when he said, 'Come *ye* to *me*, and I will give you rest.'"

At the end of one of his early sermons in New Park Street he cries, "Whosoever believeth in the Name of Jesus shall be saved."

For him, Calvinism was a term used for shortness, a useful abbreviation for the essential gospel. "That doctrine which is called Calvinism did not spring from Calvinism. We believe that it sprang from the great Founder of all truth." He would preach it and defend it for this reason: but, as he wrote to his uncle in 1855, "I wish to live in unity with every believer, whether Calvinist, Arminian (if not impossible), Churchman, Independent, or Wesleyan." In this Spurgeon is expressing not only a proper attitude for 1855 but the proper attitude for the Christians of every generation.

The question is prompted, "What would Spurgeon do if he were alive today?" An answer, I believe, can be given. He would hold to the old Faith. He was above all a man of consistency and integrity. Where his soul first cast anchor, there he would remain. We may be equally sure, however, that he would be seeking ever new and more effective ways of commending that old Faith to this new generation. His purpose as in his own life-time, would still be the exaltation of Jesus Christ. He would still exhaust his powers in extolling the glory of the Christ Who came to save. As on a previous occasion at the end of an impassioned message, he would still cry: "Let my name perish, but let Christ's name last forever, Jesus—Jesus—Jesus—Crown Him Lord of all!" And he would surely still be able to say at the end, as he did in his last words from the pulpit of the Metropolitan Tabernacle on June 7th, 1891, "Jesus Christ is the most magnanimous of Captains. There never was his like among the choicest of princes. The heaviest end of the Cross lies ever on His shoulders. If there is anything that is gracious, generous, kind, and tender, yea, lavish and superabundant in love, you always find it in Him! His service is life, peace, joy. Oh, that you would enter it at once! God help you to enlist under the Banner of Jesus Christ."

4

JOHN OWEN ON SCHISM

D. Martyn Lloyd-Jones

I am going to speak, as you have been told, on "John Owen on the subject of Schism." Why am I dealing with this? I have a number of reasons for doing so. One is, and I make no apology for this, that it is a kind of postscript to what I was trying to say last year about 1640–1662. I have not finished with that in my mind yet, and I do not think any of us should, because, as I tried to indicate then it has a great deal to say to us at the present time. We are again in a stage of transition, in an age when these great fundamental questions are thrust before us once more; and I believe that we can obtain real guidance and help from these men of three hundred years ago who had to face a similar situation.

The term *schism* was, obviously, one that was bandied about a great deal three hundred years ago. That is not at all surprising, and the term was used by all sorts of people. The Roman Catholic Church, of course, used it with respect to all Protestants, the Church of England included. Then, the Church of England began to use it with respect to the Presbyterians. And then both the Church of

83

England and the Presbyterians used it with respect to the Independents. In other words, this is a term that is almost invariably used by any church or body from whom a number go out to form a new church. It is a term that is bandied about freely and loosely, and it was because of that that John Owen took up the subject.

I call attention to it because it is already being bandied about, and we can be quite certain that if the Ecumenical Movement ever develops "the great world church" that they so delight to talk about, well then this is the term that will be hurled against everybody who refuses to be part and parcel of that mammoth organization. I feel therefore that it is our duty to prepare our own minds beforehand. Whatever may be the truth now, it will certainly be the case then that we shall be charged with schism, and it is right that we should be clear about it, and that we should instruct the people to whom we are privileged to minister concerning this all-important matter. Schism is a very great sin, it is a very serious matter. Nobody should be guilty of the sin of schism, and it is very vital therefore that we should be clear in our minds as to what exactly it is.

John Owen dealt with this subject many times. I propose to deal with the main treatises in which he did so. There is one which is just called *Of Schism*. Then he had to defend that—*A Review of the True Nature of Schism*. Then he had to answer various people who attacked him very bitterly on this subject. There is also a very interesting treatise of his called *A Brief Vindication of the Nonconformists from the Charge of Schism*. That was Owen's reply to a sermon preached by Dr. Stillingfleet, who was at that time Dean of St. Paul's and later became the Bishop of Worcester. Stillingfleet charged Nonconformists with being guilty of schism in a sermon which he preached on Philippians 3:15–16. Owen, having here a foeman worthy of his steel, and not merely a carping critic like a certain Mr. Cawdrey, a Presbyterian, who simply abused him and vilified him—produced this most interesting treatise in answer to that sermon. But then, in addition to that, there is one called *A Discourse Concerning Evangelical Love, Church Peace and Unity*. Another has the title *An Inquiry into the Origin, Nature, Institution, Power, Order, and Communion of Evangelical Churches*. Again there is

An Answer to Dr. Stillingfleet's Book of the Unreasonableness of Separation. And finally—and greater, perhaps, than all of them—was his treatise on *The Nature of a Gospel or a New Testament Church.* John Owen, you see, was very concerned about this matter because he regarded schism as being a most serious charge in view of the character of the sin involved in it.

His main object was to defend himself and the Independents from this particular charge, and as he does so, he incidentally helps to clear the Presbyterians also from the charges of the Church of England, and the Church of England in turn from the charges of the Roman Catholics. But he had a deeper motive than that; he was concerned about the truth concerning the nature of the Church. That was the thing that, ultimately, was his great concern. And that, I suggest, should be our great concern also at the present time.

I have decided that Owen himself should do the speaking, and if I can succeed somehow in conveying the spirit and the method of John Owen to you I shall be more than satisfied. With such a wealth of material, selection has been difficult, but I have tried to distill the essence of his teaching.

Owen's Approach to Schism

We start with Owen's method, his whole approach; and I am really more concerned about this than about any particular thing that he said. Owen never dealt with a problem, as it were, immediately and directly, he always put it into its context. He did not "rush" at a question that was put to him, or at a charge that was brought against him, and just answer immediately and directly with a kind of "quid pro quo." He was not interested in polemics as such, his whole nature indeed rebelled against that.

In dealing with any problem his first question always seems to have been—"Well now, what is the principle involved here? Where does this come in in the whole doctrine and teaching of the Bible? Let us settle that first." So Owen did not meet this charge of schism directly and merely in and of itself. He could hear people hurling this charge against each other, bandying it about, and each one feeling that he was right in doing so. But it was obvious on the surface that they could not all be right, because they were all bringing the charge against one another. There was something wrong therefore, and Owen came to the conclusion that it was all due to the fact that none of them had really stopped to ask the question—"How do we decide what schism is? What is our authority and what are our terms of reference?" So he turns to the Scriptures and he sees at once that certain great questions are involved.

But even before we examine his particular method, let us look at the spirit in which he approached the question. Here is no bitter partisan or narrow-minded sectarian or dry-as-dust academic theologian. Out of his heart he writes,

> I confess I would rather, much rather, spend all my time and days in making up and healing the breaches and schisms that are amongst Christians than one hour in justifying our divisions, even therein wherein, on the one side, they are capable of a fair defence. But who is sufficient for such an attempt? The closing of differences amongst Christians is like opening the book in the Revelation—there is none able or worthy to do it, in heaven or in earth, but the Lamb: when He will put forth the greatness of His power for it, it shall be accomplished, and not before. In the meantime, a reconciliation amongst all Protestants is our duty, and practicable, and had perhaps ere this been in some forwardness of accomplishment had men rightly understood wherein such a reconciliation, according to the mind of God, doth consist. When men have laboured as much in the improvement of the principle of forbearance as they have done to subdue other men to their opinions, religion will have another appearance in the world.

Let us say, "Amen."

Now that is the sort of thing I am anxious to convey to you. Many people think of this man as a dry-as-dust theologian. It is a foul aspersion upon him. Listen to this further quotation in which Owen shows us how he ever became an Independent. For John Owen was not born an Independent, he was born into the Church of England. He says about his father, interestingly enough: "As I was bred up from my infancy under the care of my father, who was a Nonconformist all his days"—that does not mean that he was an Independent, remember—"and a painful labourer in the Vineyard of the Lord, so ever since I came to have any distinct knowledge of the things belonging to the worship of God I have been fixed in judgment against that which I am calumniated withal. . . ."

Owen, in his younger days, had once published a book on the whole question of the nature of the Church and in it he was favorable to the Presbyterian point of view. When he published this treatise on schism, therefore, a certain Mr. Cawdrey, a Presbyterian from Northampton, attacked him violently, saying that he was contradicting entirely what he had said in that previous book. Owen felt this charge very deeply. He does not however reply in any spirit of bitterness, but he does take the trouble, in replying to Cawdrey, to tell us how he ever became an Independent. In looking at this we shall see something of the greatness of this man. The trouble, as he points out repeatedly, over the whole question of schism is that people will defend the position that they are in. They shut their minds, they are not ready to listen, to be instructed, and to change. Owen was big enough to change his opinion and to move from one position to another.

This is his account of how it came about: "Indeed, not long after, I set myself seriously to inquire into the controversies then warmly agitated in these nations. Of the congregational way I was not acquainted with any one person, minister or other; nor had I, to my knowledge, seen any more than one in my life. My acquaintance lay wholly with ministers and people of the presbyterian way. But sundry books being published on either side, I perused and compared them with the Scripture and one another, according as I received ability from God." What an excellent way that is! You read right around the subject and compare it with the Scripture.

Owen continues, "After a general view of them, as was my

manner in other controversies, I fixed on one to take under peculiar consideration and examination, which seemed most methodically and strongly to maintain that which was contrary, as I thought, to my present persuasion." Of the multiplicity of books he picks out one which he regards as the best, to see what it has to say to him. "This was Mr. Cotton's book of the Keys," he tells us. That is a reference to the famous John Cotton, a Church of England clergyman and a godly man. For many years Cotton was vicar of Boston in Lincolnshire and then moved over, about 1634 if I remember rightly, to Boston in Massachusetts. As the result of his thinking and meditation and reading in this country—and still more after his arrival in New England—he became a convinced Independent, and so wrote his book *The Keys.*

This is how John Owen describes the effect that the reading of this book had upon him:

> The examination and confutation hereof, merely for my own particular satisfaction, with what diligence and sincerity I was able, I engaged in. What progress I made in that undertaking I can manifest unto any by the discourse on that subject and animadversions on that book, yet abiding by me. In the pursuit and management of this work, quite beside and contrary to my expectation, at a time and season wherein I could expect nothing on that account but ruin in this world, without the knowledge or advice of, or conference with, any one person of that judgment, I was prevailed on to receive that and those principles which I had thought to have set myself in an opposition unto. And, indeed, this way of impartial examining all things by the Word, comparing causes with causes and things with things, laying aside all prejudicate respects unto persons or present traditions, is a course that I would admonish all to beware of who would avoid the danger of being made Independents.

I trust that we get the full implication of that. If you approach this subject quite honestly, comparing and contrasting all teaching with the Scriptures and especially "laying aside all prejudicate respects unto persons or present traditions," you will find it very difficult to avoid becoming an Independent, says Owen. However, that is the way in which he approached it. He set out to read this book in order that he might answer it, but he was so honest that, comparing it with the Scripture, he was persuaded. The result was that he became a convinced Independent.

Now that is surely one of the great lessons we learn from this man. Whatever else we may think, whatever our disagreements, surely we must all agree with this spirit and with this method. Most of our differences, I think, arise from the fact that we, all of us in one way or another, are unprepared to do that. The first thing you must do is to bring everything to the bar of Scripture. Here, Owen lays down the rule with respect to Scripture that we have been reminded of several times already in this Conference. He says, "And by the Scripture as our rule, we understand both the express words of it, and whatever may, by just and lawful consequence, be educed from them."

In other words he says that the whole trouble, in a sense, arises in this way, that men start from fixed positions, from things as they are, and then regard any departure from that as schism: and so hurl that charge at any who disagrees with them. We must not do that, says Owen, but go back to the fount and to the origin. We must start with Scripture itself—which is the rule we find taught in the Scripture. When we thus go to the Scripture, what do we find? How do they define what is meant by "schism"? This is how he puts it: "The thing whereof we treat being a disorder in the instituted worship of God, and that which is of pure revelation, I suppose it a modest request, to desire that we may abide solely by that discovery and description which is made of it in Scripture,—that that alone shall be esteemed schism which is there so called, or which hath the entire nature of that which is so called. Other things may be other crimes; schism they are not, if in the Scripture they have neither the name nor nature of it attributed to them."

Having arrived at it in that way, this is now Owen's definition of schism.

He points out that this is really only dealt with actually in 1 Corinthians. It is very interesting to observe how he works. He gives a good general bird's-eye view of the whole subject as it is dealt with there, and then points out that the other document dealing with more or less exactly the same subject, that comes down to us from the early ages, is an epistle from Rome to the Church at Corinth by Clement at a later date. But to continue: "The schism, then, here described by the apostle, and blamed by him, consists (and here is the vital definition) in causeless differences and contentions amongst the members of a particular church, contrary to that exercise of love, prudence, and forbearance, which are required of them to be exercised amongst themselves, and towards one another."

His whole point is this: that the only schism that is described in the New Testament is division, causeless divisions, within the Church. The people guilty of schism in the Church of Corinth had not left the Church of Corinth. The New Testament definition of schism is "causeless divisions" within the body of a particular church. Having laid that down he then goes on to indicate in various ways what is meant by schism. But listen to this: "But now this foundation having been laid, that schism is a causeless difference or division amongst the members of any particular church that meet together, or ought so to do, for the worship of God and the celebration of the same numerical ordinances, to the disturbance of the order appointed by Jesus Christ, and contrary to that exercise of love in wisdom and mutual forbearance which is required of them, it will be easy to see wherein the iniquity of it doth consist, and upon what considerations its aggravations do arise."

Schism then, means this: "Despising of the authority of Jesus Christ. It is an offence against His wisdom, whereby He hath ordered all things in the Church on set purpose that schism and divisions may be prevented." They despised that. Thirdly: "The grace and goodness of Christ are also ignored and are offended."

That, then, leads him to say this: "Let, then, the general demand be granted, that schism is 'the breach of union,' which I shall attend with one reasonable postulatum—namely, that this union be a union of the appointment of Jesus Christ." He keeps on repeating that—it must be the breaking of a union appointed by the Lord Jesus Christ.

The consideration, then of what or what sort of union in reference to the worship of God, according to the gospel, is instituted and appointed by Jesus Christ, is the proper foundation of what I have farther to offer in this business. Let the breach of this, if you please, be accounted schism; for being an evil, I shall not contend by what name or title it be distinguished. It is not pleaded that any kind of relinquishment or desertion of any church or churches is presently schism, but only such a separation as breaks the bond of union instituted by Christ.

Now, this union being instituted in the church, according to the various acceptations of that word, so it is distinguished. Therefore, for a discovery of the nature of that which is particularly to be spoken to, and also its contrary, I must show—

1. The several considerations of the church wherein and with which union is to be preserved.
2. What that union is, and wherein it doth consist, which, according to the mind of Christ, we are to keep and observe with the church, under the several notions of it respectively.
3. And how that union is broken, and what is that sin whereby it is done.

The Nature of the Church
You notice that he approaches his subject in such a way, that you come at once to the great doctrine of the nature of the Church. You cannot decide what schism is until you have decided what the Church is. That must be the first great question. Roman Catholics say that "all Protestants are schismatics." Why? "Because they have left us." But then the question to ask them is, "Who are you?" "What are you?" "Are you a church?"—and this question must always be asked. You cannot define schism unless you are clear about your doctrine of the nature of the Church; and Owen,

of course, gives the definition of the Church that we would expect of him as an Independent.

In this connection he says a very interesting thing which some of us need to remember at this present time: "Let none mistake themselves herein; believers are not made for churches, but churches are appointed for believers." That is reminiscent, is it not, of what our Lord said about the Sabbath. There are many people, it seems to me, who think that believers are made for churches. They are not. Churches are made for believers. "Their edification, their guidance and direction in the profession of the faith and performance of divine worship in assemblies, according to the mind of God, is their use and end; without which they are of no signification. The end of Christ in the constitution of His churches was, not the moulding of His disciples into such ecclesiastical shapes as might be subservient unto the power, interest, advantage, and dignity, of them that may in any season come to be over them, but to constitute a way and order of giving such officers unto them as might be in all things useful and subservient unto their edification; as is expressly affirmed in Ephesians 4:11–16." The Church was made for us, not us for the Church.

Now there he lays down a great postulate. Again, his whole point is, that that is the Church which was instituted by the Lord Jesus Christ Himself, and by Him alone. Owen brings out this point:

> There is, indeed, by some pleaded a subordination of officers in this church, tending towards a union on that account; as that ordinary ministers should be subjected to diocesan bishops, they to archbishops or metropolitans, they again to patriarchs, where some would bound the process, though a parity of reason would call for a pope: nor will the arguments pleaded for such a subordination rest until they come to be centred in some such thing.

The logical end of that argument, he says, is to have a pope of some sort or kind.

But first, before this plea be admitted, it must be proved that all these officers are appointed by Jesus Christ, or it will not concern us, who are inquiring solely after His will, and the settling of conscience therein. To do this with such an evidence as that the consciences of all those who are bound to yield obedience to Jesus Christ may appear to be therein concerned, will be a difficult task, as I suppose. And, to settle this once for all, I am not dealing with the men of that lazy persuasion that such affairs are to be ordered by the prudence of our civil superiors and governors; and so seeking to justify a nonsubmission to any of their constitutions in the things of this nature, or to evidence that the so doing is not schism. Nor do I concern myself in the order and appointment of ancient times, by men assembled in synods and councils; wherein, whatever was the force of their determinations in their own seasons, we are not at all concerned, knowing of nothing that is obligatory to us, not pleading from sovereign authority or our own consent: but it is after things of pure institution that I am inquiring. With them who say there is no such thing in these matters, we must proceed to other principles than any yet laid down.

The great point is that we are only to be concerned about that which is instituted by the Lord Jesus Christ Himself. In this connection we have got to look for a moment at what he says about the general councils, because they have come so much into this argument. Owen says that we must be concerned about nothing but that which we can establish has been instituted by the Lord Jesus Christ Himself. But then the argument comes in— What about the authority of the general council? Owen takes that up and this is what he says:

> The Church of England, as it is called (that is the people thereof) separated herself from the Church of Rome. To free herself from the imputation of schism in so doing, as she (that is, the learned men of the nation) pleaded the

errors and corruptions of that church, under this especial consideration of their being imposed by tyrants; so also by professing her design to do nothing but to reduce religion and the worship of God to its original purity, from which it has fallen. And we all jointly justify both her and all other reformed churches in this plea.

In her design to reduce religion to its primitive purity, she always professed (this is the Church of England) that she did not take her direction from the Scripture only, but also from the councils and examples of the first four or five centuries, to which she laboured to conform her reformation. Let the question now be, whether there be not corruptions in this Church of England, supposing such a national church-state to be instituted? What, I beseech you, shall bind my conscience to acquiesce in what is pleaded from the first four or five centuries, consisting of men that could and did err, more than that did hers which was pleaded from the nine or ten centuries following? Have not I liberty to call for reformation according to the Scripture only? or at least to profess that my conscience cannot be bound by any other? The sum is—the business of schism from the Church of England is a thing built purely and simply on political considerations, so interwoven with them, so influenced from them, as not to be separated.

That is his attitude toward the general councils; but he has something still more drastic to say about them, and as we are likely to hear a good deal about this sort of thing in the coming years I think we must pay heed to what he says:

But a general council is pleaded with the best colour and pretence for a bond of union to this general and visible church. In consideration hereof I shall not divert to the handling of the rise, right use, authority, necessity, of such councils; about all which somewhat in due time towards satisfaction may be offered to those who are not in bondage to names and traditions—nor shall I remark what hath been the management of the things of God in all ages in those assemblies; many of which have been the stains and ulcers of Christian religion—nor yet shall I say with what little disadvantage to the religion of Jesus Christ I suppose a loss of all the canons of all councils that ever were in the world since the apostles' days, with their acts and contests might be undergone—nor yet shall I digress to the usefulness of the assemblies of several churches in their representatives, to consider and determine about things of common concernment to them, with their tendency to the preservation of that communion which ought to be amongst them—but as to the present instance only offer—

That such general councils, being things purely extraordinary and occasional, as is confessed, cannot be an ordinary standing bond of union to the catholic church. And if any one shall reply, that though in themselves and in their own continuance they cannot be so, yet in their authority, laws, and canons they may; I must say, that besides the very many reasons I have to call into question the power of law-making for the whole society of Christians in the world, in all the general councils that have been or possibly can be on the earth, the disputes about the title of those assemblies which pretend to this honour, which are to be admitted, which excluded, are so endless; the rules of judging them so dark, lubricous, and uncertain, framed to the interest of all contenders on all hands; the laws of them, which "de facto" have gone under that title and name, so innumerable, burdensome, uncertain, and frivolous, in a great part so grossly contradictory to one another, that I cannot suppose that any man upon second thoughts can abide in such an assertion. If any shall, I must be bold to declare my affection to the doctrine of the Gospel maintained in some of those assemblies for some hundreds of years, and then to desire him to prove that any general council, since the apostles fell asleep, hath been so convened and managed as to be enabled to claim that authority to itself which is or would be due to such an assembly instituted according to the mind of Christ.

He is challenging the whole authority of these general councils, but he admits with his customary honesty, his intellectual honesty and his largeness of heart:

> That it hath been of advantage to the truth of the Gospel that godly learned men, bishops of churches, have convened and witnessed a good confession in reference to the doctrine thereof, and declared their abhorrence of the errors that are contrary thereunto, is confessed. That any man or men is, are, or ever were, intrusted by Christ with authority so to convene them, as that thereupon and by virtue thereof they should be invested with a new authority, power, and jurisdiction, at such a convention, and thence should take upon them to make laws and canons that should be ecclesiastically binding to any persons or churches, as theirs, is not as yet, to me, attended with any convincing evidence of truth. And seeing at length it must be spoken, I shall do it with submission to the thoughts of good men that are in any way acquainted with these things, and in sincerity therein commend my conscience to God, that I do not know anything that is extant bearing clearer witness to the sad degeneracy of Christian religion in the profession thereof, nor more evidently discovering the efficacy of another spirit than that which was poured out by Christ at His Ascension, nor containing more hay and stubble, that is to be burned and consumed, than the stories of the acts and laws of the councils and synods that have been in the world.

He continues with his denunciation of these general councils, and especially of the claim that they had authority and power to legislate with regard to these various additions in the matter of offices and forms of worship in connection with the life of the

Church. Owen rejects all these claims and having done so, he makes the following positive statement:

> I now descend to the last consideration of a church, in the most usual acceptation of that in the New Testament— that is, of a particular instituted church. A church in this sense I take to be a society of men called by the Word to the obedience of faith in Christ, and joint performance of the worship of God in the same individual ordinances, according to the order by Christ prescribed. This general description of it exhibits its nature so far as is necessary to clear the subject of our present disquisition.

But he not only contends that the general councils are not to be authoritative in this matter, he goes further. He says:

> We deny that the apostles made or gave any such rules to the churches present in their days, or for the use of the churches in future ages, as should appoint and determine outward modes of worship, with ceremonies in their observation, stated feasts and fasts, beyond what is of divine institution, liturgies or forms of prayer, or discipline to be exercised in law courts, subservient unto a national ecclesiastical government. What use, then, they are or may be of, what benefit or advantage may come to the church by them, what is the authority of the superior magistrate about them, we do not now inquire or determine. Only we say, that no rule unto these ends was ever prescribed by the apostles; for—
>
> 1. There is not the least intimation of any such rule to be given by them in the Scripture.
>
> 2. The first churches after their times knew nothing of any such rule given by them: and, therefore, after they began to depart from the simplicity of the Gospel in any things, as unto worship, order, and rule, or discipline, they fell into a great variety of outward observances, orders, and ceremonies, every church almost differing in some

thing or other from others, in some such observations, yet all "keeping the unity of the faith in the bond of peace." This they would not have done if the apostles had prescribed any one certain rule of such things that all must conform unto, especially considering how scrupulously they did adhere unto every thing that was reported to be done or spoken by any of the apostles, were the report true or false.

Then he goes on to say something that is most interesting at the present time, because of the proposal to fix Easter. His third argument is this:

3. In particular, when a difference fell out amongst them in a business of this nature, namely, in a thing of outward order, nowhere appointed by the authority of Christ—namely, about the observation of Easter—the parties at variance appealed on the one side to the practice of Peter, and on the other to the practice of John (both vainly enough): yet was it never pretended by any of them on either side that the apostles had constituted any rule in the case; and therefore it is not probable that they esteemed them to have done so in things of an alike nature, seeing they laid more weight on this than on any other instance of the like kind.

4. It is expressly denied, by good and sufficient testimony among them, that the apostles made any law or rule about outward rites, ceremonies, times, and the like.

The Nature of the Union

Now there again is something that is of importance for us to bear in mind. But I must hurry on, and, leaving out much interesting material, let me quote Owen on the nature of the union. The Church he defines in terms of that which is clearly instituted by Christ, which is this particular church that meets together for the ends and the objects that he has been indicating. Now he comes to deal with the nature of the union that should obtain in these churches, and how this union is to be maintained. His great point is that it is always a spiritual union, it is a union in the Spirit. He quotes, to that end, the familiar passage in Ephesians 4, and he works it out and shows how this is the controlling principle. Let me just give you his headings.

"First, that unity which is recommended unto us in the Gospel is spiritual.

"Secondly, unto this foundation of Gospel unity among believers, for and unto the due improvement of it, there is required a unity of faith" —(It is a spiritual union; secondly, it is a unity of faith)—"or of the belief and profession of the same divine truth; for as there is one Lord, so also there is one faith and one baptism unto believers." So he emphasizes these two.

"Thirdly, there is a unity of love"—and

"Fourthly, the Lord Christ, by His kingly authority, hath instituted orders for rule, and ordinances for worship, Matthew 28:19–20; Ephesians 4:8–13 to be observed in all His churches."

That is the nature of the union. Next the question arises: How is this union to be preserved? Here he has some excellent things to say.

"Now, that this union be preserved, it is required that all those grand and necessary truths of the Gospel, without the knowledge whereof no man can be saved by Jesus Christ, be so far believed as to be outwardly and visibly professed, in that variety of ways wherein they are or may be called out thereunto." There is no union unless there is agreement about the truths of the Gospel. It is a spiritual union, but it is also a union of faith. If there is disagreement about the faith, there is no union. There can be no union, therefore, between an Evangelical and a man who denies the essentials of the Evangelical faith. It is impossible.

"Secondly, that no other internal principle of the mind, that hath an utter inconsistency with the real belief of the truths necessary to be professed, be manifested by professors." Not only must there be no open, explicit disagreement, there must be no implicit disagreement either.

"Thirdly, that no thing, opinion, error, or false doctrine, everting or overthrowing any of the necessary saving truths professed as above, be added in and with that profession, or deliberately be professed also. This principle the apostle lays down and proves, Galatians 5:3–4. Notwithstanding the profession of the Gospel, he tells the Galatians that if they were bewitched to profess also the necessity of circumcision and keeping of the law for justification, Christ or the profession of Him would not profit them."

Breaking the Union

In that way he lays down his great cardinal principles as to the nature of the union and how it is to be preserved. Then, he proceeds to deal with the question of how this union can be broken. Here, in a very wonderful way he quite conclusively proves without any difficulty at all, that on these principles, the first church to be guilty of schism was the Roman Catholic church. By additions, and innovations, and contradictions of basic New Testament teaching involved in, and implied by, teaching concerning the sacraments and other matters, the Roman Catholic church has been more guilty of the sin of schism than any other church that the world has ever known.

Owen has some very wonderful things to say on this whole subject of the preservation of union. Here is something of what he has to say:

> We do confess, that because the best of men in this life do not know but in part, all the members of this Church are in many things liable to error, mistakes, and miscarriages; and hence it is that, although they are all internally acted and guided by the same Spirit in all things absolutely necessary to their eternal salvation, and do all attend unto the same rule of the Word, according as they apprehend the mind of God in it and concerning it, have all, for the nature and substance of it, the same divine faith and love, and are all equally united unto their Head, yet, in the profession which they make of the conceptions and persuasions of their minds about the things revealed in the Scripture, there are, and always have been, many differences among them. Neither is it morally possible it should be

otherwise, whilst in their judgment and profession they are left unto the ability of their own minds and liberty of their wills, under that great variety of the means of light and truth, with other circumstances, whereinto they are disposed by the holy, wise providence of God. Nor hath the Lord Christ absolutely promised that it shall be otherwise with them; but securing them all by His Spirit in the foundations of eternal salvation, He leaves them in other things to the exercise of mutual love and forbearance, with a charge of duty after a continual endeavour to grow up unto a perfect union, by the improvement of the blessed aids and assistances which He is pleased to afford them. And those who, by ways of force, would drive them into any other union or agreement than their own light and duty will lead them into, do what in them lies to oppose the whole design of the Lord Christ towards them and His rule over them. In the meantime, it is granted that they may fall into divisions, and schisms, and mutual exasperations among themselves, through the remainders of darkness in their minds and the infirmity of the flesh.

This is most important. It explains the differences even among us in this very conference. That is a perfect account of it. Our Lord, he says, as it were makes provision for this, anticipates that it is going to happen: "In the meantime, it is granted that they may fall into divisions, and schisms, and mutual exasperations among themselves, through the remainders of darkness in their minds and the infirmity of the flesh, Romans 14:3; and in such cases mutual judgings and despisings are apt to ensue, and that to the prejudice and great disadvantage of that common faith which they do profess. And yet, notwithstanding all this (such cross-entangled wheels are there in the course of our nature), they all of them really value and esteem the things wherein they agree incomparably above those wherein they differ." (Thank God we can still say that!) "But their valuation of the matter of their union and agreement is purely spiritual, whereas their differences are usually influenced by carnal and secular considerations, which have, for the most part, a sensible impression on the minds of poor mortals."

Let every man examine himself! That is my interjection. But you notice what Owen says: "Their evaluation of the matter of their union and agreement is purely spiritual, whereas their differences are usually influenced by carnal"—What church were we born in? where were we brought up?—"and secular considerations"—What happens to me if I make a change?—"and secular considerations, which have, for the most part, a sensible impression on the minds of poor mortals." We are all guilty! That is also my comment, not John Owen's. We are all guilty. He proceeds:

> But so far as their divisions and differences are unto them unavoidable, the remedy of farther evils proceeding from them is plainly and frequently expressed in the Scripture. It is love, meekness, forbearance, bowels of compassion, with those other graces of the Spirit wherein our conformity unto Christ doth consist, with a true understanding and the due valuation of the "unity of faith," and the common hope of believers which are the ways prescribed unto us for the prevention of those evils which, without them, our unavoidable differences will occasion. And this excellent way of the Gospel, together with a rejection of evil surmises, and a watchfulness over ourselves against irregular judging and censuring of others, together with a peaceable walking in consent and unity so far as we have attained, is so fully and clearly proposed unto us therein, that they must have their eyes blinded by prejudices and carnal interests, or some effectual working of the god of this world on their minds, into whose understandings the light of it doth not shine with uncontrollable evidence and conviction.

Then in another place he points out that in Philippians 3 Paul says: "Nevertheless, whereto we have already attained, let us walk by the same rule." "And if," he says (in v. 15) "in anything ye be otherwise minded, God shall reveal even this unto you." They were not to quarrel or part over minor matters. "Go on together," he says, "and pray together, and God will reveal the truth concerning those matters also." Paul teaches that that is the way in which this union is to be maintained.

Schism and Separation

Now there is one other aspect of the subject that we must just notice. Owen draws a distinction between schism and separation, and teaches quite definitely that at times separation is demanded of us, that it is indeed a duty at such times: "What may regularly, on the other hand, be deduced from the commands given to 'turn away from them who have only a form of godliness,' 2 Timothy 3:5; to 'withdraw from them that walk disorderly,' 2 Thessalonians 3:6; not to bear nor endure in communion men of corrupt principles and wicked lives, Revelation 2:14; but positively to separate from an apostate church, Revelation 18:4; that in all things we may worship Christ according to His mind and appointment; that is the force of these commands."

Then he gives these commands. In so doing he gives a very good account of the reasons which led the Church of England to leave the Church of Rome. Here he again has a command with regard to this question.

> I deal, as I said, with them who own reformation; and I now suppose the congregation, whereof a man is supposed to be a member on any account whatever, not to be reformed—in this case, I ask whether it be schism or no for any number of men to reform themselves, by reducing the practice of worship to its original institution, though they be the minor part lying within the parochial precincts, or for any of them to join themselves with others for that end and purpose not living within those precincts? I shall boldly say this schism is commanded by the Holy Ghost, 1 Timothy 6:5; 2 Timothy 3:5; Hosea 4:15. Is this yoke laid upon me by Christ, that, to go along with the multitude where I live, that hate to be reformed, I must forsake my duty and

despise the privileges that He hath purchased for me with His own precious blood? Is this a unity of Christ's institution, that I must for ever associate myself with wicked and profane men in the worship of God, to the unspeakable detriment and disadvantage of my own soul?

I suppose nothing can be more unreasonable than once to imagine any such thing.

He continues his argument along those same lines.

> It is usually objected about the church of Corinth, that there was in it many disorders and enormous miscarriages, divisions, and breaches of love; miscarriages through drink at their meetings, gross sins, the incestuous person tolerated, false doctrine broached, the resurrection denied;— and yet Paul advises no man to separate from it, but all to perform their duty in it. But how little our present plea and defensative is concerned in this instance, supposed to lie against it, very few considerations will evince:
>
> First, the church of Corinth was undoubtedly a true church, lately instituted according to the mind of Christ, and was not fallen from that privilege by any miscarriage, nor had suffered anything destructive to its being; which wholly differences between the case proposed, in respect of many particulars, and the instance produced. We confess the abuses and evils mentioned had crept into the church, and do thence grant that many abuses may do so into any of the best of the churches of God.

An argument is often brought forward at this point in these terms, that if you do act on these principles, how long would it last? We cannot guarantee absolute purity even if we separate, and then even the new church may go wrong. According to Owen you must not expect anything different:

> Nor did it ever enter into the heart of any man to think that so soon as any disorders fall out or abuses creep into it, it is

instantly the duty of any to fly out of it, like Paul's mariners out of the ship when the storm grew hazardous; it being the duty of all the members of such a church, untainted with the evils and corruptions of it, upon many accounts, to attempt and labour the remedy of those disorders, and rejection of those abuses to the uttermost, which was that which Paul advised the Corinthians and some others unto; in obedience whereunto they were recovered. But yet this I say, had the church of Corinth continued in the condition before described—that notorious, scandalous sins had gone unpunished, unreproved, drunkenness continued and practised in the assemblies, men abiding by the denial of the resurrection, so overturning the whole Gospel, and the church refusing to do her duty, and exercise her authority to cast all those disorderly persons, upon their obstinacy, out of her communion—it had been the duty of every saint of God in that church to have withdrawn from it, to come out from among them, and not to have been partaker of their sins, unless they were willing to partake of their plague also, which on such an apostasy would certainly ensue.

Now, there, he points out that in certain conditions and circumstances separation is actually a duty, and he goes on in this immediate context to point out that this has reference to the reason why the Church of England left the Church of Rome.

We turn now to a very interesting point, the relevance of which will be obvious: "It may be some will yet say (because it hath been said often), 'There is a difference between reforming of churches already gathered and raised, and raising of churches, out of mere materials. The first may be allowed, but the latter tends to all manner of confusion.'" In other words, he imagines a possible objection might be made to this effect: It is all right to reform an existing church, but that does not justify you in forming, as it were, a new church, as he puts it, "out of mere materials."

I have at present not much to say to this objection, because, as I conceive, it concerns not the business we have in hand; nor would I have mentioned it at all, but that it is insisted on by some on every turn, whether suited for the particular cause for which it is produced, or no. In brief, then—

1. I know no other reformation of any church, or any thing in a church, but the reducing of it to its primitive institution, and the order allotted to it by Jesus Christ. If any plead for any other reformation of churches, they are, in my judgment, to blame.

And when any society or combination of men (whatever hitherto it hath been esteemed) is not capable of such a reduction and renovation, I suppose I shall not provoke any wise and sober person if I profess I cannot look on such a society as a church of Christ. . . .

Let me repeat that—"And when any society or combination of men is not capable of such a reduction" (that is to say, to the primitive institution) "and renovation, I suppose I shall not provoke any wise and sober person if I profess I cannot look on such a society as a church of Christ." A church that cannot reform itself in that way is not a church of Christ. He goes on:

. . . and thereupon advise those therein who have a due right to the privileges purchased for them by Christ, as to Gospel administrations, to take some other peaceable course to make themselves partakers of them.

2. Were I fully to handle the things pointed to in this objection I must manage principles which, in this discourse, I have not been occasioned to draw forth at all or to improve. Many things of great weight and importance must come under debate and consideration before a clear account can be given of the case stated in this objection, such as:

(1) The true nature of an instituted church under the Gospel, as to the matter, form, and all other necessary constitutive causes, is to be investigated and found out.

(2) The nature and form of such a church is to be exemplified from the Scripture and the stories of the first

churches, before sensibly infected with the poison of that apostasy which ensued." [I urgently commend the consideration of those words at this present time. We must study the Scriptures and also the history of the first three centuries of the Christian Church.]

(3) The extent of the apostasy under Antichrist, as to the ruining of instituted churches, making them to be Babylon, and their worship fornication, is duly and carefully to be examined. Here lie our disorder and division; hence is our darkness and pollution of our garments, which is not an easy thing to free ourselves of: though we may arise, yet we shall not speedily shake ourselves out of the dust." [That is the chief difficulty for every one of us; we are all bound by what has gone before us.]

(4) By what way and means God begat anew and kept alive his elect in their several generations, when antichristian darkness covered the earth and thick darkness the nations, supposing an intercision of instituted ordinances, so far as to make a nullity in them as to what was of simple and pure institution; what way might be used for the fixing of the tabernacle of God again with men, and the setting up of church worship according to His mind and will.

(5) What was the way of the first Reformation in this nation, and what principles that godly learned men of those days proceeded on; how far what they did may be satisfactory to our consciences at the present, as to our concurrence in them, who from thence have the truth of the Gospel derived down to us; whether ordinary officers be before or after the church, and so whether a church-state is preserved in the preservation of officers, by a foreign power to that church whereof they are so, or the office be preserved, and consequently the officers inclusively, in the preservation and constitution of a church—these, I say, with sundry other things of the like importance, with inferences from them, are to be considered to the bottom

before a full resolution can be given to the inquiry couched in this objection, which, as I said, to do is not my present business.

All that means this: Before you rush off to start a new church, consider all these subjects very seriously and very deeply. It is not a matter to be rushed into, it is all to be examined in the light of Scripture and the early history of the Christian Church.

What then is the conclusion of all this? Owen sums it up himself in these words:

> Let us now see the sum of the whole matter, and what it is that we plead for our discharge as to this crime of schism, allowing the term to pass in its large and usual acceptation, receding, for the sake of the truth's farther ventilation, from the precise propriety of the word annexed to it in the Scripture. The sum is, we have broken no bond of unity, no order instituted or appointed by Jesus Christ—have causelessly deserted no station that ever we were in, according to His mind; which alone can give countenance to an accusation of this nature. That on pure grounds of conscience we have withdrawn, or do withhold ourselves from partaking in some ways, engaged into upon mere grounds of prudence, we acknowledge.
>
> And thus, from what hath been said, it appears in what a fair capacity, notwithstanding any principle or practice owned by us, we are in to live peaceably, and to exercise all fruits of love towards those who are otherwise minded.

He feels that he has thus clearly absolved himself from the charge of schism.

Owen's Appeal to Us

Finally, let me put before you the great appeal which, it seems to me, Owen addresses to us who are here gathered at this present time as reformed evangelical Christians. Let us listen to his moving words:

> The truth is, if God would be pleased to help us, on all hands, to lay aside prejudices, passions, secular interests, fears, and every other distempered affection, which obstruct our minds in passing a right judgment on things of the nature treated on, we should find in the text and context spoken unto a sacred truth divinely directive of such a practice as would give peace and rest unto us all; for it is supposed that men, in a sincere endeavour after acquaintance with the truths and mysteries of the Gospel, with an enjoyment of the good things represented and exhibited in them, may fall, in some things, into different apprehensions about what belongs unto faith and practice in religion. But whilst they are such as do not destroy or overthrow the foundation nor hinder men from pressing "toward the mark for the prize of the high calling of God in Christ Jesus," that which the apostle directs unto them who are supposed to be ignorant of or to mistake in the things wherein they do differ from others, is only that they wait for divine instruction in the use of the means appointed for that end, practising in the meantime according to what they have received. And as unto both parties, the advice he gives them is, that "whereunto they have attained," wherein they do agree—which were all those principles of faith and obedience which were necessary unto their acceptance with God—they should "walk by the same rule, and mind the same thing"; that is, "forbearing one another" in the things wherein they differ: which is the substance of what is pleaded for by the Nonconformists.

But consider further:

> It is not impossible that some may, from what hath been spoken, begin to apprehend that they have been too hasty in judging other men. Indeed, none are more ready

to charge highly than those who, when they have so done, are most unable to make good their charge. What real schisms in a moral sense have ensued among brethren, by their causeless mutual imputation of schism in things of institution, is known. And when men are in one fault, and are charged with another wherein they are not, it is a ready way to confirm them in that wherein they are. There is more darkness and difficulty in the whole matter of instituted worship than some men are aware of; not that it was so from the beginning, whilst Christianity continued in its naked simplicity, but it is come occasionally upon us by the customs, darkness, and invincible prejudices that have taken hold on the minds of men by a secret diffusion of the poison of that grand apostasy. It were well, then, that men would not be so confident, nor easily persuaded that they presently know how all things ought to be, because they know how they would have some things to be, which suit their temper and interest. Men may easily perhaps see, or think they see, what they do not like, and cry out schism! and separation! but if they would a little consider what ought to be in this whole matter, according to the mind of God, and what evidences they have of the grounds and principles whereon they condemn others, it might make them yet swift to hear, but slow to speak, and take off from the number of teachers among us. Some are ready to think that all that join not with them are schismatics, and they are so because they go not with them; and other reason they have none, being unable to give any solid foundation of what they profess. What the cause of unity among the people of God hath suffered from this sort of men is not easily to be expressed.

In all differences about religion, to drive them to their rise and spring, and to consider them as stated originally, will ease us of much trouble and labour.

We have to go back beyond the seventeenth century, beyond the sixteenth century; we have got to go back to the beginning.

Now that is an exhortation we all need. We all suffer from the tendency to defend inherited positions and our own particular history. We must go back to the very beginning, to the rise and spring of it all in the first century. He then goes on to say:

> Perhaps many of them (i.e. the differences) will not appear so formidable as they are represented. He that sees a great river is not instantly to conclude that all the water in it comes from its first rise and spring; the addition of many brooks, showers, and land-floods have perhaps swelled it to the condition wherein it is. Every difference in religion is not to be thought to be as big at its rise as it appears to be when it hath passed through many generations, and hath received additions and aggravations from the disputings and contendings of men, on the one hand and on the other engaged. What a flood of abominations doth this business of schism seem to be, as rolling down to us through the writings of Cyprian, Austin, and Optatus, of old, the schoolmen, decrees of popish councils, with the contrivances of some among ourselves, concerned to keep up the swelled notion of it! Go to its rise, and you will find it to be, though bad enough, yet quite another thing than what, by the prejudices accruing by the addition of so many generations, it is now generally represented to be.
>
> The great maxim, "To the law and to the testimony," truly improved, would quickly cure all our distempers.

May I be allowed to say that this is my profound belief also. I believe our present day distempers also could be cured if only we obeyed this injunction. Owen felt that. He proceeds:

> In the meantime, let us bless God that though our outward man may possibly be disposed of according to the apprehension that others have of what we do or are, our consciences are concerned only in what He hath appointed. How some men may prevail against us, before whom we

must stand or fall according to their corrupt notion of schism, we know not. The rule of our consciences in this, as in all other things, is eternal and unchangeable. Whilst I have an uncontrollable faithful witness that I transgress no limits prescribed to me in the Word, that I do not willingly break or dissolve any unity of the institution of Jesus Christ, my mind as to this thing is filled with perfect peace. Blessed be God, that hath reserved the sole sovereignty of our consciences in His hand, and not in the least parcelled it out to any of the sons of men, whose tender mercies being oftentimes cruelty itself, they would perhaps destroy the soul also, when they do so to the body, seeing they stay there, as our Saviour witnesseth, because they can proceed no further! Here, then, I profess to rest, in this doth my conscience acquiesce: Whilst I have any comfortable persuasion on grounds infallible, that I hold the head, and that I am by faith a member of the mystical body of Christ; whilst I make profession of all the necessary saving truths of the Gospel; whilst I disturb not the peace of that particular church thereof by my own consent I am a member, nor do raise up nor continue in any causeless differences with them, or any of them, with whom I walk in the fellowship and order of the Gospel; whilst I labour to exercise faith towards the Lord Jesus Christ, and love towards all the saints —I do keep the unity which is of the appointment of Christ. And let men say, from principles utterly foreign to the Gospel, what they please or can to the contrary, I am no schismatic.

Perhaps the discovery which hath been made, how little we are many of us concerned in that which, having mutually charged it on one another, hath been the greatest ball of strife and most effectual engine of difference and distance between us, may be a means to reconcile in love them that truly fear God, though engaged in several ways, as to some particulars. I confess I have not any great hope of much success on this account; for let principles and ways be made as evident as if he that wrote them carried the sun in his hand, yet whilst men are forestalled by prejudices, and have their affections and spirits engaged suitably thereunto, no great alteration in their minds and ways, on the clearest conviction whatever, is to be expected. All our hearts are in the hand of God; and our expectations of what He hath promised are to be proportioned to what He can effect, not to what of outward means we see to be used.

Last of all here is a very beautiful passage from Owen's treatise on Christian love and peace:

> Herein, therefore, lies the fundamental cause of our divisions; which will not be healed until it be removed and taken out of the way. Leave believers or professors of the Gospel unto their duty in seeking after evangelical unity in the use of other means instituted and blessed unto that end—impose nothing on their consciences or practice under that name, which indeed belongs not thereunto; and although, upon the reasons and causes afterward to be mentioned, there may for a season remain some divisions among them, yet there will be a way of healing continually ready for them, and agreed upon by them as such.

Oh, that we might all give that a hearing and our careful attention! "Where, indeed, men propose unto themselves different ends, though under the same name, the use of the same means for the compassing of them will but increase their variance: as where some aim at evangelical union, and others at an external uniformity." There is our exact position at the present time. Some of us are aiming at evangelical union; others are aiming at "external uniformity": " . . . both under the name of unity and peace, in the use of the same means for these ends, they will be more divided among themselves." (If the aim is different, we are only going to increase the division). "But where the same end is aimed at, even the debate of the means for the attaining of it will insensibly bring the parties into a coalition, and work out in the issue a complete reconciliation."

If we all as evangelicals are out to defend the faith, and to show men clearly the way of salvation, then, Owen says that we shall be brought together. If that is our real objective.

> . . . In the meantime, were Christians duly instructed how many lesser differences, in mind, and judgment, and practice, are really consistent with the nature, ends, and genuine fruit, of the unity that Christ requires among them, it would undoubtedly prevail with them so to manage themselves in their differences, by mutual forbearance and condescension in love, as not to contract the guilt of being disturbers or breakers of it; for suppose the minds of any of them to be invincibly prepossessed with the principles wherein they differ from others, yet all who are sincere in their profession cannot but rejoice to be directed unto such a managery of them as to be preserved from the guilt of dissolving the unity appointed by Christ to be observed. And, to speak plainly, among all the churches in the world which are free from idolatry and persecution, it is not different opinions, or a difference in judgment about revealed truths, nor a different practice in sacred administration, but pride, self-interest, love of honour, reputation, and dominion, with the influence of civil or political intrigues and considerations, that are the true cause of that defect of evangelical unity that is at this day amongst them; for set them aside, and the real differences which would remain may be so managed, in love, gentleness, and meekness, as not to interfere with that unity which Christ requireth them to preserve. Nothing will from thence follow which shall impeach their common interest in one Lord, one faith, one love, one Spirit, and the administration of the same ordinances according to their light and ability. But if we shall cast away this evangelical union among the disciples and churches of Christ—if we shall break up the bounds and limits fixed unto it, and set up in its place a compliance with, or an agreement in, the commands and appointments of men,

making their observations the rule and measure of our ecclesiastical concord—it cannot be but that innumerable and endless divisions will ensue thereon. If we will not be contented with the union that Christ hath appointed, it is certain that we shall have none in this world. . . .

I believe that evangelicalism is being challenged in these days along that very line. If we do not face the challenge of the ecumenical movement at the present time and achieve this evangelical union, I prophesy that we shall never have it. Our divisions will only be greatly increased:

> If we will not be contented with the union that Christ hath appointed, it is certain that we shall have none in this world; for concerning that which is of men's finding out, there have been, and will be, contentions and divisions, whilst there are any on the one side who will endeavour its imposition, and on the other who desire to preserve their consciences entire unto the authority of Christ in His laws and appointments.
>
> There is none who can be such a stranger in our Israel as not to know that these things have been the great occasion and cause of the divisions and contentions that have been among us near a hundred years, and which at this day make our breaches wide like the sea, that they cannot be healed. Let, therefore, those who have power and ability be instrumental to restore to the minds of men the true notion and knowledge of the unity which the Lord Christ requireth among His churches and disciples; and let them be left unto that liberty which He hath purchased for them, in the pursuit of that unity which He hath prescribed unto them; and let us all labour to stir up those gracious principles of love and peace which ought to guide us in the use of our liberty, and will enable us to preserve Gospel unity—and there will be a greater progress made towards peace, reconciliation, and concord, amongst all sorts of Christians, than the spoiling of

the goods or imprisoning the persons of dissenters will ever effect. But it may be, such things are required hereunto as the world is yet scarce able to comply withal; for whilst men do hardly believe that there is an efficacy and power accompanying the institutions of Christ, for the compassing of that whole end which He aimeth at and intended—whilst they are unwilling to be brought unto the constant exercise of that spiritual diligence, patience, meekness, condescension, self-denial, renunciation of the world and conformity thereunto, which are indispensably necessary in church guides and church members, according to their measure, unto the attaining and preservation of Gospel unity, but do satisfy themselves in the disposal of an ecclesiastical union into a subordination unto their own secular interests, by external force and power— we have very small expectation of success in the way proposed. In the meantime, we are herewith satisfied: Take the churches of Christ in the world that are not infected with idolatry or persecution, and restore their unity unto the terms and conditions left unto them by Christ and His apostles, and if in any thing we are found uncompliant therewithal, we shall without repining bear the reproach of it, and hasten an amendment.

May God grant unto us, every one of us, the spirit of John Owen in this matter.

I trust that I have been able to show that John Owen speaks very directly and immediately to our situation at this very moment. May God give us grace to ponder these things. But above all may He give us great wisdom, and beyond everything, may He give us great love and charity in our hearts, and patience with one another, so that, as men professing the same faith, we may present it together to an apostate church, though she be "a world church," and to lost men and women everywhere.

Part 2

Able Ministers of the New Testament

1964

5

JOHN CALVIN'S DOCTRINE OF GOD

R. A. Finlayson

It has been claimed that the first word in the Calvinistic system is God; that John Calvin began where Scripture begins: "In the beginning God. . . ."

What does that mean? For John Calvin it meant everything, inasmuch as he viewed everything on earth and in heaven, in this life and the life to come, in its light. Calvin relates everything to God, and specifically to the God whom he discovered in the Scriptures.

The central fact of the system called by his name is, therefore, its vision of God. It has indeed been said, with some truth, that Calvin as a theologian is Calvin looking Godwards and telling the world what he sees, and doing it without personal bias or predilection, doing it in a manner that fills his own soul with awe and perhaps with shrinking. That is the distinctive feature of Calvin's theology that marks it as different, that sets it apart from other systems, that it not only holds that God is God, but that it reckons with the fact in the entire practice of life. Though other systems give prime place to the doctrine of God, Calvinism accepts the implications of the doctrine in every sphere of thought and life more completely and consistently than any other system.

This was strikingly true of Calvin himself. If at any time he arrived at a conclusion from which, for personal reasons, he might shrink, he did not fail to state the conclusion, and, if he found it in Scripture, to stick to it. At the close of his life, shortly before he drew his last breath, he made the moving statement: "I never knowingly corrupted or distorted a single passage of Scripture."

We make the claim, therefore, that of all the systems of theology, the one labelled Calvinistic seeks to do full justice to all, and not merely a part, of what it finds in its doctrine of God. Others may, and do, stop short when they find that the implications of the doctrine baffle their understanding, or offend their pride, or limit their autonomy. They thus tend to subordinate one truth to some other truth more congenial to their system. Calvin shows no such inhibitions. He constructs his system from the Scriptures with a vigorous logic that leads from consequence to consequence, from postulate to postulate, issuing often in a sense of antinomy, in antithesis and apparent contradiction. These great antinomies, great affirmations in the face of other great affirmations, Calvin holds in balance, recognizing that the seeming contradiction is due to our limited understanding, to our defective intelligence. He accepts the mystery, and holds in correct balance such seeming contradictions as divine sovereignty and human responsibility, God's predestination and man's free will, the divine election and the free gospel offer.

This balance introduces into Calvin's system an invaluable principle, that of conformity within the analogy of faith. If the system is accepted as in conformity with Scripture, then dogma must be formulated, and Scripture itself interpreted, so as not to overthrow or contradict our system of revealed truth. There is thus a rule of faith that is normative for the whole system, and if it does not always teach us what to say, it teaches us what not to say. Modern theology has no analogy of the faith to safeguard, because it has no credal content. Anything goes!

Many attempts have been made to decide on a principle of

Calvinism which unifies the whole, whether predestination, or particular redemption, or human depravity, or divine sovereignty. Calvin himself claimed that he merely sought to interpret the Scriptures—"to open up the understanding of the Scriptures" was how he put it in the preface to the first edition of *The Institutes*— and it is agreed that Calvin's Commentaries, if not as readily accessible as *The Institutes,* provide as authoritative a source for the understanding of his theology. We could claim that the motto that dominates the whole Reformation movement, *Soli Deo gloria,* provides the key to Calvin's theology. It is the glory of God that He is God and cannot be less than God. It is this that has led so many to discover the principium of Calvin's theology in divine sovereignty. It were perhaps more truly described as the God who is sovereign—sovereign in all His manifestations and relationships.

We claim, however, that if divine sovereignty be accepted as the formative principle in his system, it is because the Church and theology needed Calvin to restore the doctrine of God's sovereignty to the fundamental position it holds in the Bible. However we define it, it is God, the centrality of God, that is preeminently the basis of Calvin's system.

Count Zinzendorf of the Moravians referred to Calvin's theology slightingly as "the theology of the Father," owing to the supreme place that it gave to the First Person as the representative of the honor and majesty of the Deity. Too often the demand for what is called a Christocentric theology has been but an attempt to evade this centrality of God. It is done in the spirit of compromise as a means of getting rid of some of the less comfortable aspects of the doctrine of God. The Apostles' Creed confesses: "I believe in God the Father Almighty," before it confesses: "And in Jesus Christ His Son." That was the true Christian approach in every age. The theology of Schleiermacher was the first to be labelled Christocentric, and it soon became apparent that it was in reality anthropocentric. It forgot that man exists for the glory of God.

Calvin's attitude to this preoccupation with man, even with his salvation, is tersely expressed in his Epistle to Sadoleto: "It savours little of the true theologian to attempt to compare man to himself so much rather than to command and instruct him that the beginning of directing his life aright is to increase and show forth the glory of God. It is for God above all things," he concludes, "that we are born and not for ourselves." Not without reason, therefore, was the Reformation spoken of as the discovery of God in His sovereign holy centrality.

It cannot be said that Calvin made any very original contribution to the doctrine of God in general beyond what he had inherited from Athanasius, Augustine, and Anselm. It is in the application of his doctrine of God that he broke new ground, or rather, shed fresh light on ground already traversed. It has to be borne in mind that *The Institutes,* like the Westminster Confession of a later day, was designed as a manual of religion rather than a textbook of theology. This was the authentic Reformation outlook: it was a "rediscovery of Christianity as religion," as Warfield expresses it.

In most systems of theology our knowledge of God is generally distributed under the headings of His Being or Substance; His Character or Attributes; His Will or Purposes; and His Manifestation or Works. It is not at all easy to adopt this arrangement in dealing with Calvin's doctrine of God for the reason, already indicated, that he is concerned with God as the object of religious reverence, rather than as the object of speculative thought, as for example in the case of Zwingli.

The General Doctrine of God

We may look in passing, and it is no more than a cursory glance, at three sections of his doctrine of God—His Nature, His Character, and His Will—that we may be the better able to study how he applied that doctrine to the various spheres of human knowledge and conduct.

God's Nature or Subsistence

In dealing with the nature of God Calvin disclaims the "presumptuous curiosity to attempt an examination of His essence which," he adds, "is rather to be adored than curiously investigated." He regards consideration of the nature and attributes of God as more a matter of the heart than of the understanding. And so he leaves the great topics of the existence, the nature, and the attributes of God without formal or detailed discussion in *The Institutes.* In the depth of His being God is to man past finding out. "His essence," he says, "is incomprehensible, so that His divinity wholly escapes all human senses."

Concerning the essence of God, Calvin mentions only two qualities which Scripture attributes to Him, immensity and spirituality. He speaks of God as "of eternal infinite spiritual essence," and adds, "who also alone has in Himself the power of existence from Himself and bestows it upon His creatures."

The depersonalized God of modern theology, however, has absolutely nothing in common with Calvin to whom God is Lord and Father to His creatures. He would be the first to recognize that without personality in God religion would be impossible, and in any case a God who is not a person, who lacks the attributes of personality as we know them, is inferior in the scale of being to man himself: he is a mere impersonal concept which we have generated from our own imagination, an idol of our own creation, Calvin would undoubtedly call it.

It has, however, to be recognized that in the exposition of the subsistence of God Calvin put the finishing touches to the formulation of the doctrine of the Trinity undertaken by Origen, Tertullian, Athanasius, Augustine, Anselm, and Aquinas. It has been supposed, and often asserted, that the Reformers, and especially Calvin and Melanchthon, were indifferent to the doctrine of the Trinity and passed it over lightly as something of an embarrassment. This is wrong. The doctrine had been inherited from the unbroken Church and was not in dispute.

To Calvin the doctrine of the Trinity meant the completeness and all-sufficiency of God. It meant that God was complete in Himself and required nothing outside Himself in order to have perfect realization and fulfillment. In Himself as Father, Son, and Holy Spirit, He possesses the highest form of communion, self-revelation, and self-giving. He is not a unipersonal Being, aloof and alone, but a tripersonal Being in the active life of an eternal fellowship, to which neither the creation of the world nor the salvation of man can add anything.

This is what makes Calvin suggest that *vitality* is given to God only by the trinitarian conception of Him. And so he insists on teaching the doctrine "vitally" rather than scholastically. To him tripersonality was another "special note" of God to be placed alongside His immensity and spirituality, not as something by way of addition, but as entering into the very idea of God. Hence in Calvin's opinion there can be no such thing as a monodistic God, for a divine monod is to him less conceivable than a divine Trinity.

Calvin eschewed the speculation and illustration of so many of the Early Fathers, but insisted, in his Catechism of 1532, that "our intelligence is not able to conceive the Father without at the same time comprehending the Son in whom His living image is repeated, and the Spirit in whom His power and virtue are manifested." To illustrate this, we note that Calvin starts with the creation of heaven and earth as the foundation of all revelation. But he makes this the introduction to two further articles of faith when he asserts for Christ and the Holy Spirit the category of creator. Hence the activities of God in redemption and regeneration partake of the absoluteness of His activities in creation.

Where Calvin makes a valuable contribution to the doctrine is when he insists, in opposition to the subordinationism introduced by the Eastern theologians, on the perfect and complete equality, of the Three Persons within the being of the Godhead, and the self-existence of each of them as Father, Son, and Spirit, thus attributing perfect and absolute divinity to the Son and the Spirit as to the Father. The doctrine of the Trinity was to Calvin, Warfield says, a "postulate of his profoundest religious emotions and was given indeed with his experience of salvation itself."

God's Character or Attributes

With regard to the second head of the doctrine of God—the divine character, or what is commonly called His attributes—Calvin is, in this also practical rather than speculative.

Though the attributes of God are made the main subject of

two chapters in *The Institutes,* one discussing in detail the revelation of the divine perfections in His works and deeds, the other the revelation He made of them in His Word, it is true that neither in Calvin nor in Zwingli do we meet with a formal doctrine of the attributes or with any attempt at classification. It is significant, perhaps, that in the first edition of *The Institutes* Calvin did attempt a classification of the ethical attributes, but they fell out of the further editions and were never afterwards developed. Calvin does not so much neglect the attributes as deal with them in a practical way so as to focus attention on what God is to us. As Thornwell has put it in this very connection: "What He is in Himself is past finding out, what He is to us has been made manifest."

What we call the attributes of God became to Calvin the sum of our knowledge of Him. And so the attributes are rather mentioned in connection with God's works and manifestations in the world below. For example, He "sustains the world by His immense power, governs it by His wisdom, preserves it by His goodness, rules over the human race especially by His righteousness and justice, bears with it in His mercy, defends it by His protection."

Two terms Calvin uses frequently of God are "severity" and "clemency," severity in God's attitude as Judge of the world, and clemency toward the penitent sinner, inculcating in His creatures the response of fear and trust. Lord and Father are the designations Calvin most frequently applied to God, and it is not too much to say that for him true religion involved the recognition of God, not only as Lord, but as Father also. The sense of the divine Fatherhood is as fundamental to Calvin's conception of God as is that of divine sovereignty. Indeed his doctrine is outstanding among Reformed statements in the commanding place it gives to the divine Fatherhood. A sovereign is how Calvin conceived of God, and in his view God's Fatherhood and love did not divest Him of those fundamental attributes which constitute Him the upholder and vindicator of moral law in the universe.

But, let it be emphasized again, Calvin is insistent that God is not properly conceived of unless He is conceived of in all His perfections. This for him preserves the unity of God. While we recognize that God in Himself is more than the aggregate of all His perfections, (His revealed attributes tell us what God is to us,) and that, according to Calvin, is all we need to know. But God is wholly in each of His attributes. Every attribute of man is limited by the finitude of his nature, so much justice, so much mercy, so much love. But in God each attribute is the perfect and complete expression of His nature. It would be legitimate, even, to conceive of God as just possessing one attribute, say holiness or goodness. Whether it manifests itself in justice or love or compassion or mercy, it is just the holiness or goodness of God manifested in the particular situation that it meets with. It must, therefore, be a legitimate inference to draw from Calvin that whatever attribute in God we may recognize or designate in a given situation, it is the nature of God manifesting itself in circumstances in which a particular aspect of His character comes more clearly to view.

Thus we see that the entire discussion of the character of God is directed in Calvin toward a religious, rather than a philosophical, end.

God's Will or Purpose

To Calvin, as to the biblical writers, the will of God is the expression of His character. What God is determines what God does and how He does it. In other words, there is nothing arbitrary in any of God's acts: they are the free expression of His nature and character.

To say, as is frequently done, that Calvin reduces God to the bare notion of arbitrary will without ethical content is, therefore, untrue to Calvin's teaching and is based, probably, on a misunderstanding of his use of the term "the will of God." Here Calvin differed from the Schoolmen. The opinion held by Aquinas and Duns Scotus that an expiatory sacrifice for sin, for example, might, if God had so chosen, have been dispensed with, found no countenance with the Reformers who took their stand on the immutable character of the divine righteousness, and on the idea of the Moral Law as founded, not in the mere will of God, but in His essential nature.

There is in Calvin, in any case, no reduction of God into pure and naked will. Nor does he teach that the divine will is the only and sufficient cause in the universe, though he does assert that all that takes place must take place in accordance with the divine will. This he explains by saying that whatever God has willed will certainly come to pass, although it comes to pass "in such a manner that the cause and matter of it are found in second causes." So little is he inclined to reduce the Father in Heaven to bare will that he speaks of "the fiction of absolute power which, as it is profane, so ought to be deservedly detestable to us," and again he speaks of those who are "profanely safeguarding His righteousness from His power." Thus the will of God is to Calvin the complete expression of the divine perfection, and for him there is no belief in the true and living God without belief in the predestinating will of God.

This raises Calvin's treatment of the doctrine of the divine predestination. The doctrine itself is not included in the Geneva Catechism, and it is only at the end of the third book of *The Institutes*—what may be called the last book of his theology proper—that Calvin discusses predestination. In the first edition of 1536 the doctrine is not dealt with as a special topic: it appears, as if it were incidentally, in three or four passages in connection with the negation of human merit. The first direct exposition of the doctrine appears in 1537 and then as the development *a posteriori* of an experiential fact. In 1539 *The Institutes* contain a chapter devoted to predestination—the eighth chapter out of a total of seventeen. The doctrine thus stated met with objections which called for more exact statement, and in the last edition in 1539 he arrives at his doctrine of Double Predestination, that of the righteous and that of the wicked. It is now recognized that if it is not the foundation of his theology, and we hold that it is not, it is certainly the keystone which sustains the edifice. Its affirmations rest firmly and squarely on the sovereignty of God

By the sovereignty of God, we understand, put in very simple terms, that God makes His own plan and carries it out in His own time and way.

If God is intelligent—and He is Supreme Mind—He must plan. That plan Calvin expounds as the decree of God. As all God's acts constitute one system, so all God's decrees constitute one purpose. While we are wont to speak of decrees in the plural, because with our finite understanding we grasp God's plan only partially and in fragments, it is in reality only one decree constituting one plan. God's decree is eminently rational, the outworking of the Supreme Mind, and the product of all His attributes.

Then, if God is almighty —and He is Unlimited Omnipotence—He must carry out His plan. The sovereignty of the eternal Throne is engaged in the execution of the will of God.

And if God is all-wise—and He is Infinite Wisdom—He must carry out His plan in His own time and way. Any change would be a reflection on the wisdom of His design as well as on His power of execution.

It is, thus, not possible to conceive of anything interfering with the complete and perfect exercise of the divine sovereignty. The least interference or interruption would reflect on His intelligence, or His power, or His wisdom, and He would no longer be God.

The Doctrine of God Applied

I now propose to examine how Calvin applies the ruling principle of divine sovereignty in three spheres that are relevant to our study—the spheres of knowledge, of salvation, and of providence. In the sphere of knowledge, it is the sovereignty of divine revelation; in the sphere of salvation, the sovereignty of divine election; and in the sphere of providence, the sovereignty of divine foreordination.

The Sphere of Knowledge: Revelation

We believe that self-revelation is a quality of the divine nature, and that it is as natural for God to reveal Himself as it is for the sun in the heavens to shine. But we do not have, therefore, to believe that God was under necessity to reveal Himself either in the creation of the universe or in the "garnishing of the heavens." Self-revelation belongs to the ineffable fellowship of the Blessed Trinity and can be perfectly fulfilled in the interrelations that we believe to exist within the Trinity. God is thus self-sufficient and He does not need to bring any of His ideas into outward realization by means of a universe.

Yet in sovereign grace God chose to let His self-manifestation flow beyond Himself so that the universe now reflects His nature and His character. This is Calvin's starting point in dealing with the knowledge of God. "There is not an atom of the world," he says, "in which you cannot behold some brilliant sparks at least of His glory . . . for the exact symmetry of the universe is a mirror in which we may contemplate the otherwise invisible God." This is what has been called Calvin's philosophy of nature: It would be better termed his theology of God and of His creature man.

"Our doctrine," Calvin remarks, "in so far as it ought to be deemed true and solid wisdom consists almost entirely of two parts, the knowledge of God and of ourselves." To Calvin the capacity to know God is man's great spiritual endowment. All men everywhere and at all times, have been endowed with the capacity to understand and develop an acquaintance with God. This is what he calls the *semen religionis* which is inherent in the very constitution of man's nature. Thus the revelation and the response are alike of God's creation. God, who is the fount of being, is also the source of knowledge, and the very principles by which man is capable of knowing anything have their termination in God the Creator. While we could legitimately define religion as man's response to the self-manifestation of God, Calvin would rather say that the capacity for religion is inherent in man, and is aided from without by the creation in which, as in a mirror, the perfections of God may be contemplated.

By thus placing the origin of the whole revelational process historically in the creative act of God, Calvin teaches that the sovereignty of God is perfect and absolute. As this applies to the general revelation of God, so it applies to the special revelation. Recognizing that all have "degenerated from the true knowledge of God" and that it is a false God that sinful man now conceives of and worships, Calvin adds: "it remains for God Himself to give a revelation concerning Himself from Heaven." In Scripture we have this revelation. "It must be considered as a fixed principle," he says, "that in order to enjoy the light of true religion, we ought to begin with the doctrine of Heaven and that no man can have the least knowledge of true and sound doctrine without having been a disciple of the Scriptures." Scripture, quite apart from its doctrine of redemption, was necessary even to give us "a just and lively description of God as He appears in His works." How much clearer is the face of God in Christ the Mediator!

Calvin does not make the sharp distinction that later theologians make between the content of general revelation and that of special revelation. Both are of God, both are equally valid and authoritative, and Calvin asserts that "the qualifications thus enumerated (in the Scriptures) are just those which we saw shining in the heavens, and on earth, compassion, goodness, mercy, justice, judgment, and truth." He thus takes pains to make clear the harmony of the description of God given in the Scriptures with the conception of Him we may draw from His works, the Scriptures being but a plainer republication of the general revelation of God given in His works and deeds.

This is in line with Calvin's later teaching which links redemption also with the general character of God. Though he gives soteriology a prominent place, he claims that it is not the whole of theology. The self-revelation of the Infinite must be regarded as the foundation of theology. Even in special revelation, it is still the sovereign Creator that Calvin is speaking about. In order to make the divine revelation effective, God not only presented us with this supreme objective evidence of Himself in Scripture, but He gave the creative Spirit, who acted as the author of Scripture, to enlighten men's hearts and minds to understand and appropriate to themselves the revelation of Himself. It was needful, he points out, "that the same Spirit who spake by the mouth of the prophets should come into our hearts and touch them to the quick." Elsewhere he states his position even more clearly: "Accordingly we need not wonder if there are many who doubt as to the author of Scripture, for although the majesty of God is displayed in it, yet none but those who have been enlightened by the Holy Spirit have eyes to perceive what ought, indeed, to have been visible to all, and yet is visible to the elect alone."

Thus Calvin attributes to the creative sovereignty of God the revelation of Himself, the entire character of Scripture in which the saving revelation is given, and the quickening of the human heart to respond to it. It is this sovereignty, testified by the Spirit in our hearts, that gives supreme authority to the revelation.

To Calvin all revelation bears on its face this mark of the divine sovereignty. This must be so in the very nature of the case. A time-conditioned creature cannot think in terms of eternity: the only source of man's true knowledge of eternal things is from God, Who alone can think in eternal categories, and so reveal the truth to us in the measure in which, by His enabling grace, we can bear it.

The Sphere of Salvation: Election

It is in the third book of *The Institutes* that Calvin deals with election and reprobation, and then only as deductions from a consideration of the extent of the Spirit's work in regeneration. Since the work of Christ is not efficacious for all men, although Christ is freely offered to them in the gospel, the reason for this must be in the predestination of God. This is different from foreordination. The predestination of God is His eternal decree by which He has determined in Himself what He would have become of every individual of mankind. All are not created for the same destiny. Some are predestinated to eternal life, some to eternal death. The election of the one class leads to eternal life by the effectual calling and saving work of the Holy Spirit, the destruction of the other class is secured by their own wickedness. By their faith the one class make evident their election, by unbelief the other class make evident their reprobation. Here we have the clearest application of the divine sovereignty.

Salvation entails on the part of God the full choice of the objects of His mercy, and this choice is an eternal election from God's side. That means that what God does in time in the salvation of souls, He willed to do in eternity. This is really a tracing of the experience of salvation back to its roots in the sovereignty of divine grace. In this connection it is interesting to note that the term elect is applied to none in the Scripture except those who are in Christ, and Calvin himself, as already indicated, places his exposition of this doctrine in book 3, after he had dealt with the doctrine of salvation in Christ. Election is thus viewed and interpreted in the light of an experience of salvation, the context in which it becomes meaningful.

It is in light of the fact that all are not put in possession of salvation that Calvin expounds the corollary of election, reprobation. On both he is equally emphatic as disclosures of the will of God given in Scripture. "The predestination by which God accepts some to the hope of life, and adjudges others to eternal death, no man who would be thought pious ventures to deny," he affirms with perhaps a confidence that not all the pious nowadays share. Notwithstanding, he makes an essential difference between election and reprobation. While "unconditional" is a term applied to both, since both proceed from the free and sovereign will of God, the distinction lies in the fact that while men are saved by an act of absolutely free and unmerited grace, without regard to faith or good works, men are condemned on the ground of their own sin. This is in line with Paul's argument that while the vessels of mercy were afore prepared by God unto glory, the vessels of wrath were fitted for destruction, fitted not by God but by their own character and conduct.

While it is clear that Calvin attributes their reprobation to the decree of God, he does not suggest that the decree is the ground of condemnation, or the cause of their corrupt state. He indeed teaches a positive decree of reprobation involving more than mere preterition, involving a foreordination to damnation, but it must be remembered that Calvin does not present foreordination as the cause of acts in the sphere of human responsibility, even when the decree makes their occurrence certain. In other words, the judicial reprobation need not be viewed as merely a purpose formed in eternity and therefore unconditional, but as having its termination in time as the inescapable sequel to a career of impenitence and sin.

Uneasiness has been expressed by many true Calvinists that in Calvin himself, and in many of the formularies based on his system, notably the Irish Articles and the Westminster Confession of

Faith, the decree of salvation is referred wholly to grace, while the decree of reprobation is referred wholly to justice, and to God's inscrutible sovereignty. Two considerations have to be borne in mind. It must not be overlooked that within the decree of reprobation, so to speak, there is the operation of kindness, goodness, forbearance, and mercy to those who persist in rejecting the overtures of peace, and that there must be somewhere, in the light of their refusal, a place or point where forbearance goes no further and holy equity takes over and the rebel is abandoned to his deserts. And then, as already indicated, the whole nature and character of God must be seen to be expressed in this manifestation of justice, and not merely one attribute of His being. The whole wealth of His nature is poured out in this administration of His justice, and good and gracious and holy ends are, we doubt not, being served by it. It is a vindication of all that He is as a great God and a Savior.

In short, we do not know why the elect are chosen, but we know why the reprobate are condemned, and Calvin would have us rest there. "Wherefore," he says, "let us in the corruption of human nature contemplate the evident cause of condemnation rather than enquire into a cause hidden and almost incomprehensible in the predestination of God." Of the doctrine of reprobation he uses words, often quoted against him: "It is an awful decree, I confess," with the variant renderings of "a dreadful decree," and "a horrible decree." The actual words of Calvin—*decretum horrible*—are capable of a better translation. The Latin *horribilis* is a derivative of the verb *horreo,* meaning "to tremble," or "to stand in awe." The words of Calvin could, therefore, be appropriately translated "an awe-inspiring decree." And that eminently suits the subject.

The decree of election, on the other hand, he expounds, not only in the interests of his leading principle, the glory of God, but for the comforting and strengthening of God's people. In one of his sermons on Ephesians he observes, "There are two principal reasons why this doctrine should be proclaimed and why it has great utility for us . . . one is that God may be magnified as He deserves, the second is that we may be certified of our salvation in order that we may invoke Him our Father in full liberty." He concludes: "if we have not these two things, woe to us, for we have neither faith nor religion."

Thus the doctrine of predestination in its aspects of election and reprobation has the double significance that it affirms the divine independence and at the same time assures the believing soul of his salvation.

What is important to note, as we conclude this section, is that the sovereignty of a holy God, showing favor to some, and injustice to none, does not reflect a parsimonious heart, but can be viewed in the wider perspective of the salvation of a multitude which no man can number as the consummation of His sovereign purpose. Calvin somewhere introduces the thought of Augustine approvingly to this effect: "It is judiciously remarked by Augustine," he says, "that there is the brightest example of gratuitous election in the Head of the Church Himself, that it may not perplex us in the members. He did not become the Son of God by living a righteous life, but was gratuitously invested with this high honour that He might afterwards render others partakers of the gifts which were bestowed on Him." This would point to Christ the Elect of God as the Head and Representative of a new humanity who should be members of His body and partakers of His gifts.

This is the thought elaborated by Abraham Kuyper and B. B. Warfield. "The sovereignty of God," says Warfield, "lays the sure foundation for the salvation of the world. God and God alone saves now, and in His own good time He will bring the world in its entirety to the feet of Him whom He presents to us as the Saviour of the world, of whom He has disclosed that He has made propitiation, not for our sins only, but for the sins of the whole world." Warfield concludes in these heart-lifting words: "Christ has been made head over all things to His Church, and the rate of the Church's progress to its goal, the nature of the progress, the particular individuals who are to be brought into it, are in His hands and under His control. . . . His people may be few today, the world will be His people tomorrow." Calvinism can accept this, in the face of every evidence to the contrary, because it rests utterly and completely on the sovereign grace of Almighty God, not as a parsimonious gift to the few, but as the outpouring of the bounty and unlimited wealth of the divine nature.

The Sphere of Providence: Foreordination

Calvin explains his doctrine of providence thus: "By providence we mean, not an unconcerned sitting of God in heaven, from which He merely observes the things that are done in the world; but that all-active and all-concerned seatedness on His throne above by which He governs the world which He Himself has made." And so he concludes: "That Providence, therefore, which we ascribe to God, pertains as much to His operating hands as to His observing eyes."

Here, then, the transcendence and immanence of God meet in the history of the world and the experience of individual men and women.

The transcendence of God means that God unceasingly rules by His providence in pursuance of a purpose. There we enter the field of foreordination, rather than that of predestination. The world in all its parts and processes and stages and forms of life is the outcarrying in time of one divine plan, conceived in the eternal reason of the Godhead and realized by creative power, wisdom, and love. The relation of this divine purpose in eternity to its execution in time is the dominant thought in Calvin's theology in general, and in His doctrine of providence in particular.

On the other hand he proclaims the immanence of God who, as he puts it, "everywhere diffuses, sustains, dominates, and quickens all things in heaven and in earth," who "circumscribed by no boundaries, by transfusing His own vigour into all things, breathes into them being, life and motion." Thus God acts in all things, acting from within outwards, from the center of every atom and from the innermost springs of life and thought, of feeling and will, a continuous sequence of cause and effect.

Calvin's doctrine of providence singles out what he terms "three distinct elements in regard to the government of the world." These he calls, respectively, general providence, particular providence, and special providence.

By general providence Calvin means that by which "God directs all creatures according to the condition and property which He has given to each in forming them." This direction is no other, Calvin adds, "than that which we call the order of nature," which gives to human nature itself its plenitude and completion.

Particular providence, by which God works in His creatures to subserve His goodness, justice, and judgment, directs the effects of general providence on human nature.

Special providence is the operation of saving grace, so that human nature is restored and brought into obedience.

In all this the action of God is absolutely sovereign, for all the means to execute His desires and to accomplish them in and through His creatures are at His disposal. God having fixed the laws of the universe, and given life to His creatures, makes use of these laws and these creatures to accomplish His will and realize His plan.

If it be conceded that, in the familiar words of the Westminster Shorter Catechism, God "foreordains whatsoever comes to pass," or in Calvin's own words, that "He so overrules all that nothing occurs without His command," and that nothing in heaven or earth falls outside His ordination, then there must be some explanation of evil and its entrance into and operation in the world, that shall safeguard the divine character. Calvin deals with this. The will of God he holds to be the necessity of all things, yet God is not the author of evil. The wicked can do nothing without His appointment, yet His holiness is not tarnished by their evil deeds. Calvin's statement is clear in itself, if not in its application: "God works His purposes by means of the wicked, so that the sanctity which is in Him does not justify them at all, while the infection that is in them does not contaminate Him at all."

Lecerf has stated the Christian position tersely thus: "For the Christian who has been apprehended by the sovereign God, there is no such thing as the problem of evil; there is only the mystery of evil." This I presume means God's sovereignty solves or evaporates the problem, but does not illumine the dark mystery.

There is the further difficulty of reconciling the expressions of God's desire for men with God's absolute decree concerning man. It would seem clear that God wills with genuine desire when

He does not will by executive purpose. This has led theologians to make use of the two terms, the decretive will and the preceptive will of God, or, His secret and His revealed will. For example, it is revealed that God would have all men to be saved and come to a knowledge of the truth, while He has not decreed universal salvation. Commenting on 2 Peter 3:9, Calvin says: "But it may be asked, If God wishes none to perish, why is it so many perish? To this my answer is, that no mention is here made of the hidden purpose of God according to which the reprobate are doomed to their own ruin, but only of His will as made known to us in the gospel. For God there stretches out His hand, without a difference, to all, but lays hold only of those, to lead them to Himself, whom He has chosen before the foundation of the world."

Thus it cannot be said that God merely desires the ultimate salvation of all men without also desiring their repentance and faith and sanctification: for, as Calvin says, that would mean "to renounce the difference between good and evil." The position could thus be more clearly put as meaning that God desires all men to be righteous in character and life and to use the means He has appointed to that end. It is in harmony with the revealed will of God that without the use of the means appointed by Him the end shall not be attained. As a holy God, the Creator commands all His moral creatures to be holy, and He cannot be conceived as in any way obstructing their pursuit of holiness by His decree.

There is room left, also, for the full exercise of human responsibility in regard to one's own salvation and that of our fellow men. Calvin affirms in clearest language the reality of human freedom as a natural endowment of man, and of man's responsibility for his voluntary actions.

But this freedom is only one factor in the complicated web of human life. There is always the other factor of external providence which has a profound bearing on human choices and often decides the line of action which man deems it right to take. And providence is the sphere of divine foreordination. There is thus in every human act a concurrence of two lines, divine sovereignty and human responsibility, appearing to move along parallel lines, but meeting, as all parallel lines do, in infinity. God is the highest cause of everything that happens. In His plan He uses angels and demons, sinful men and regenerate men. In His infinite wisdom He treats every agent according to its nature, doing violence to none, predestinating and preserving man's responsibility and accountability. "It does not prevent," as Calvin puts it, "each creature whether in heaven or on earth from having and retaining its quality and nature, and following its own inclinations." Thus each realizes his nature and his destiny fully, in accordance with eternal law. This is as true of the wicked as of the righteous, of angels as of devils. An angelic nature brings forth angelic fruit and enters upon an angelic destiny; a devilish nature brings forth devilish fruit and enters upon a devil's destiny. It is so because in the nature of things it cannot be otherwise. God is responsible for the law that governs the case in each instance; He is not responsible for the fruits.

In the light of all this, it may perhaps be legitimate to sum up, as A. A. Hodge does, that God can determine any action without causing it, and that while His decree determines everything, it causes nothing.

Modern indeterminism would seem irreconcilable with Calvinistic foreordination. But indeterminism, as now proclaimed, merely goes to say that events are not predictable because the laws of behavior are not determinable. But that brings us only so far as human knowledge and observation and experiment go. They do not reach as far as the law and will of God go. To human observation and experiment many phenomena are indeterminable, but that is because observation and experiment cannot penetrate far enough. It is true that this argument of indeterminism may be pressed into the service of the autonomy of man and the freedom of human will and action as uninfluenced by anything outside man himself.

While Calvin accepts the freedom of man to make his choice and determine his course of action in the line of his personal choice and, therefore, of his nature, that does not leave him truly free. He is still at the command of his nature and very often its mere slave, and in the doing of evil the nature is not uninfluenced by forces from without. Christian liberty, however, is of a different order since grace acts from within. It is a misconception to suppose that by irresistible grace is meant an *ab extra* coercing influence. Calvin, like Augustine, delights to present it as the law written on the mind and the heart, indicating that grace acts from within, so that there is no longer any resistance or any desire to offer it. To be made willing in a day of God's sovereign power is the highest liberty, enlisting all the faculties of mind, heart, and spirit. As a bird is free in the air and a fish in the sea, each in his own native element, so man is truly free in the will of his God.

Thus divine providence presents to us the only constant and immutable thing in the universe, the will of God. What is known to us as natural law, or the law of human thought, is constant only insofar as it is an expression of the will of God. The will of Almighty God is the dominant factor in every situation, the only source and pledge of fulfillment for the entire nature of man, and for the destiny of the universe.

It is true, as the late Daniel Lamont once pointed out, that the word sovereignty does not fully define the gracious relation of God to man. That is, he thought, why so many shy at the word, and rest content with the assurance that God is love. But, as he pointed out, the love of God detached from the conviction of His sovereignty, wields no power. It is in the context of sovereignty that the Bible speaks of His love. It is the love of the Lord God, of the Sovereign Father. That sovereignty in its many-sidedness sweeps the entire moral universe and shall one day sweep it clean of all taint of moral evil. True, it does not in the here and now shed light on everything we want to know. There are hidden depths, as Professor Lamont remarked, in the counsels of the Godhead. The greatest Christian thinkers in every age have tried, not to probe the mysteries of the divine will—Calvin has sufficiently warned us against that presumption—but to find a resting place for their minds in the presence of these mysteries. And like Paul the Apostle they found rest at the place of wonder, adoration, and praise, as with him they exclaim: "Oh, the depth both of the wisdom and knowledge of God. How unsearchable are His judgments and His ways past finding out. For of Him, and through Him, and to Him are all things, to whom be glory for ever and ever, Amen."

6

JOHN CALVIN
THE MAN

O. R. Johnston

Exactly when and by whom the stereotype of Calvin's character was fixed it is not my purpose to examine. Certainly Bolen's work of 1577 contributed largely. But a stereotype there undoubtedly is, and a glance at a few typical twentieth-century sources will remind us of what is usually accepted.

In a brilliant Dutch history of western culture by no means hostile to the Christian faith, the illustrated *Atlas of Western Civilization,* we meet Calvin directing his "iron theocracy"[1] as "the hard and penetrating Calvin." If we take a standard reliable Church History we discover a certain reticence. From Williston Walker's eleven pages on Calvin's life and work we can cull only two adjectives that come anywhere near to a personal portrait—earnest and erudite. Walker's final comment on Beza, Calvin's successor, as "a man of more conciliatory spirit and gentler ways" certainly implies rigidity and harshness in Calvin.[2] And

141

this, let us remember, from Williston Walker, a man who had himself written a full-scale biography of Calvin! *The Oxford Dictionary of the Christian Church* depicts Calvin as "without the human attractiveness of the German Reformer [Luther]. He was disinterested, simple and austere in his private life, but his vindictiveness and his claim to be the supreme authority to decide what is true Christianity and what is not was resented even by his followers." As on other occasions when it deals with Reformation topics, we find this particular work a monument of erudite prejudice.

Turning to a writer more sympathetic to the Calvinist heritage, we may glance at J. S. Whale's book *The Protestant Tradition,* in which there is a section on Calvin's thought and influence. His fifty-two pages on Calvin contain little material to enable us to form a picture of the Genevan Reformer's personality. He is described as "fitted by faith, temperament and intellect to be a great theologian and a great churchman[3] . . . a man of precise notions and constructive action[4] . . . a practical man. He never avoided awkward issues[5] . . . a man of order, strong as iron in his certainty of the majesty, the sole causality, the glory of God."[6] Whale asserts that Calvin "hotly repudiates" or "warmly and bitterly disavows" unfair charges, despite the fact that "his legal training confirmed his native caution."[7] He can display "grim humour"[8] but is chiefly distinguished by his "pitiless logic"[9] or "unflinching logic."[10] This and no more do we learn of the man from Whale's pages. To be fair, it must be said that Whale is writing principally of the Protestant tradition rather than of the Reformers themselves, but the picture is scarcely even an outline— John Calvin: courageous, direct, cautious but heated in controversy, systematic to the point of ruthlessness. Such are the lineaments of the character drawn for us by some typical works of reference.

Four things are striking about the picture which has begun to emerge. First, there seems little doubt about the stature of Calvin. His scholarship is quite outstanding, based on vast linguistic and theological erudition; his style is incomparable, both in use of language (Latin or French) and in sense of form; his influence, both during his lifetime and subsequently, has been tremendous. On all hands it is agreed that we are looking at a great man.

The second fact which seems clear is that any outline of Calvin's character has to be carefully and delicately sketched in because the direct personal evidence available to the vast majority of those who have written about him is so scarce. We have no Table Talk as we have for Luther, and what indications we have from Calvin's works must be pieced together with great sensitivity like small pieces of an intricate mosaic. With Luther the task is more like that of putting together a simple jig-saw; there is only one proper place for each piece.

Third, it is worth pointing out that because of the relatively small amount of direct evidence, it is easy to build an outline model of Calvin's character and then to color it in with one's own surmises and conjectures. The nature and effect of this coloring will depend not so much on objective evidence, which is scanty, but to a great extent upon the biographer's own reaction to the Reformer's life work and doctrinal position, particularly those doctrines which have been in a special way connected with his name, such as the divine sovereignty, predestination, election, total depravity, scriptural revelation, and so on. Widely differing pictures can thus be built up around the same slender scaffolding of material.

Finally, it is interesting to note that there has been no great change in the image of Calvin as a person, even in the world of theological studies. Here again we discover a contrast with Luther, whose image has received considerable correction during the last forty years. Early undisguised vilification by Roman Catholic writers had been succeeded in the late nineteenth and early twentieth centuries by a smear campaign suggesting mental unbalance or similar aberration. However, beginning with Karl Holl in Germany (1932) right through to the works of our own Professor Rupp (1951 and 1953), scholarship has filled in the character of Luther fully, reliably, and in nearly every facet to the credit of the German reformer. Yet for most of us Calvin remains at best strangely elusive, at worst coldly repulsive, notwithstanding the monumental labors of Doumergue.

Early Influences on Calvin

John Calvin was born on July 10, 1509, at Noyon in Picardy, fourth son of the first wife of a minor legal official in the service of clergy and magistrates. The ancient and influential cathedral of Noyon dominated the town in more ways than one; Calvin's father was for four years the bishop's secretary. John was taught first by tutors and then later at a local boys' school—in both cases with the sons of the local aristocracy. Showing early promise of academic brilliance, he was sent to the Collège de la Marche in Paris at the age of 14 (1523) and destined for a clerical career. His father financed his education by obtaining for him a cathedral chaplaincy and later two other benefices—none of which involved any duties whatsoever. It was at the Collège de la Marche under the tutorship of Mathurin Cordier, a distinguished classicist, that Calvin began to take real delight in learning and to acquire what McNeill calls "that unfailing sense of style and diction that marks all his writings."[11] He later transferred to the more rigorous and conservative Collège de Montaigu, notorious, thanks to Erasmus's biting publicity, for its bad food and the bad health of its students in consequence.

What may be said of the young man during this early period of his studies? A hostile historian speaks of him as mentally alert and vigorous though given to much fasting, serious, reticent, and notably solitary. "He was never seen," comments Florimond de Raemond, "amongst groups of his fellows, always retiring, of a melancholy disposition . . . sharing his thoughts with few people, not taking pleasure in any company other than that of his own thoughts, a lover of seclusion." Cadier accepts this testimony.[12] But the least that can be said is that it needs some modification. Is this not the stereotype in its early stages? There is evidence pointing in a different direction. For example there is now no ground for believing the once popular epigram that Calvin was called by his fellow undergraduates "the accusative case." Doumergue has shown that the man who is supposed to have reported this said nothing of the kind. Admittedly Beza tells us that Calvin was critical of student vices, but given the demands of study (and they were heavy) and a real zeal for knowledge, given too a general adherence to

Christian morality, what is more probable than that Calvin should turn with some impatience from student buffoonery and licentiousness? Not every student takes part today in rag-day processions, but doubtless there can still be found those who will designate nonparticipants as solitary, overserious, and supercilious.

Other facts show Calvin in quite a different light; McNeill lists them for us: "He maintained good relations with his former schoolfellows of the de Hangest families, with three of whom, and their tutor, he had come to Paris. He was closely associated with his scholarly cousin, Olivétan, three years his senior, whom he had known also in Noyon. He became a welcome guest in the homes of two of the greatest men of the University, Guillaume Cop, a medical scholar, and Guillaume Budé, the most learned Hellenist of France. . . . Calvin formed close ties with the sons of these distinguished men, and later both families were represented among French religious refugees to Geneva. Through his influence a number of the de Hangest family also later became Protestants. . . . All these facts belie the picture of young Calvin as morose. It would be difficult indeed to discover a teenage student of his time who attracted so many choice friends. The fact that his friends were not the rank and file and that they were all older than he, has no doubt some significance. We may suppose that as a student he felt no attraction toward intellectual mediocrity."[13] If we may anticipate a little, and look back on the whole of Calvin's life, it is noteworthy that he very rarely severed a friendship, and in the few cases when he felt obliged to do so, it was more in sorrow than in anger. He does not overwhelm men like du Tillet and de Falais with scorn and reproach when they returned to Rome or espoused an unorthodox opinion, though he is warm in his persuasion to attempt their recovery, and betrays a certain stiffening and bitter humor in his last letters to de Falais.[14]

In 1528 Calvin's father changed his mind about his nineteen-year-old son's future and sent him to study law at Orléans. Already a licencié, Calvin then pursued his postgraduate studies (as we might call them) in law and later in literature at Orléans, Bourges, and Paris, with occasional visits to Noyon. He was at his father's deathbed in May 1531. His cousin Olivétan was at Orléans, and by now a convinced Protestant, while both at Orléans and at Bourges Calvin was taught by the classical scholar Melchior Wolmar, a German sympathetic toward Lutheranism, in whose circle Reformation ideas were often discussed. Calvin's sociability at this stage is attested in two ways—first by his election as president of the Picard students' group at Orléans (a choice scarcely open to an embittered recluse!) and second by the fact that he could still correspond with former student friends of this period right up to the end of his life. In the years 1531 and 1532 he was engaged in legal and humanistic studies leading to two publications, neither of which betrays any personal interest in matters religious, though while writing his commentary on Seneca's *De Clementia* he was lodging in the house of a Waldensian cloth merchant who was a zealous and fearless propagandist of Lutheran ideas and publications. The example of this man, Etienne Laforge, who was later to be burned at the stake for his faith, must have made some impression.

In 1533 Calvin's friend Nicholas Cop, Rector of the University of Paris, preached a sermon, parts of which bore strong resemblances to Reformation doctrine. Though not overtly anti-papal, it was a bold bid for popular support of religious reform; some sections of the sermon were Erastian, advocating a policy of Christian humanism, others more militant and based on actual sermons of German Reformers. Calvin was somehow implicated—scholars are not agreed just to what degree. But reaction came swiftly and Cop and Calvin both fled the capital. Calvin took refuge with friends in Angoulême at Claix in the house of Canon Louis du Tillet; in the months that followed he had the opportunity for quiet reading and discussion with a group of liberal clergy. In May 1534, after an interview with the aged biblical scholar Lefèvre d'Etaples, revered doyen of the moderate reforming party in France, Calvin resigned all his benefices. The break with Rome had been made.

Calvin's Conversion

We have now to consider the difficult matter of Calvin's conversion, difficult, that is, as far as the date of it is concerned. Calvin himself unambiguously refers to it as "sudden," so presumably he could date it himself. But it is the character of the conversion itself which is far more important. Calvin was always very reticent on the details of his personal life. He quietly omitted anything that might savor of self-advertisement; God must be glorified, not His worthless instrument. There is little material here for the psychologist, little of the delicate, tortuous and—let us admit this— subtly gratifying analysis of inner emotional conflict in which authors aspiring to greatness have indulged ever since Rousseau's *Nouvelle Héloïse.*

However, in the precious piece of autobiography that Calvin has left us in the Preface to his *Commentary on the Psalms* (1557), Calvin does tell us that he was stubbornly addicted to the superstitions of the papacy. This would seem to indicate that despite the discussion of Reformation issues which formed a more or less constant element in his student environment, he had never seriously considered leaving the Roman fold. Where else was there a rallying-point for Frenchmen anyway? An anguished question indeed, as M. Cadier stresses on more than one occasion. Yet there is no reason to doubt that discussion and example since his early days at Orléans in 1528 had been unconsciously working beneath the surface. So that in 1533 or 1534 it was revealed to him that he had been kicking against the goads of all these providential events, meetings, and conversations.

McNeill, rightly in my judgment, suggests that it was in all probability during the quiet days at Claix during the first half of 1534 that the light dawned. Thus Calvin's first public act of testimony to his newfound faith would be his renunciation of benefices at Noyon on May 21. God had drawn him from this deep mire, and he could no longer (if we may continue the metaphor) keep his hands soiled in the filth of blasphemy. He must refuse to retain even a nominal connection with a system that remained a public insult to the finished work of the Redeemer.

If this account is true, then Calvin again becomes in this respect also a brother of Martin Luther—both were converted in the study, poring over the Scriptures. Both seem to have sought peace of conscience in the traditional round of activities prescribed by

Roman tradition and found them wanting; both felt great reverence for the Church and at first recoiled from the way in which the new doctrines were tending, but both were made finally and utterly sure of the gospel and of their own state before God through studying the written Word.

It is surely no exaggeration to see chapters 3–5 of book 3 of *The Institutes* as an extended biblical commentary on Calvin's experience. He can write with such certainty and power about false and true repentance, the folly and confusion of papal notions of contrition, satisfaction, auricular confession, and similar unscriptural inventions not only because he has found the profound yet simple Bible teaching on true repentance, but also because this has been burned in upon his own heart by the Holy Spirit. Reticent though he was about his own particular pilgrimage, it is difficult not to hear the voice of a man who has lived in bondage. Among the scholastic authors, says Calvin, "there is indeed much talk concerning contrition and attrition. They torture souls with many misgivings, and immerse them in a sea of trouble and anxiety. But where they seem to have wounded hearts deeply, they heal all the bitterness with a light sprinkling of ceremonies."[15]

The Romanists set conditions which are complex, based on definitions which are obscure, contradictory, and sometimes impossible. Yet, Calvin goes on, "if there is anything in the whole of religion that we should most certainly know, we ought most closely to grasp by what reason, with what law, under what condition, with what ease or difficulty, forgiveness of sins may be obtained! Unless this knowledge remains clear and sure, the conscience can have no rest at all, no peace with God, no assurance or security; but it continually trembles, wavers, tosses, is tormented and vexed, shakes, hates and flees the sight of God. . . . Therefore, when consciences have for a long time wrestled with themselves, and exercised themselves in long struggles, they still do not find a haven in which to rest."[16]

The other aspect of Calvin's conversion to which I wish to allude is one which is too well known to spend much time on, but too important to omit entirely. It is the fact that Calvin always refers to his entry on the Christian life as a sovereign act of God's free grace, arresting him on the path to ruin and as it were forcibly halting his headlong career toward perdition. His heart was hardened, his will was stubborn, he was not easily drawn from the mire. But God subdued his heart and made it docile. It was Calvin's unswerving conviction from that moment onward that he was not his own; God's hand was upon him. "He could not explain in terms of human motivation how it happened that he resisted no longer: at once he found himself docile, tractable, obedient, alert to do the will of God."[17]

The other image which Calvin uses is the common scriptural picture of the opening of the eyes of the blind, the light given to those in darkness. The minister in Calvin's *Reply to Cardinal Sadoleto* (1539) speaks thus of his conversion: "Thou didst shine upon me with the brightness of thy Spirit, that I might detest these things [i.e. papal superstitions as the way of salvation] and recognize how impious and injurious they were; Thou didst bear the torch of Thy word before me that I might loathe them as they deserve; Thou didst arouse my soul." In this passage we find a personal expression of what had surely been Calvin's own experience, an expression of those principles which he puts in more strictly theological form in *The Institutes* in such words as these: "this bare and external proof of the Word of God should have been amply sufficient to engender faith, did not our blindness and perversity prevent it. But our mind has such an inclination to vanity that it can never cleave fast to the truth of God; and it has such a dullness that it is always blind to the light of God's truth. Accordingly, without the illumination of the Holy Spirit, the Word can do nothing."[18] Or again, "we shall possess a right definition of faith if we call it a firm and certain knowledge of God's benevolence towards us, founded upon the truth of the freely given promise in Christ, both revealed to our minds and sealed upon our hearts through the Holy Spirit."[19]

In this double aspect of mind and heart we see the total character of Calvin's own conversion. His fine intellect was illuminated by the Word of God and by grace perceived the mighty unity of all God's teaching about His gracious provision for sinners; on the other hand Calvin's intense and ardent nature found the seal of ownership and control set upon the *heart;* he was tamed, mastered, and directed, his energies henceforth set upon the glory of God alone.

The *Institutes* and Geneva Ministry

Whether Calvin had already started to plan and write his small introduction to Christian doctrine before the event of the placards against the Mass in October 1534 is not known. Certainly the situation of French Protestants became serious from this date, and the first edition of Calvin's doctrinal treatise, with its masterly apologia addressed to Francis I King of France, was ready by the summer of 1535. It was the book which was to go on growing, finally to become the large work which we now read as *The Institutes.* The work was designed both as a compendium of the doctrines of the Christian religion and as a confession offered to a persecuting king on behalf of the author's fellow believers. The excesses of Anabaptists in Germany and even within France were also in Calvin's mind; he felt it his duty to distinguish Reformation believers of the main stream from iconoclasts or those with extreme revolutionary intentions.

In 1534 Calvin had been successively at Noyon, Paris, Poitiers, Angouléme, and Orléans. After the affair of the placards he travelled beyond the borders of France—Metz, Strasbourg, and Basel, where the first edition of *The Institutes* appeared. We find him then in Ferrara, where for a short time Frenchmen of unorthodox views were welcomed by the liberally minded French princess Renée, who had married the Duke Hercule d'Este, a son of Lucretia Borgia. But persecution threatened even there, and Calvin took advantage of a temporary amnesty offered to religious exiles by visiting Paris in June 1536 to settle some property matters. He then intended to go to Strasbourg, and it seems no injustice to what we know of his temperament and gifts to assume that his aim was (as one biographer puts it, "to resume the life of a scholarly interpreter and inspirer, from a quiet nook, of the movement in which he preferred to let others take the posts of danger and of power."[20] What occurred on that fateful journey is well known even to those who have no more than a nodding acquaintance with Reformation history.

Forced by the renewed hostilities between the Emperor Charles V and Francis I to take another road to Strasbourg, Calvin found himself staying for one night at Geneva en route. His companion du Tillet let it be known that the brilliant young author of the *Institutio* was in the city, and the leading Reformer of the place, a powerful red-bearded gospel preacher by name Guillaume Farel (1489–1565), called upon him first imploring and then thundering at Calvin to remain and help to organize the work of Reformation then proceeding, and to teach the people. Shaken by Farel's solemnity and urgency, he complied. In his own words: "Master Guillaume Farel held me back in Geneva, not so much by his advice and urgent exhortation as by a fearsome adjuration, as if God from on high had stretched out His hand to stay me . . . after he heard that I had some particular study for which I wished to keep myself free, when he saw he could get nowhere by prayer he even went as far as a curse, that it might please God to curse my rest and the tranquillity for study that I was seeking, if in so great necessity I were to withdraw and refuse to give my help."[21] Shattered and somewhat ashamed, Calvin stayed. He was never to set foot on French soil again, and Geneva was to be the scene of his labors from that day in 1536 until his death in May 1564, nearly twenty-eight years later, apart from a period in Strasbourg from 1538 to 1541 in which he was the pastor to the French refugee congregation.

While in Strasbourg as well as fulfilling his pastoral duties, Calvin took part in several ecumenical conversations. Even this work was undertaken against all that Calvin had planned, for after his banishment from Geneva in 1538 he had gone to Basel to work away quietly at another edition of his *Institutes*. But the Strasbourg Reformers—Butzer, Capito, and Sturm—employing something like Farel's technique two years earlier, solemnly admonished him that he was evading a responsibility for which he had been called and equipped, and once more Calvin acquiesced. He spent three happy years at Strasbourg. The senior Reformer there,

Butzer, was a man of wide sympathies eighteen years older than Calvin who was not yet thirty. The city was politically less inflammable than Geneva, and Calvin's pastoral charge was not an overheavy burden. In May 1539 there came hints that he was thinking of marriage, and in August of the next year he married the widow of an artisan from Liège. The happiness of their marriage was disturbed only by the continual ill health of both husband and wife. They were to enjoy each other's company for only nine years; a son born in 1542 died in infancy. The loss both of his son and of his wife seven years later caused Calvin great grief, and he determined thereafter to lead a solitary life. Even in these events he saw the hand of God, "a severe wound," he wrote of his infant son's death, "but our Father knows what is best for his children."

Calvin's recall to Geneva came in October 1540. The decision to go back was not taken without considerable inner struggle. His Strasbourg friends did all that they could to dissuade him, but Calvin knew where his God-given duty lay. "There is no place under heaven that I am more afraid of," he wrote to Viret. Calvin so often asserts his own innate timidity that in any assessment of the Reformer's character we must take this seriously. He hated the limelight and he hated responsibility, at any rate in public office. Unlike Knox and Luther, he was by temperament a quiet and sensitive man to whom any kind of struggle but a literary one was repulsive. Yet this was the man who returned to Geneva, to endure the constant strain of hostility, apathy, immorality, and ignorance on all hands.

He confessed that the first few months almost wore him out. Nor was relief to be given speedily. It was fifteen years before the anti-Calvin party was removed from its supreme position. During those fifteen years church discipline was resented, and Calvin was insulted in the streets and attacked from the pulpit by unorthodox teachers. Important and influential families were ranged against him. He winced from violence and was constantly subject to attack, either in his good name, his theology, or his policies for the well-being of Geneva. Luther seemed to thrive on opposition. Calvin was slowly worn down, sustained only by the hidden resources of the spirit.

This is not the place to chronicle his tribulations at Geneva, but it might be useful to note that Calvin's control of Geneva, if such it may be called, was without any of the apparatus that we associate with the modern word "dictator." He "used lawful means, went unarmed and unguarded, lived modestly and without display, sought advice from many, claimed no authority save as a commissioned minister of the Word, assumed no title of distinction or political office." It was not until Christmas Day 1559, after he had been instrumental in the admission of hundreds of refugees to citizenship, that he himself, on the invitation of the magistrates, became a citizen.[22] The dominance of Calvin's views on *all* matters was never achieved, and when he had espoused a particular cause on principle, it was often only after years of tenacious campaigning, preaching, and persuading that he won his point in the city's assemblies.

Calvin's Character

We have already mentioned that Calvin never enjoyed robust health in manhood. From about the age of thirty we are told that he suffered from headaches, catarrh, asthma, and indigestion. On occasions he could not see his lecture notes because his vision was so impaired by migraine. After 1558, when he had an attack of quartan fever, he was never anything but an invalid, stricken with arthritis, hemorrhoids, and then pleurisy leading to tuberculosis. He was ceaselessly in pain, and had finally to be carried to the cathedral to preach.

Any more thorough assessment of Calvin's character must be made in the light of these disabilities—the deterioration in physical health due to disease, and no doubt aided by the state of more or less continuous exhaustion in which he must have lived. It is not easy to imagine the toll on his time and energies taken by lecturing and preaching, writing and correcting new editions of older works, corresponding with old friends and influential leaders all over Europe, keeping his doors open to entertain strangers and refugees from many lands. Under these circumstances, it is not surprising that a naturally sensitive man should prove quick-tempered, and certainly Calvin does give us on occasion the impression of being irascible, "touchy" as we should now put it. Before his opponent has finished speaking, a stinging retort is on its way back. The early pages of his *Reply to Cardinal Sadoleto* contain a passionate and detailed justification of his behavior in his first years at Geneva. Is this personal apologia perhaps somewhat overelaborate, the defense excessively concerned with Calvin's own reputation? Is there room for another Galatians after the death of the Apostles? It is hard to be certain, but one cannot help asking these questions.

In controversy Calvin was accustomed to use strong words distasteful to us today. Yet there is another factor which must be taken into account here. Just as in the case of Servetus, while admitting the wrong that was done, we go on to point out that in that particular age such—and often worse—was the usual fate of the heretic (one pile of faggots here, for instance, contrasted with more than 300 in the five years' reign of our own Mary Tudor), so in the case of Calvin's vituperative language. One wonders whether those who are so ready to castigate Calvin's intemperate idiom in controversial matters have steeped themselves in the literary battles of the sixteenth century to such an extent that they can say, not simply that Calvin is bitter and intolerant, but that he far outstrips his contemporaries in bitterness and intolerance. It is this kind of perspective that we must seek in order truly to evaluate the temper of the Reformer's writings. Judged by the standards of his age, I should venture to say that an impartial investigation would not justify our calling Calvin's wording excessive.

It is only fair however to consider whether there has not been a degree of whitewashing on the side of Calvin's friends. Let us take, for example, Beza's *Discours,* usually referred to as Beza's *Life of Calvin.* It is certainly fulsome, for it is the voice of a man who has just lost a leader and a dear friend. "Never did Calvin have an enemy," he writes, "who in assailing him was not making war against God." He concludes his brief account of some of Calvin's adversaries thus: "In short, I think that you will not find any heresy, ancient, lately renewed or reforged in our time, which he [Calvin] has not destroyed to its very foundations." Later he defends Calvin from cruelty and excessive severity; no adulterer was ever executed in Geneva, he points out, and only one heretic was burned, and that with general approval.

However, even Beza, when he comes to Calvin's irritability, is forced to comment: "I do not wish to make an angel out of a man. Notwithstanding, because I know how God has wonderfully used even this vehemence, I must not be silent. Besides his temperament which was naturally inclined to anger, his quick mind, the indiscretion of several people, the many and infinitely varied business of the Church of God, and—towards the end of his life—illnesses both ordinary and serious had made him morose and difficult. But far from taking pleasure in this fault, no one saw it better than he did, nor counted it so great." As to his vehemence in public pronouncements and writings, Beza sees it as prophetic and majestic; religion, he reminds us, is no cold matter—it must be fiery if it is true faith. Beza, then, extenuates but does not attempt to deny Calvin's irascibility in his later years. Nor did Calvin struggle with this temptation only in his declining period; in Strasbourg he had lost his temper in Zell's house over the attempts of Caroli to drive a wedge between himself and the other Reformation leaders there. In a letter to Farel about the incident he admitted "I sinned gravely."[23]

We can moreover go some way toward counterbalancing the hard and sometimes intemperate language with which Calvin assails his enemies in matters theological. He was in many ways a tolerant man. Though he was absolutely certain of the broad lines on which Christian theology must move if it is to be true to itself, in detailed exegesis he is constantly cautious. Readers of the Commentaries will know how careful he is to give the various views, not always pontificating but time and time again telling us, after reviewing the linguistic and patristic interpretations, which sense he is inclined to attribute to the verse in question. His words in the first preface to Olivétan's French Bible are worth quoting here. Having commended the translator in general terms, he continues, "However, there are, I have no doubt, passages which will not please everyone because of the diversity of our apprehension or because in a work of such a length we sometimes fall asleep. I invite the readers if they meet with passages of this nature not to bite a man who is a worthy servant of the sacred word, not to attack him, but rather to inform him of his lapses in moderate language."[24] Furthermore, Calvin would not consent to overnarrow definitions of the doctrinal terms on which communion might be taken. On some points we are ignorant, and there may well be disagreement on nonessentials.

If we may quote McNeill's summary: "He favoured a liberal practice of intercommunion between churches, even where minor divergencies existed in doctrine, discipline and worship. In 1554 he besought the English refugees at Wesel not to desert the communion of the Lutheran church there because of dissatisfaction with its worship. Fellowship with Lutherans, Anglicans, Waldenses, Bohemian brethren as well as with the national branches of the Reformed, was cherished by him. . . . He unhesitatingly admits that some within the Church of Rome are God's elect. His passion for ecumenical unity induced an ecclesiastical tolerance that was unusual in his day and is still distasteful to many who profess themselves Christians."[25]

How else may we attempt to fill in this picture of Calvin as a whole man? Perhaps this is the place to say something of Calvin's appreciation of beauty, both in nature and in art. He had a deep wonder and gratitude for all the glories of the natural world, sun, moon, stars, birds, trees, and flowers. Not only does he constantly turn to them for illustrative material, but he also takes a genuine pleasure in these things for their own sake, or rather for what they are in themselves as creatures of God. "Wherever you cast your eyes," he says, "there is no spot in the universe wherein you cannot discern, at least some sparks of His glory. You cannot in one glance survey this most vast and beautiful system of the universe in its wide expanse without being completely overwhelmed by the boundless force of its brightness."[26] Or again, it is fitting "for man seriously to turn his eyes to contemplate God's works, since he has been placed in this most glorious theatre to be a spectator of them."[27] Heaven and earth form "a magnificent theatre . . . crammed with innumerable miracles."[28]

Most impressively of all, perhaps, in his *Preface to the New Testament* of 1535: "The little singing birds are singing of God; the beasts cry unto Him; the elements are in awe of Him, the mountains echo His name; the waves and fountains cast their glances at Him; grass and flowers laugh out to Him." Beauty, in fact, is different from mere utility; it need not be confused with the use to which created things may be put. "Has the Lord," asks Calvin, "clothed the flowers with the great beauty that greets our eyes, the sweetness of smell that is wafted upon our nostrils, and yet will it be unlawful for our eye to be affected by that beauty, or our sense of smell by the sweetness of that odour. . . . Did he not, in short, render many things attractive to us apart from their necessary use?"[29]

Again, although music serves our enjoyment rather than our need, "it ought not on that account to be judged of no value still less should it be condemned."[30] In the Strasbourg church under Calvin's ministry, the congregational singing in which all could join moved a student visitor to tears in 1545 as he saw each one praising the Lord with a book of music in his hand. The book had been compiled and published by Calvin himself. Music, he wrote, in his additional preface to the edition later published (1545) in Geneva, is one of God's first gifts to man for his recreation and pleasure. It has power for good—principally in worship—and for great evil. It may affect the heart to edification or lure toward moral ruin. Like Plato, Calvin was conscious that music had to be watched, but he felt no need to deny that it was a good gift from the Creator.

Likewise with the plastic arts. Admittedly it is unlikely that any scholarly figure in Renaissance Europe should be ignorant or unappreciative of the artistic heritage of civilized man; happily Calvin leaves us in no doubt about his position: "Because sculpture and painting are gifts of God, I seek a pure and legitimate use of each, lest those things which the Lord has conferred upon us for His glory and our good be not only perverted by misuse but also turned to our destruction . . . God must not be represented. . . . Therefore it remains that only those things are to be sculptured or painted which the eyes are capable of seeing."[31] Within the limitations he considers Scripture imposes, Calvin sees a broad field of activity open for the artist. Conclusive on this matter, however, is the very style of Calvin himself. It is sensitive, pointed, entirely adequate for every demand made upon it; it can be rich and colorful, humorous, scornful, earnest, solemn, persuasive. The view that Calvin was aesthetically blind, or a foe of the arts, is another side of the caricature that has often passed for a picture of the Reformer's personality.

With his intense and single-hearted devotion to the cause of God Calvin had a heavy burden to bear; besides the work in Geneva there was, in the words of the Apostle, "the care of all the churches." We see this travail in his immense correspondence and in his gracious reception of the unending streams of visitors and refugees. It seems under these conditions to be almost ludicrous to ask how Calvin spent his leisure! However there are some few indications here too which leave us in no doubt that Calvin was a whole man, and only the fearful responsibility which God had undoubtedly laid upon him prevented him from relaxing more often. Beza asserts that he was good company at the meal-table, and we know that he sometimes enjoyed a game of quoits. McNeill also tells us that "another game he enjoyed—an excellent one for ready relaxation, as those who have played it will agree—consisted of tossing a bunch of keys so that they slide over a table and approach as closely as possible to the farther end without falling off."[32] A letter to de Falais even mentions—but why should I concede this word "even"?—Calvin's delight in playing with babies.[33]

Though it speaks of his deep emotion and thus, in a way, of his humanity, Calvin's use of satire has sometimes been criticized. B. B. Warfield provides an interesting defense here. This use of satire, Warfield maintains, "was not merely a result of native temperament with him but a matter of deliberate and reasoned choice. Of course he had nothing in common with the mere mockers of the time—des Periers, Marot, Rabelais—whose levity was almost as abominable to him as their coarseness. Satire to him was a weapon, not an amusement. The proper way to deal with folly, he thought, was to laugh at it. The superstitions in which the world has been so long entangled were foolish as truly as wicked; and how could it be, he demanded, that in speaking of things so ridiculous, so intrinsically funny, we should not laugh at them 'with wide open mouth'? Of course this laugh was not the laugh of pure amusement; and as it gained in earnestness it naturally lost its lightness of touch. It was a rapier in Calvin's hands, and its use was to pierce and to cut." Warfield then takes as examples Calvin's parody of the Sorbonne articles against Reformation teaching, his treatise on relics, and his tract against the Nicodemites (secret believers who remained Romanists in their outward conformity). He concludes thus: "Literature this all is, doubtless, and good literature; and by virtue of it 'Calvinistic satire'—Calvin, Beza and Viret were its first masters—has a recognized place in the history of French satire. But it is not primarily or chiefly literature, and it had its part to play among the moral and religious forces which Calvin liberated for the accomplishing of his reforming work."[34]

The secularization of satire since Calvin's time has proceeded so far that few Christians in our own day feel able to employ or to enjoy the use of this weapon, though the *Honest to God*[35] debate provided us with distant echoes of what this kind of controversy must have been like.

Calvin's Correspondence

Our treatment of Calvin has thus far touched upon the more public sources for the most part—the tracts, treatises, commentaries, and *The Institutes*, besides references to the positions he filled and the policies he pursued. There is one other activity which is worthy of our consideration as we draw toward the conclusion of our short estimate of Calvin the man—his correspondence. More even than a theologian, Calvin saw himself as a pastor, an undershepherd of God's flock. Souls—precious immortal souls—had been committed to his charge. Time and again he found himself forced into the limelight, forced to take up his pen or to raise a voice from the pulpit simply that the people of God might not be misled, disastrously deceived by some satanic error. The other side of this pastoral solicitude is to be seen in his huge correspondence. Here equally the care of souls lies upon him as a solemn responsibility.

Calvin had a deep sense of the worth of the individual soul, and men knew that he cared for them and valued them profoundly. This value to Calvin was because Christ had died for them, not in any way for what they were in themselves. In this atmosphere respect and compassion flourished, and men could confide. "You brought me to birth in Christ," writes one correspondent. "I opened my heart to him as a child would to a father," wrote a minister of his letters exchanged with the Reformer. An imprisoned aristocrat under sentence of death thanks him for not having abandoned him, and for consolation and food for his soul gleaned from Calvin's letters, a former student testifies that thanks to Calvin he had not given in to despair. Another assures him that he knows nothing apart from the Bible more calculated to strengthen his faith than the friendly letters in which Calvin exhorts and warns him. "The most despised of men," writes another friend, "can address himself familiarly to you as to an angel of God and a true servant of Jesus Christ."[36]

Many of Calvin's letters were addressed to prisoners and to those soon destined for martyrdom. It was a bleak and bitter age for the French. Pastors were trained at Geneva and then went back into France to accomplish what ministerial charge they could, their heroic pastorate often ending in arrest, prison, and the stake. As soon as Calvin heard of their arrest he would write to them to testify to the anxious care of the church at Geneva, to encourage them, and to prepare them to face death for the gospel's sake. These letters are among the most moving of any written by the Reformer. We have some knowledge of how they were received; Louis de Marsac, soon to suffer at the stake at Lyons, was imprisoned there in company with another young man, Denis Peloquin, also destined to be burned not long after. The former of these two managed to get a reply to Calvin, which read thus: "Sir and brother, I cannot relate the great comfort that I have received from the letters that you have sent to my brother Denis Peloquin, who found a way of getting them to one of our brothers who was in a cell above me and who read them to me, since I couldn't read them; I could see nothing in my cell. I beg you to continue always to help us with like consolations in the situation we are in, which invites us to weep and to pray."[37]

The first element in all these letters, Benoit notes, is true compassion, the sympathy which sets the Reformer down with the afflicted in their situation; he endures their suffering at their side, he is a prisoner with them. Thus as he joins them in heart and mind—and as he suffers too, for this is real identification, not mere verbiage—the captives are conscious even in their prison cells of the reality of the communion of the saints, the body of Christ. In such a letter, for example, we read: "Although we are not at the moment in a similar condition to yours, we do not cease to strive in prayer, in anxious thought and in compassion as being your members, since it has pleased our heavenly Father in His infinite kindness to unite us in one body under His Son who is our Head."[38]

To those about to be "interrogated" (grim word!) Calvin has much to say; where necessary he would get a letter back suited to the particular needs of each accusation. But in the last resort nothing was as telling as a simple personal testimony. Calvin had such confidence in the work of the Holy Spirit on such occasions that he refused to draw up a confession of faith that the martyrs would simply have to learn and repeat. "I am not sending you such a profession of faith as our good brother Peloquin asked for," he writes, "for God will use the one which He will give you according to the measure of the Spirit which He has imparted to you, to much greater effect than anything which might be suggested by anyone else."[39]

In the same way he would not correct a confession submitted to him by a prisoner; he would neither add nor delete a single word, not wishing to lessen the authority and efficacy of the divine inspiration, though he confessed that he (Calvin) would have couched it in rather different terms. Such humility needs no comment.

Calvin's Greatness and Humility

It is perhaps not unfitting that we should note this quality last of all. Here surely is the strangest of all the things we find in Calvin—strange, that is, when compared with the stereotype of that haughty, scornful, ruthless, power-loving, aristocratic disposition . . . his humility! If we set aside his attitude on the occasions when scriptural doctrine appeared to him to be threatened, Calvin was beyond any doubt humble and did not hesitate to confess his faults. Writing to the church of Geneva after his banishment, he clears his own conduct and that of Farel (also temporarily exiled), but goes on: "I have no doubt that God has humiliated us in this way to show us our ignorance, rashness and other weaknesses which I for my part have been very conscious of, and I have little difficulty in confessing them before the Church of the Lord."[40] On his death bed he was to sound precisely the same note to the Genevan elders: "I have had much infirmity with which you have had to bear, and even the total of all I have done has been worth nothing. Evil men will take this word up, but I still say that all I have done has been worth nothing, and that I am a miserable creature. But I can say that I desired your good, that my vices have always displeased me and the root of the fear of God was in my heart. . . ."[41]

Here we must finish our brief and disjointed portrait of Calvin the man. I have embarked upon no original research for this paper, and all that I have found to put before you has already been found by others. My sources, apart from *The Institutes,* the letters, and the little *Life* of Beza, are all secondary sources—and even in some cases, I suspect, tertiary or even quaternary. Such things are not unknown, even in the austere world of Puritan and Reformed scholarship, and it would be unfair to conceal this fact from you. How much more I owe to McNeill and Cadier than is directly indicated in the text some of you may be interested to discover if this paper should be printed. The only responsibilities I do bear are those of selection and arrangement of the material. I believe that what I have put before you is reliable and relevant to my theme, and I believe the way in which we have looked together at the various sides of Calvin's character has not been seriously misleading, even if it has been in the last resort inadequate. It is not easy to make a man live in the minds of others, especially at a distance of four hundred years.

What we can perceive, albeit dimly, across those four centuries is first, a man, with his own particular nature and temperament. Sensitive and in many respects timid, intense and quick-tempered, ardent in controversy and in friendship, sympathetic, a lover of beauty and of books, humble yet hard as steel, Calvin was subject both to the infirmities and temptations of his own inherited disposition and to the narrowness and blindness of his age on some scores. He of all men would not have us deny this. Second, we see a Christian, tamed and enslaved by the hand of God, made docile by grace, and thrust out of the study into the street, there to be fashioned into a mighty instrument of spiritual reformation and public reconstruction. Amid nearly thirty years of constant struggle with men, with error, and with disease—never a note of self-pity.

And finally, a mouthpiece and an example to succeeding generations. It is probable that if Calvin himself could hear of this paper, he would deplore the attempt which it represents. For he wished to be forgotten; his gravestone bore no inscription and the place of his burial is now unknown. He tried—and by grace was largely able—to *live* the message which he preached, taught, and wrote. This is what he would have us remember. If we have not fully grasped his character, the main lines of that message are clear. The man becomes transparent, as he would have wished. Of him more than of almost any other saint it may truly be said: "He, being dead, yet speaketh."

7

JOHN CALVIN: A SERVANT OF THE WORD

J. I. Packer

It is now four hundred years since John Calvin died. Why should we concern ourselves with him today? Why should we regard him as a man worthy of commemoration at the present time?

It would be answer enough to this question simply to point out that his influence on history was so immense that you cannot begin to explain modern Britain—England, Wales, Scotland, Ireland—nor modern Europe, nor modern America, nor indeed any English-speaking country anywhere, without making reference to him. You cannot leave him out of the story of any part of the Western world.

It is not always realized, but it is true none the less, that for a century and more after his death John Calvin was quite literally the world's most influential man, in the sense that his ideas made more history than did the thoughts, or actions, of anyone else who was alive at that time. The epoch from the middle of the sixteenth century to the beginning of the age of Newton, in the last quarter of the century following, was in truth the age of Calvin.

For proof of this, think of some of its great men and movements. Think of the shaping of the churches of England and Scotland in the second half of the sixteenth century. Think of Jewel and Knox. Think of the Puritans in England, the heroes of the "second reformation" and the Covenanters in Scotland, the Huguenots in France, the Pilgrim Fathers in New England, the "Beggars" in Holland. Think of the revolt of the Netherlands, the English Civil War, and the continental wars of religion. Think of William the Silent, Gaspard de Coligny, Oliver Cromwell, John Owen, John Milton, and Richard Baxter. Think too of some of the great ideals for which men fought in those days. Think of the ideal of the Christian commonwealth, in which the national church and the civil government stood independent of each other, yet recognized each other's divine authority and supported each other within their own spheres. Think of the ideals of toleration, of representative democracy, of establishing the rights and liberties of subjects, of constitutionalizing monarchy. Think of the ideal, dear to all the Puritans, of a universal Christian culture, in which the secular is seen to be sacred, and arts, crafts, sciences, and industries, all develop freely, harmoniously, and ethically, to the glory of God the Creator. The inspiration of all these movements and ideals, and of the men whom we have mentioned and many more like them, flowed directly from Calvin.

Without Calvin, Protestantism might well not have survived beyond the middle of the seventeenth century; for it is a matter of simple fact that the only Protestants who were prepared to stand and fight, to the last ditch if necessary, against Roman and Erastian tyranny, were the Calvinists. If we look at more recent history, and think of men like Edwards, Brainerd, Whitefield, Howell Harris, Wilberforce, Spurgeon, Carey, Henry Martyn, Moffat, Paton, McCheyne, we see at once that the evangelical movement which began with revival in the eighteenth century, and the social and missionary movements which overflowed from it throughout the nineteenth century, could not have been what they were without

John Calvin; for these great leaders, and a host of others who stood with them, were all Calvinists in their basic creed.

Thus we may fairly say that if we are going to understand our religious and cultural heritage in this mid-twentieth century, it is absolutely essential that we should know something about Calvin. And that in itself would be sufficient reason for commemorating him now.

But my main reason for asking you to join me at this time in thankful recollection of John Calvin is that he is in a real sense a prophet for today, a man with a message for us and for our times. In his own life, he was God's man for a crisis, ministering to a Europe that was in turmoil. And, though comparisons between one age and another are notoriously risky, and can easily mislead those who make them, I think it is quite certainly true that, so far as basic attitudes are concerned, no age since has been more like Calvin's than is our own. At a deep level, our times are like his, and his teaching speaks directly to our own present need. An American tribute to Calvin, published in 1959, was entitled *John Calvin: Contemporary Prophet.*[1] This estimate of Calvin's significance for us is, in my judgment, sober truth.

Let me specify some of the main likenesses between Calvin's day and ours that I have in mind.

First: we live today in a world torn by political unrest, the world of the iron and bamboo curtains, a world of upsurging rival nationalisms directed by absolute rulers. Ours is a world of wars and rumors of wars, a world of strain and tension and unrest and fear. And so was Calvin's. The Europe of Reformation days was literally torn apart by the disruptive forces of nationalism. The background of the movement was a sequence of international crises, generated by European monarchs playing the Russian-roulette game of power politics. At the Eastern gates of Europe stood the Turks, the heralds of Islam, ready, it seemed, to pounce as soon as the Western states had weakened themselves sufficiently by internal strife. Martin Luther, surveying the times, was convinced that the second coming of Christ was imminent! Such was the world to which Calvin spoke: a world uncannily similar to our own.

Again: we face today a situation in which an inherited pattern of Christian civilization is disintegrating before our eyes. The ideal of a Christian commonwealth is giving way—in some parts of the world, it has long since given way—to that of a secular state. Christianity has come to be classed as a merely private interest, one which none should be hindered from following if they want to, but which has not the least claim to be treated as universal truth for the guidance of rulers and nations, and of public and corporate life. Christian standards and values, both personal and social, are being superseded by a "new morality"—or should we say a new immorality?—based on the essentially pagan ideal of self-realization and living "naturally." Is this situation unprecedented? Not entirely. John Calvin faced something very similar in the Renaissance Europe of Reformation days. There, too, an inherited form of Christian civilization, that of the Middle Ages, was breaking up, and cultural and moral disorders were flooding in as a result. It is, incidentally, a striking fact that then, as now, impetus toward the break up was coming from members of a class of men who claimed the name "humanists." I do not suggest that the outlook of a sixteenth-century Renaissance humanist and that of a twentieth-century scientific humanist correspond in detail: far from it. The few Italian humanists of Renaissance days who were forthrightly "secularist" and "new-moralist" in their attitudes were not typical of the champions of the "new learning" as a body. But I do suggest nevertheless that at the level of motivation, the motivation from which their name derives—that is, their anthropocentric preoccupation with releasing the powers and realizing the possibilities of man—the affinity between humanists ancient and modern is obvious.

Then there is a third basic likeness between Calvin's age and ours. Today we face, in addition to political and cultural tensions, religious confusion which is deep and widespread. Disillusioned with the church as they have known it, and bewildered by a clamor of conflicting voices, all claiming to speak for Christianity, the minds of professed Christians are in a state of utter muddle concerning the things of God. This confusion centers upon three basic issues over which sharp conflict rages: the authority of the

Bible, the grace of the gospel, and the unity of the church. John Calvin faced similar confusion, centering upon the same three issues, and it is striking to see how little, at the level of basic principles, the terms of the debate have changed since Calvin's day.

Thus, the dispute over *biblical authority* remains approximately where it was. None of the modern developments in biblical study, important as they are in other ways, have altered the fundamental issues. All affirm that Holy Scripture is in some sense the inspired Word of God; so they did in Calvin's day. But still, now as then, the Church of Rome tells us that the only way to be sure what Scripture means is to let her interpret it to us by the light of her own tradition. And still the principle of the ancient Anabaptists is maintained by modern liberal and postliberal Protestants. These moderns all hold in some form the position that the divine truth by which we must live consists of those convictions which we reach, or which reach us, when we go to the Bible asking whether its various teachings are right and true, and refusing to commit ourselves to them further than independent experience or reflection has led us to feel that they are valid. This formulation, dynamically interpreted, covers the diverse approaches of Barth, Brunner, Niebuhr, Tillich, and "honest John" Robinson, no less than the more old-fashioned liberalism of such men as Weatherhead, Soper, and Fosdick. But such approaches do not seem to differ in principle from the Anabaptist doctrine of the "internal word," the word of God revealed in the heart and the conscience, which (it was claimed) is the God-given truth whereby we must judge the external word of Scripture; for, on the Anabaptist view, the external word was no further authoritative than the internal word confirmed it. Thus it appears that the basic terms of the three-cornered debate between what we may call "evangelical," "traditionalist," and "subjectivist" views of biblical authority, have hardly changed at all—nor, be it said, have *Institutio* 1.9 and 4.8 lost any of their relevance and cogency for settling it.

The situation is similar with regard to the second issue, concerning *grace and salvation*. Still, as in Calvin's day, those who maintain the Reformation understanding of the gospel, the understanding set forth in the slogans *sola Scriptura—solo Christo—sola fide—sola gratia* (by Scripture alone—by Christ alone—by faith alone—by grace alone) find themselves obliged to fight on two fronts. Rome stands against them on the one hand, proclaiming, now as then, that the way of salvation in and through Christ is to commit oneself to Rome's own sacramental system. On the other hand, they also have to counter the Christological inadequacies of such versions of the gospel as were put out in Calvin's day by rationalists and mystics among the Anabaptists. Moralistic re-hashes of justification by works still pass for Christianity in many quarters, while self-styled radicals dilate on salvation as a state of new and authentic being, springing from some God-given inner illumination which, though linked with the Jesus of history, is not related in any direct way to His atoning work on the cross. This is the "existentialist" gospel of Bultmann and his followers. It is dressed up in Teutonic jargon to look like the last word in uninhibited modernity; yet in fact many Anabaptists in Calvin's day, using a slightly different jargon, were saying just about the same thing. As John Wesley observed in another connection, we are but where we were.

On the third issue, concerning *church unity*, essentially the same question is being put to evangelical Protestants today as was put to their ancestors in Calvin's day. It is asked: Is not all separation between organized Christian bodies sinful and schismatic? Does not the very nature of Christ's church require immediate reunion?—and does not the duty to reunite require us to shelve our historic doctrinal debates as matters of secondary importance, more especially those which keep "protestants" and "catholics" apart? This, for substance, was the question put by Rome to the Protestant world of Calvin's day, as she summoned the "separated brethren" to "come home" (see, for instance, Sadolet's Letter to Geneva, with Calvin's answer). Nowadays, it is our own fellow Protestants who pose the question; but Rome stands in the background, nodding approval, and it is clear where a journey which begins with an affirmative answer to this question will end.

Note, then, these striking correspondences between the situation which faced Calvin and that which faces us; and note, too, that Calvin coped with this crisis situation successfully, kept European Protestantism steady, and charted a straight course for the people of God amid all the storms and contrary winds that blew. It is no exaggeration to say that he saved Protestantism in his own day. Nor do I think it is exaggeration to say that he can save it again in ours, forlorn though our present prospects are (make no mistake about that!)—if only Protestants today will heed his message. We are going to look in a moment at some of the basic principles which guided Calvin, and by which he would guide us. God grant us ears to hear as we sit under the teaching of our great "contemporary prophet."

Calvin's Penetrating Mind and Humble Heart

Calvin held that the hand of God had been upon his life throughout. Reviewing it, one cannot but agree. The providential way in which he was brought to the post which he was so uniquely qualified to fill is particularly striking. The story is well known. In July, 1536, the month of his twenty-seventh birthday, and four months after the first appearance of the *Institutio*, Calvin, a Protestant refugee, left his native France for good: he sold up, and headed for Strasbourg, a Protestant center, intending to settle there. But a local war compelled him to take a long way around, and travel via Lyons and Geneva. He put up for a night at the Bear Inn in Geneva, meaning to travel on next day. From his language describing the incident, one would gather that he was incognito, and had no intention of making himself known to anyone in that city. But an old Protestant friend bumped into him, and passed the word around that the author of the famous *Institutio* was in town.

As a result, that evening, as he sat in his room, Calvin had a visitor: a huge red-bearded man, twenty years older than himself, with fierce eyes and a loud voice. This was Guillaume Farel, pioneer of the Reformation in Geneva, and senior minister there. He put it to Calvin quite bluntly that the latter ought to stay in the city and become his colleague in the work of reform. Calvin explained that he was temperamentally unfitted for public life, being nervous and shy, and that he needed leisure from regular employment to pursue academic projects that he had in mind. Farel rose to the occasion with imprecatory prayer, which turned Calvin's dream of becoming a Protestant Erasmus into a nightmare. "After he heard" (Calvin wrote, twenty years after) "that I had some particular study for which I wished to keep myself free, when he saw that he could get nowhere by appeal, he even ventured upon a curse, that it might please God to curse my rest and the tranquillity for study that I was seeking if in such great need I should withdraw and refuse to give my help and assistance. This word frightened and shattered me so much that I set aside the journey I had planned. . . ." He felt, he tells us, "as if God from on high had stretched out his hand to stay me." He remained at Geneva, first as Farel's assistant, until they were both banished in 1538, and then, after his own recall in 1541, as senior pastor, till his death in 1564.

Calvin brought to his work at Geneva qualifications of mind and heart which made possible a unique ministry of amazing usefulness. I want to say a little here about the two key qualities which, as I see it, were together the real secret of his power and achievement. The first was his natural gift of *penetration;* the second, the supernatural gift to him of *humility.*

A word, first, about the former. Often when I hear and read what people say about Calvin's outstanding intellectual abilities, I am left dissatisfied; they seem not to stress the right thing. It is not enough to say that Calvin had a razor-sharp mind, ready speech, and a fine literary style, true though all this is. What made Calvin great as pastor, teacher, theologian, controversialist, and church leader, the quality without which he could not have been great in any of these capacities, was his gift of penetration. It is this that needs to be emphasized. Penetration is more than a clear head and a good style. You can have these, and still lack penetration, just as you can be clever without being wise. Penetration is an aspect of intelligence. It is the power to see into people and get inside their minds. It is the power to see into situations and assess them realistically. It is the capacity to get to the bottom of things. This capacity Calvin had in full measure. It was this gift that fitted him for training as a lawyer, and no doubt his legal education at Orleans served to sharpen it. When he became a pastor, his gift of penetration was the first vital factor in his success.

It was this gift which, under God, made him great as an *expositor*. When he went to the Bible, he was able to see straight into the minds of the writers whose words he was reading, hence he could enter into their meaning, and bring it out, with an accuracy and point that was unsurpassed in his own day, and has given his commentaries an honored place on the shelves of theologians and pastors from that day to our own.

Again, it was this gift which, under God, made him great as a *spiritual guide* and as a *controversialist*. When men opened to him their confusion and perplexity of soul and conscience, he could always see what was at the root of their trouble, and speak to their condition, and, as we say, "sort them out" by bringing the Word of God to bear on them at the point of their real need. As his pastoral letters show, he was a superb physician of the soul, unerring in diagnosis and supremely skillful in applying the remedies of the gospel. Similarly, when he was involved in theological debate and, as was often the case, his adversaries were men of hazy minds and muddled thoughts, who put out their ideas in an imprecise and disorderly way, he could always see what they were really driving at and in his reply go straight to the heart of the matter in dispute. The secret of his ability to settle issues was his power to clarify them. He was an adversary to be feared, for he could always pick out the proper target to shoot at, and he never misfired.

Again, it was his gift of penetration that made Calvin great as a *theologian*. It was this that both prompted and enabled him to analyze every issue of truth in terms of the will and work and rule and glory of God. It was this that kept him consistently theocentric in his thinking, following out the viewpoint of the Bible. These are the first essentials of theological greatness, to which men without the gift of penetration, sanctified by the Holy Spirit, do not attain.

Calvin's gift of penetration, though sanctified and informed by a regenerate heart, was in origin a natural qualification; his amazing power of insight would have made him a great man, even if he had not been a Christian at all. But this is not true of the second key to his power, the grace of humility. This quality was not natural to him in any sense; just the reverse. He was an intellectual, and as with many intellectuals, the natural temper of his mind was proud and arrogant. He was not humble by nature, but was made humble by grace. He saw his conversion as a humbling. "By a sudden conversion," he wrote, "God subdued my heart and brought it to docility, though it was more hardened against such things than was to be expected of my youthful age." Prior to this, he tells us, he was obstinate and opinionated—"passionately devoted to the superstitions of the papacy"—but in his conversion he was humbled and made teachable by sovereign divine grace.

What did it mean for Calvin to be humbled? It did not mean that from then onward Calvin pretended that his natural gifts and abilities were less than they were in fact. There is nothing unrealistic about humility, and such a pose, had Calvin affected it, would not have been humility. In fact, he knew his own ability, and never pretended otherwise. He always found it hard to suffer fools gladly, and to be patient with those who seemed stupid and slow— though the measure of patience which God wrought in him impressed those who knew him best as one of the most Christlike things about him. The mark of Calvin's humility was not, then, any disclaiming of ability, but rather the submissive and receptive temper which his conversion wrought in him. "God *subdued my heart*"—the word suggests putting a bridle on an untamed horse. "God brought (my heart) to *docility*"—that is, God made him teachable. Submissiveness and docility, both in the highest degree, were the essential aspects of Calvin's humility.

Conversion made Calvin *submissive*—so that when God called him to the Geneva ministry in 1537, though this call ran clean contrary to his natural hopes and wishes, and his natural ideas as to what he was suited for, he nevertheless submitted. And when, after three years of exile in pleasant company at Strasbourg, he was summoned back to his thankless Swiss pastorate, he submitted again. He did not want to return to Geneva—"I should prefer a hundred other deaths rather than this cross on which I should have to die a thousand times a day," he wrote when the invitation came. But he did not play Jonah, running away from the call of God. To Farel, who had pressed on him the duty of returning, he wrote: "If I had any choice I would rather do anything than give in to you in this matter, but since I remember that I no longer belong to myself, I offer my heart to God as a sacrifice." So back he went, for twenty-three more years of unremitting labor, till, worn out with illness and overwork, he died, in harness, as the sun went down on May 27, 1564. His seal showed a heart held by a large hand, with the motto *Prompte et sincere*—and his life was a sustained display of promptness and sincerity in submitting to the God who had made Himself the master of Calvin's heart. Without complaint, discontent, or self-pity, he submitted to the rigors of health, circumstances, and the crushing load of spiritual responsibility, that God put upon him, and bore these burdens patiently till God gave him release. This was one side of his humility before God.

Conversion also made him *docile*. This, too, was a crucial element in Calvin's humility. We are thinking of Calvin as a servant of God's Word—and a man must be divinely humbled before he becomes capable of this service. Proud man naturally leans to his own understanding; he would far rather speculate and follow his own ideas than listen to God speaking in Holy Scripture. Calvin, however, was humbled and made teachable by divine grace, and from then onward his overmastering intellectual concern was to learn the truth taught by Scripture; to function as a faithful echo of Scripture in his own teaching; and to make an accurate application of Scripture to men and situations. There never was a less speculative, less opinionated thinker than John Calvin. No theologian or preacher has ever been more consistently and exclusively dependent on Holy Scripture. Thus, though the *Institutio* is a work of tremendous power, learning, and ability, a book which reveals a truly staggering intellectual grasp at every point, one cannot read a page of it without realizing that, for all its positiveness of assertion and sharpness in controversy, it is fundamentally a humble book. Though learned, it is the very opposite of sophisticated; it reveals its author as a man of a simple, childlike spirit. For Calvin never says: this is my idea. He only ever says: this is what Scripture teaches. The author of the *Institutio* displays no other intellectual interest than to echo and explicate the written Word: in other words, to be a loyal servant of the Word of God.

Such, then, was John Calvin, the brilliant boy from Noyon, transformed by conversion into a God-centered, God-mastered, God-honoring man who bowed humbly to God's will and listened humbly to God's Word, and whose tremendous powers of penetration and insight were put wholly at the service of the Scriptures. This was the man whom God could and did use to preserve Protestantism.

Calvin's Greatest Accomplishment

If we ask: What was the greatest thing that Calvin accomplished? our answer must, I think, be: he wrote a book—the *Institutio*. He never did anything greater or more significant for the cause of God and the welfare of the church than that. Though he produced commentaries on almost all the books of the Bible, and separate tracts and treatises on almost every major issue in theology, Calvin was essentially a one-book man. He worked steadily on the *Institutio* for nearly a quarter of a century, from the first edition of 1536 to the sixth edition in 1559, revising, augmenting, rearranging, perfecting. All that he knew went into it, in the same way that all Dickens knew went into *Pickwick Papers*. The final product is a supreme masterpiece of theological and expository writing.

What is the *Institutio*? It offers itself to us as a compendium of Christianity. Its title proclaims it as not simply a book of theology, but also, and indeed primarily, a course in practical Christian living, a primer on godliness. Here is the full title of the first edition: *Instruction* (institutio) *in the Christian religion, containing virtually the whole sum of godliness* (pietatis, "Christian practice") *and all that needs to be known in the doctrine of salvation. A work very well worth reading for all Christians with a zeal for godliness.* As Calvin developed it through successive editions, it became, as well as a handbook for the Christian, a textbook for the theological student, an introduction to Calvin's own commentaries, and an apologia for every aspect of the Reformation. William Cunningham, that great light of the Free Church of Scotland a century ago, whom Charles Hodge regarded as the finest Reformed theologian in the world, called the *Institutio* "the most important work in the history of theological science"—and it does not appear that anything has happened in the last hundred years to challenge Cunningham's opinion.

What do we find in the *Institutio?* Calvin would have answered that question biblically, and told us that we find there a summary statement of biblical theology and biblical religion, presented in order from the Bible's own point of view. I would not dispute this claim—indeed, I would defend it—but for our purpose it is more helpful to answer the question historically, and to say that in the *Institutio* we find an integrating and systematizing of the total Reformation understanding of Christianity. In it, Calvin appears less as an innovator than as a consolidator. He comes on the scene as a second-generation Reformer, and he sees his task as the conserving and confirming of the gains of the first generation. To his mind, all the main truths of biblical theology had already been drawn out and dealt with, more or less fully and more or less adequately, by his great predecessors, Luther, Zwingli, Bucer, and their associates. What was needed now was to synthesize their findings. That was what the *Institutio* set out to do.

The integrating concept which Calvin used to bind all this material together was one which unites in itself the whole of Christian doctrine, experience, and behavior—namely, the biblical concept of *knowledge of God.* The *Institutio* offers itself as a treatise on knowledge of God, dealing with both the knowing of God, which is religion, and what is known of God and about God, which is theology. Both these (Calvin holds) are directly correlative to God's own Word written in Holy Scripture. They belong together; they should be treated together; and Calvin's great book brings and holds them together.

To the question: What does it mean to know God?—what, in other words, is religion?—the *Institutio* replies somewhat as follows. Knowing God (it says, in effect) means this: to acknowledge Him as He has revealed Himself in Scripture; to worship Him and give Him thanks for all things; to abase oneself before him as a sinner, and to learn of Him as He speaks of salvation; to believe on the Christ whom He has set forth to be our Savior; to love the Father and the Son with a love answering the love that they have shown to us; to live by faith in the promises of divine mercy which have been given us in Jesus Christ; to sustain the hope of a joyful resurrection; to obey God's law, and to seek God's honor in all human relationships and all commerce with created things. This view of the life of knowing God is expounded in detail throughout the book.

To the parallel question: What is the intellectual basis on which this practical knowing of God rests?—what, in other words, do we know about God? the *Institutio* replies by subdividing the contents of biblical theology under four heads, and expounding them in four books. Book 1 deals with knowledge of God the Creator; book 2 with knowledge of Christ the Mediator; book 3 with knowledge of the grace of Christ in human life, through the work of the Holy Spirit; book 4 with the church, the sacraments, and civil government, which Calvin views as a means of grace. In this arrangement, Calvin is consciously following the order of the Apostles' Creed—"I believe in God the Father . . . Jesus Christ . . . the Holy Ghost . . . the holy catholic church." Under these heads, he claims to deploy the whole of biblical teaching. Having lived for fifteen years with the *Institutio* never far from my desk, and having observed, almost with awe, how constantly Calvin's exposition anticipates, and in principle settles, theological and pastoral problems which are represented as novel, and peculiar to our times, I have learned to respect Calvin's claim. The *Institutio* is emphatically a book for today—more so, I think we may safely say, than most of the religious books that will be published in 1965.

A Concern for God's Truth

I have said that Calvin has a message for us, and for our time. Let me now focus this by asking: if Calvin were here today, standing where we stand on the Christian battlefield, facing the problems and pressures of the modern world, what are the chief concerns which he would feel, and which he would want to see us share? Our answer to this question can only, of course, be speculative; we can only derive it by reflecting on the thrusts and emphases of Calvin's historic teaching as he spoke to his own times, and by seeking—as indeed we did earlier in this address—to see our times as he would have seen them. But nonetheless I think we may say with some confidence that Calvin, were he back among us now, would give us counsel on at least the following points.

First, he would urge us to share his *concern for God's truth*—that is, for the inspiration, sufficiency, clarity, and authority of Holy Scripture, the written divine Word of which he was a servant, and which he describes as "the sceptre of God," whereby God through Christ rules His church. Be jealous, Calvin would say, for Holy Scripture.

How did Calvin regard Holy Scripture? His understanding of this subject has been much muddied and misstated by oversubtle modern scholars, but in itself, as any reader of *Institutio* 1.6–9 and 4.8–9 will soon see, it is plain and clear. It focuses on two related ideas. The first is *os Dei*, "the mouth of God," whereby in condescension He speaks to us, using words which we can understand. The second is *doctrina*, "doctrine" or "teaching," the instruction conveyed by God's verbal utterances. "Teaching from the mouth of God," or, more simply and dynamically, "God *speaking*"—"God *teaching*"—"God *preaching*": this is the essence of Calvin's concept of Holy Scripture.

Commenting on 2 Timothy 3:16 ("all scripture is given by inspiration of God, and is profitable for doctrine, for reproof, for correction, for instruction in righteousness"), Calvin crystallizes his view as follows:

> He (Paul) commends the Scripture, first, on account of its authority, and, second, on account of the utility that springs from it. In order to uphold the authority of Scripture, he declares it to be divinely inspired *(divinitus inspiratam);* for if it be so, it is beyond all controversy that men should receive it with reverence. . . . Whoever then wishes to profit in the Scriptures, let him first of all lay down as a settled point this—that the law and the prophecies are not

> teaching *(doctrinam)* delivered by the will of men, but dictated *(dictatam)* by the Holy Ghost. . . . Moses and the prophets did not utter at random what we have from their hand, but, since they spoke by divine impulse, they confidently and fearlessly testified, as was actually the case, that it was the mouth of the Lord that spoke *(os Domini loquutum esse)* . . . we owe to the Scripture the same reverence which we owe to God, because it has proceeded from Him alone, and has nothing of man mixed with it *(nec quicquam humani habet admixtum)*.

With this we may compare Calvin's reference to the prophets as having "obediently followed as their leader the Spirit, who ruled in their mouth as in his own sanctuary" (commentary on 2 Peter 1:20), and some famous sentences from the *Institutio:*

"The full authority which they (the Scriptures) obtain with the faithful proceeds from no other consideration than that they are persuaded that they proceeded from heaven, as if God had been heard giving utterance to them" (1.7.1).

"Clear signs that God is its speaker *(manifesta signa loquentis Dei)* are seen in Scripture, from which it is plain that its teaching *(doctrinam)* is heavenly" (1.7.4).

"Being enlightened by him (the Holy Spirit) . . . we are made absolutely certain . . . that it (Scripture) has come to us by the ministry of men from God's very mouth" *(ab ipsissimo Dei ore ad nos fluxisse)* (1.7.5).

"The apostles were the certain and authentic amanuenses of the Holy Spirit and therefore their writings are to be received as oracles of God; but others have no other office than to teach what is revealed and deposited in the Holy Scriptures" (4.8.9).

Such was Calvin's understanding of the nature of Scripture and the meaning of inspiration. Did your cyebrows go up at his reference to its being "dictated by the Holy Ghost," and to the apostles as the Spirit's amanuenses—that is, secretaries? This language is frowned on today, yet Doumergue, Warfield, and others have shown that when Calvin and other sixteenth-century divines, both Protestant and Roman, used it, it was not intended to imply a psychological theory of the mode of inspiration, but was simply a theological metaphor conveying the thought that Holy Scripture comes to us from God uncorrupted, in just the form in which God meant us to have it: for what is written in Scripture bears the same relation to the mind of God which was its source as a letter written by a good secretary bears to the mind of the man who dictated it—a relation, that is, of complete correspondence, and thus of absolute authenticity. This, as our quotations showed, is the point which Calvin was concerned to make when he employed "dictation" language with reference to Holy Scripture.

What Calvin is saying can be put thus: that all Scripture has the character of the prophetic oracles, in the sense that all Scripture has a dual authorship. The prophets began their sermons by announcing: "thus saith the Lord" (literally, "oracle of Jehovah!"). This was to say, in effect, that the words which they spoke were to be heard and received as words from God: what came from their mouth was actually coming from God's mouth. So it is, says Calvin, with all Scripture; not only the prophets, and the law, and those other passages where the claim to divine authorship is explicit, but also the psalms and the wisdom writings and the history books of both Testaments and the New Testament epistles, and indeed all sixty-six books of the Bible. All Scripture has the same double aspect: it consists of words of men which are also words of God, and so is to be received, every particle of it, as having proceeded from God's very mouth. It is God's *doctrina,* divine teaching all of it, given for our instruction. Over and over again Calvin uses *doctrina* as a synonym for "the Word of God," "the teaching of the Holy Scriptures."

Affirming the identity of what God said, and says, with what the biblical authors wrote, Calvin could hardly do other than maintain that everything written in Scripture is true, or, putting it negatively, inerrant. Nor in fact did he. It is true that biblical inerrancy is not a topic which he ever discussed directly; but then, he did not need to, for it was a matter of general agreement in his day, and therefore something which he could take for granted. Why should he waste time breaking down open doors? We cannot, therefore, reasonably extract from his lack of emphasis on this issue the conclusion that he was either unclear about it or indifferent to it. This conclusion, however, is drawn by modern scholars. Many since Doumergue have sought to play down Calvin's identification of the words of Scripture with the Word of God, and to find room in his thought for the possibility that biblical assertions err in points of detail. Such a view, as recent debates have no doubt made us realize very vividly, is the thin end of the "liberal," "subjectivist" wedge, and involves in principle the abandonment of the concept of inspiration which Calvin set forth; and if we can see that, it would have been strange had Calvin himself been blind to it. The fact that those who have fathered on to Calvin a willingness to admit errors in Scripture have been, without exception, scholars who had already given up Calvin's concept of inspiration on other grounds, may fairly put us on our guard. But when we look at the evidence, all doubt vanishes. The attribution to Calvin of a willingness to admit error in Scripture rests on a superficial misreading of what he actually says.

The handful of passages in his commentaries which have on occasion been taken as affirming or implying that he thought particular biblical writers had gone astray prove on inspection to fall into the following categories. (1) Some are reminders of points where God has accommodated Himself to rough-and-ready forms of human speech, and tell us only that in such cases God is evidently not concerned to speak with a kind or degree of accuracy which goes beyond what these forms of speech would naturally convey. Thus, for instance, Calvin warns us that we must not expect to learn natural science (he specifies astronomy) from Genesis 1, which is written in popular phenomenal language. (2) Others say only that particular texts show signs of having been altered in the course of transmission. Thus, for instance, Calvin tells us that "by mistake" Jeremiah's name has somehow "crept in" (*obrepserit,* his regular word for unauthentic textual intrusions) in Matthew 27:9. There is a similar comment on "Abraham" and the seventy-five souls in Acts 7:14–16. (3) Others deal with cases where apostolic writers quote Old Testament texts loosely; Calvin's point in this group of comments is invariably that the apostles quote paraphrastically precisely in order to bring out the true sense and application—a contention strikingly supported by the modern discovery that this was standard practice among the rabbis at that time. (4) Others deal with a few points of what we might call formal inaccuracy by suggesting that in these cases no assertion was intended, and therefore no error can fairly be said to have been made. The inference is clearly unexceptionable if the premise can be established, for where no assertion is intended the question of falsehood and error cannot arise.

An example of this class of statements is Calvin's denial that the evangelists meant at every point to write narratives which were chronologically ordered, leading to the claim that since they did not intend to connect everything chronologically, but on occasion preferred to follow a topical or theological principle of arrangement, therefore they cannot be held to contradict each other when they narrate the same events in a different sequence.

Another example (which Professor John Murray, perhaps rightly, thinks unhappy and "ill-advised," but which clearly comes in this category) is Calvin's suggestion that in Acts 7:14 (the seventy-five souls) and Hebrews 11:21 (Jacob's staff) the writer may have chosen to echo the Septuagint's mistranslation rather than correct it, lest he disconcert his readers or distract them from the point he was making, which was not affected by the mistranslation one way or the other. In these cases, Calvin implies, alluding to the incidents in the familiar words of the Greek Bible would not involve asserting either that the Septuagint translation was correct or that it expressed the true facts at the point where it parted company from the Hebrew. On neither of these issues would the New Testament writer be himself asserting anything, and consequently his formal inaccuracy in echoing the substantial inaccuracy of the Septuagint would not amount to error (false assertion) on his part.

Whether this line of explanation be accepted or not, it is clear that, so far from admitting that biblical authors fell into error, Calvin's concern in his treatment of all these passages is to show that they did no such thing; and this is what matters for us at present.[2]

Rupert Davies, a liberal scholar who is not himself in sympathy with Calvin's basic position, concludes his survey of the passages in question by saying that the most they can possibly prove is that Homer may have nodded—in other words, that in the course of thirty years of theological writing so prolific as to fill fifty-nine large volumes of the *Corpus Reformatorum* Calvin may on three or four occasions have broached a suggestion about a text which did not fit his doctrine of Scripture quite as well as he thought it did. "The instances quoted by Doumergue," writes Davies, "are but drops in a bucket of unquestioning reverence for the words of Holy Scripture, and indicate at most that he was very occasionally in a long career untrue to one of his most dearly-cherished ideas."[3] This in itself should be enough to dispose of the assumption, made too readily by Doumergue and others, that these few passages are significant for Calvin's view of inspiration; at most, they merely show even Calvin could on occasion fail to be quite consistent with himself. And even this may be thought to concede too much. It might be rash to affirm that Calvin's handling of all four groups of texts which we mentioned was right in every particular, but I do not think it would be hard to maintain that it does involve not the least inconsistency with his doctrine of inspiration.

How, in the light of all this, should the authority of Scripture be conceived? Well, says Calvin, the first thing to be clear on as we approach this question is that the claim of Scripture to be believed and obeyed does not derive from the say-so of the church. When Augustine declares that had he not been moved by the authority of the church, he would not have believed, all he means is that the spectacle of the church's faith prepared his mind to receive Christian truth on its own terms. Rome's claim that the proper object of faith is her teaching, as such, and that canonical Scripture is to be received as such on her authority, is no less presumptuous than the parallel claim that canonical Scripture must be interpreted according to Roman tradition. Then, secondly, Calvin continues, the authority of Scripture does not rest on any judgment passed by the inquiring intellect. Rational arguments drawn from the remarkable qualities of Scripture—its majesty, consistency, antiquity, preservation, and so forth—can perform a real service in preparing us to acknowledge its inspiration and authority, and by showing such acknowledgment, which is an act of faith, to be eminently reasonable. But the true ground on which the authority of the Bible rests, Calvin maintains, is its divine authorship, the fact that it came from the mouth of the Lord. Its claim to rule our minds and lives is absolute, just because it is the Word of God.

Scripture is, in the last analysis, self-authenticating, says Calvin, as divine realities always are: those who have faith recognize its divine character in the immediate, unanalyzable way in which one recognizes a color, or a taste, by physical sense. About this perception of the divinity of Holy Scripture no more can be said than that it happens, and that inner certainty on the point is the sure sign that it has happened. If we ask: What brings it about? Calvin's answer is: The inner witness of the Holy Spirit. Calvin's conception of the inner witness is not of a particular kind of experience or feeling, as such, but of work of inward enlightenment whereby, through the medium of external verbal testimony, divine realities come to be recognized and embraced for what they are. Thus, it is through this inward enlightenment that we perceive the truth of the deity and mediation of Jesus, as set forth in the external witness of the gospel, and receive Him as the Savior of our souls. And it is through this same inward enlightenment that we recognize the divinity of the Scriptures, as witnessed to by Christ, prophets, psalmists, and apostles, and receive them, according to their own claims, as the Word of God to rule our lives.

In a well-known sentence from the *Institutio,* which we quoted in part before, Calvin writes: "Enlightened by Him (the Spirit) we no longer believe that Scripture is from God either on our own judgment or on that of others; but, in a way that surpasses human judgment, we are made absolutely certain, just as if we beheld there the majesty *(numen)* of God Himself, that it has come to us by the ministry of men from God's very mouth" (1.7.5). The inner witness of the Spirit opens the blind eyes of the heart and gives us understanding, and in consequence we recognize and bow to the divine authority—the right to rule, the claim to dominate—which is inherent in the Scriptures, as the Word of the speaking God.

What has Calvin to say about the interpretation of Scripture? This: that, being as truly human as it is divine, it must be understood literally—that is, in the plain natural sense intended by the human writer; for it is by getting into the minds of the biblical authors that we get into the mind of God, from whom ultimately their writings came. We must first grasp their meaning, therefore, and then seek to apply what they say to ourselves and our own situation. In both stages of the interpreter's task, but particularly in the second, we need the help of the Holy Ghost. Calvin's handling of Scripture exemplified his principles perfectly. He approached his text asking, first, what its true sense was, and, second, what effect God meant its teaching to produce on himself and his hearers and readers. It was by persistently asking these two questions—surely the right questions—of every passage of Scripture with which he dealt, that Calvin became a biblical interpreter of such supreme quality.

Today, the ideas of biblical revelation, of inspiration, of interpretation, of the authority of Scripture, are back in the melting pot. On these issues, world Protestantism presents a picture of seemingly inextricable confusion. Subjective and skeptical principles effectively hinder many of our fellow churchmen (and chapelmen!) from receiving Holy Scripture as God's Word and bowing without reserve to its authority. The crowning irony, and indeed tragedy, of this situation is that these Protestant brethren of ours actually invoke the leading of the Holy Spirit as justifying their departure from the teaching of Holy Scripture!

Calvin would answer them as he answered the Anabaptists, whose position was similar, by maintaining that the Holy Spirit does not contradict Himself. The Spirit's work now, said Calvin, is to lead us to acknowledge the divine authority of the Scriptures which He inspired long ago; to interpret them to us, and to convince us of their truth, and to work in us a response to what they say. The spirit that leads men to disregard and contravene the inspired Scriptures is not the Spirit of God. So if we would be led by the Spirit, we must allow ourselves to be led to the written Word, to believe it, study it, preach it, defend it, and be subject to it ourselves. Contend for the authority of Scripture, Calvin would say to us. Revere Holy Scripture, and learn from it. All that is written is for our profit. Commenting on Romans 15:4 ("whatsoever things were written aforetime were written for our learning"), Calvin wrote: "There is nothing in Scripture which is not useful for your instruction, and for the direction of your life . . . there is nothing vain and unprofitable contained in the oracles of God. . . . Whatever then is delivered in Scripture we ought to strive to learn; for it would be a reproach offered to the Holy Spirit to think that he has taught us anything which it does not concern us to know; let us know, then, that whatever is taught is conducive to the advancement of piety."

Let Calvin examine us on this point. Do we profess faith in the divine inspiration and authority of Holy Scriptures? If we do, that is good; but in that case, we must ask ourselves: Do we adorn the doctrine which we profess? Do we labor to lay to heart the whole of God's revelation?—or do we content ourselves with one or two favorite passages and one or two favorite doctrines and never go outside them? If we maintain that the whole Bible is the Word of God, Calvin would say to us, let us show that we are serious in what we say by taking seriously all that the Bible teaches, lest we discredit our own position and injure our own souls.

A Concern for God's Grace

Second, if Calvin were back among us today, he would urge us to share his *concern for God's grace.* Our review of Calvin's doctrine of Scripture leads on naturally to this, for his view of Scripture was rooted in his doctrine of grace. Scripture was a gift of grace, according to Calvin, for it was precisely God's means for bringing sinners to know Him and His Son. Without Scripture, there would be no knowledge of salvation. Calvin opposed both speculative thinking about God and self-righteousness before God ("natural theology" and "merit"). To him, both were instances of the same mistake—namely, trust in human ability, in the one case intellectual, in the other moral. Just as (said Calvin) it is a mistake to think that by one's own unaided effort and free will one can gain righteousness before God, so it is a mistake to think that by one's own unaided reflection and free thinking one can know truth about God. One effect of sin is to blind our minds, so that we cannot know God truly. But Scripture is given to supply our need.

Calvin's illustration of this point is well known. We, he says, are like shortsighted people with damaged vision; there is a glorious revelation of the majesty of God in the created order, but we cannot see it without help. Scripture gives us the help we need, for it functions like spectacles. When we put on the spectacles—that is, when we learn of God from Holy Scripture—we find that we can then see the glory of God in creation; but we cannot begin to know God the Creator from our natural experiences and thoughts until we have first come to know Him through the Word.

Calvin calls us away from the delusive by-paths of natural theology, just as he seeks to divert us from the pursuit of self-righteousness and the dream of salvation by works. Realize your impotence and inability, Calvin would say to us; you cannot know God, or find salvation, without Holy Scripture. The Bible introduces us to God and leads us to Christ the Savior, who is its focal point and goal *(scopus);* and only so can we, as sinners, ever come to know God and obtain righteousness and acceptance with Him. We need the Bible in order that we may know God's grace which it sets forth. Be jealous, Calvin would say to us, for the biblical doctrine of grace.

If you asked me to put in a sentence the thrust of Calvin's concern here, I would say this: Calvin wanted men to know the grace of God as it is set forth in Romans, the epistle which he himself described as the key to Holy Scripture. In his own ministry, he was constantly laboring to inculcate this knowledge, as all his writings bear witness, and to remove two particular obstacles to it which he saw to be hindering many from grasping it.

The first obstacle, in Calvin's day as in our own, was *a shallow view of sin.* Calvin saw that shallow views of sin destroy knowledge of the glory of Christ as Savior of the helpless and the unworthy. If fallen man thinks that despite sin he is still good at heart, still free for good, free to please God, he will trust his own works for salvation, and never learn to look to Christ as his righteousness. Therefore Calvin never tires of laboring the biblical insistence on the radical damage which sin has done to human nature. Constantly he stresses the wretchedness of the fallen human condition. Men think that Calvin was malevolent and misanthropic, because he regularly made so much of human wretchedness in his preaching and teaching. But why did he do it? Simply to make men humble before God, knowing themselves to be under sin, in order that they might then go out of themselves to find salvation in trusting the blood of Christ. In other words, Calvin's motive was to lead men from Romans 1:18ff. through to Romans 3:21ff. This is not misanthropy, but true evangelism and pastoral care. All grace is found in Christ. Full atonement, plenteous redemption, perfect righteousness, is laid up for men in Him. But none receive it save those who are driven through self-despair to the Savior's feet. Calvin therefore labored the seriousness of sin in order to engender self-despair, and so shut men up to faith in Christ, the perfect Savior.

The second obstacle, then as now, to a true knowledge of divine grace was *a speculative view* of *predestination*. How ironical it is that Calvin should be thought of as the great speculator about predestination! For he actually spent much of his ministry fighting speculative views of predestination—scholastic speculations, which reduced it to ineffective foreknowledge, on the one hand, and Anabaptist speculations, which reduced it to fatalism and obscured the universality of the gospel promise and the sufficiency of the atonement, on the other.

The keynote of his own treatment of this theme is his recurring demand for reverent submission to scriptural teaching. It is supremely important, he insists, that we should resolve to know no predestination save that which Scripture teaches. Where Scripture leads, we must follow; but where Scripture is silent, we must be content not to know.

Why is it that in the *Institutio* Calvin treats of predestination and election not in book 1 where he handles divine sovereignty in creation and providence, but later on in book 3, after dealing with the cross and the gospel and faith and repentance and justification and the Christian life and prayer? The answer seems to be: Because he wants the theme to appear in the same evangelical context in which it appears in Romans. Where does the theme of election enter in Romans? In Romans 8:29–30 ("whom he did foreknow, he also did predestinate to be conformed to the image of his Son . . . whom he did predestinate, them he also called: and whom he called, them he also justified: and whom he justified, them he also glorified"). And what is the purpose of the declaration contained in these verses? Not to start a controversy; not to provoke speculation and academic debate; but to encourage the people of God, by confirming the fact that their justification and salvation sprang from the free grace of God, and therefore that God's gracious purpose will stand, and they will be preserved to the end.

If God eternally resolved on their salvation before ever they repented and believed, He will certainly not abandon them now that they have repented and believed. This is the unspeakable comfort which the doctrine of election brings in Romans 8:29–38; and it is in order that it may bring this same comfort to his readers that Calvin holds it back until he can set it in an equivalent context in the *Institutio*. A glance at the opening paragraphs of *Institutio* 3.21 shows Calvin drawing out this "unspeakable comfort," and justifying his onslaught against speculative conceptions—or, rather, misconceptions—of predestination by the need to keep this comfort intact for the people of God.

This is simply to say that the knowledge of election and predestination which Calvin sought to inculcate was not a theoretical knowledge, but the practical knowledge expressed in Murray McCheyne's words:

> Chosen, not for good in me;
> Wakened up from wrath to flee;
> Hidden in the Saviour's side,
> By the Spirit sanctified;
> Teach me, Lord, on earth to show
> By my love, how much I owe.

It is a knowledge of election as the family secret of the children of God—an open secret, certainly, but one which brings no comfort or benefit, because it has no application, until a man has come to faith in Christ and been adopted into the divine family. It is a knowledge of election which thrills and humbles, and drives a man to his knees to praise the God of his salvation as never before.

Were Calvin here today, he would tell us, I think, that most of our teaching about grace is pathetically shallow, and he would counsel us to seek a deeper view of sin and a truer view of the saving plan and action of God, and so get more realism and vigor into our Christianity, more life and more praise. And this leads straight to our final point.

A Concern for God Himself

Third, Calvin would urge us to share his *concern for God Himself:* God the Creator; God the Lord, God the Sovereign; the holy One about whom the Bible is always talking. At the heart of Calvin's Christianity there was a vision and a passion. The vision was of God on the throne, God reigning in majesty. How often Calvin uses the words "majesty" and "glory"! How often he dilates on the greatness of God! The passion corresponded to the vision. It was the passion expressed in that great phrase which has become the slogan of Calvinism—*soli Deo gloria!* It was the longing that the Almighty Creator and Redeemer, the Source and Stay and End of all things, should receive the praise and worship and adoration that were His due.

Warfield insists that this passion, with the vision from which it derives, is the formative principle of Calvinism. He stresses that the focal center of the Calvinistic outlook is not justification, or predestination, or the "five points," crucial though all these things are, but something greater still—not just a view of salvation, but first and foremost a view of God. What view of God? Well, Warfield puts it in better words than I can muster, so let me simply quote to you what he says.

> It is the vision of God and His Majesty . . . which lies at the foundation of the entirety of Calvinistic thinking. . . . The Calvinist is the man who has seen God, and who, having seen God in His glory, is filled on the one hand, with a sense of his own unworthiness to stand in God's sight as a

creature, and much more as a sinner, and on the other hand, with adoring wonder that nevertheless this God is a God who receives sinners. He who believes in God without reserves and is determined that God shall be God to him, in all his thinking, feeling, willing—in the entire compass of his life activities, intellectual, moral, spiritual—throughout all his individual, social, religious relations—is . . . by the very necessity of the case, a Calvinist.[4]

And if Calvin could come back, he would tell us, I think, that our God was too small; and he would ask us whether we had ever seen the vision of God on His throne; and he would ask us to let him show it to us. "In your world that is shaken to its foundations by political and cultural convulsions, in days when your churches are weak and starving, in a time of fear and depression and discouragement," Calvin would say to us, "this is the vision you need; and it is a vision that God will give you from His Word, as He gave it to me; all that you need is to learn to listen to what He says." And then perhaps Calvin would point us to such a passage as Psalm 93, where the whole Calvinistic vision, and with it the whole Calvinistic confidence and the whole Calvinistic passion, is summed up:

> The Lord reigneth, he is clothed with majesty;
> the Lord is clothed with strength, wherewith he hath
>   girded himself;
> the world also is established, that it cannot be moved.
> Thy throne is established of old: thou art from everlasting.
> The floods have lifted up, 0 Lord,
> the floods have lifted up their voice;
> the floods lift up their waves.
> The Lord on high is mightier than the noise of many
>   waters,
> yea, than the mighty waves of the sea.
> Thy testimonies are very sure:
> holiness becometh thine house, 0 Lord, for ever.

And let all the people say, Amen!

8

THE GROWTH OF
JOHN CALVIN'S *INSTITUTIO*

G. E. Duffield

Honesty forces scholars to admit that they simply do not know when John Calvin began to write the first draft of his *Institutio*. The years between 1533 and the publication of the first edition from the Basle press of Thomas Platter in 1536 are among the most obscure in Calvin's adult life. In the autumn of 1533 he only just escaped police arrest in Paris for his part in drawing up the famous University Rectorial address delivered by his friend Nicolas Cop. Calvin certainly had some part in it, though precisely what part remains obscure. But to understand the formative influences which shaped the volume, we must glance briefly at what is known of Calvin's earlier background.

Calvin had been educated at two different colleges in Paris

193

University. At first his father intended him for the priesthood, but then after a quarrel with the local clergy and some reflections on the economic prospects, he substituted the legal profession. As a result, Calvin transferred to the flourishing legal faculties of the Universities of Orléans and Bourges. But when his father died, he went back to Paris to pursue classical studies which had steadily attracted more and more of his attention. Then came the Cop affair and Calvin's flight.

Calvin's early experiences and training influenced his later writings. In Paris he experienced the cruel rigors of medieval education, acquired a grounding in languages, got to know the Schoolmen, encountered nominalist philosophy, and above all he made contact with those enlightened humanists who gathered around the aged Jacques Lefèvre of Etaples, Bishop Briçonnet, and the King's sister, Margaret of Angoulême. These people were reformers but not Reformers. They were fed up with medievalism, its moral corruptions, its bigotry, its poor scholarship, its wild allegorisms, and its hairsplitting disputations. They wanted to discover the world of antiquity—classical and biblical—for themselves, not have it garbled for them by the Schoolmen. That was what it meant to be a humanist, and humanists wanted ordinary people to be able to read the Bible for themselves.

Although some men in this group drew back when literary reform turned into theological Reform, the group also nurtured such future Reformers as Calvin and Farel. Under the influence of humanism Calvin acquired not only an elegant style for his own composition, but a knowledge of the Bible and the classics at first hand. He learnt to study these texts in their contexts and in the original languages. At Orléans and Bourges Calvin studied law, which further developed his prodigious memory and gave him the lawyer's incisiveness for developing arguments and stating a case clearly. During his period of legal studies Calvin kept up his contacts with humanism and in fact published his first book, a commentary on Seneca.

We simply do not know when Calvin was converted, for he is very reticent with personal details. However, we do have certain facts. He was originally a devout and conscientious Roman

Catholic with a great respect for "the Church." In Paris he must have known of Luther's writings, for his humanist friends would certainly have kept him abreast of the various reforming currents. Calvin himself states that he read Zwingli early on and was put off by Zwingli's sacramental views. His association with the Cop address shows him firmly in the reforming humanist camp, but it is not a Protestant address. Later, in the preface to his *Commentary on the Psalms,* he writes of his *subita conversio.* I am myself inclined to think his experience of the gospel may have come earlier and that this *conversio* refers to his decisive break with Rome, but I cannot go into the evidence here. But Calvin was no rebellious radical by temperament, for just as he had been put off by Zwingli's eucharistic radicalism, so his first religious book, *Psychopannychia,* was an attack on the Anabaptist doctrine of Soul-sleep.

What sort of man emerges? A talented young man who starts off a devout Roman, who is antiradical by temperament, who respects the Church, a man who has acquired a considerable knowledge of scholasticism, classical languages, and law, a man who has caught humanism's passion for a real knowledge of antiquity, a man who by that passion has been gradually led to see what Christianity is, and a man who has come to a knowledge of the gospel and a decision to break with Rome. Such a man wrote the *Institutio,* and the whole variety of his talents and learning can be seen within that book.

The 1536 *Institutes*

After the Cop incident Calvin became a fugitive. He travelled about, spending the largest amount of time in Angoulême with the Du Tillet family, his friends. In 1534 he must have been working on the book in their excellent library, but toward the end of that year an incident occurred which was to give his book a new urgency and to shape some of its subject matter. During the night of October 18 placards against the mass were posted up all over Paris, and one was even attached to the King's bedchamber door. The anonymous author proved to be Antoine Marcourt, who was minister of Neuchatel. His language was strong and polemical to say the least, and at times verging on the scurrilous.

The results of the placard incident were catastrophic. The King was incensed not so much by the theological implications as by the overtones of insurrection. He ordered public processions of penitence and prayers "to beg God that he would correct these scandalous heretical placards and books," but worse was soon to follow. Protestants were burnt at the stake. From Basle whither he had moved to seek "a quiet hiding place" for the pursuit of his studies, Calvin heard about these events in France, and like other Protestants, he was horrified. Now Francis I valued his alliance with the German Protestant princes, so he had it put about in France and Germany that the victims were seditious folk—Anabaptists, whose excesses everyone would know.

This false charge gave Calvin his immediate reason for publishing the *Institutio*. He addressed a lengthy preface to the King of France because he believed that the excuses were to shelter even greater bloodshed to come. Calvin had known some of the martyrs personally, and he could not suffer them to be misrepresented as Anabaptist rebels. He explains his twofold aim in writing: first, "to vindicate from undeserved insult my brethren whose death was precious in the sight of the Lord," and he hoped incidentally to move Protestants in other countries to help the sufferers. Second, "to serve our French people of whom I can see many who are hungry and thirsty for Jesus Christ and few who have gained a right knowledge of him."

The case of persuading the king was not as hopeless as a cynical latter day observer might suppose. For with the death of the chief persecutor, Cardinal Duprat, in July 1535 there was a lull in the persecution, and Bucer and Melanchthon had even been invited to Paris to discuss Church reform.

But the events of Munster where, after a long seige, the fanatical Anabaptist rebellion had been ruthlessly crushed in the summer of 1535, were a greater threat than persecution. All the Reformers realized the terrible danger which threatened from the Anabaptists, and Calvin was anxious not to let the Reformation get identified with them. Equation with their extremities and fanciful ideas would have sunk the Reformers.

In March 1536 the Latin *Institutio* appeared with its full title: *The Institute of the Christian Religion, Containing Almost the Whole Sum of Piety and Whatever It Is Necessary to Know in the Doctrine of Salvation: A Work Very Well Worth Reading by All Persons Zealous for Piety and Lately Published.* I am inclined to agree with Benoit in *Studies in John Calvin* which I had the privilege of editing, that most of this long title was probably added by the printer as "printer's blurb," for it is not an accurate description of the first edition, though it does describe subsequent editions much more accurately.

The word *Institutio* is interesting and important. It was a common word among the humanists for a manual or summary of instruction. Erasmus and Budé, whose family Calvin knew well and from whose linguistic erudition he had benefited, had each written an *Institutio.* There may be a fuller meaning in the title as I shall suggest a bit later.

The *libellus,* the little book as Calvin called it, of 1536 was pocket size (6 1/8 by 4 inches). It was 520 pages long, and contained six chapters, and a short index. The first four chapters follow the familiar ground of Luther's Catechism expounding respectively the Law, the Creed, the Lord's Prayer, and the two sacraments. Then the tone changes—perhaps because events in France called for something different. The fifth chapter denounces the other five "sacraments" of the medieval church. The sixth chapter discusses Christian liberty. Such then was the first edition of the *Institutio,* a *libellus* based on the plan, at least, of Luther's Catechism plus certain additions to meet the needs of the hour. Calvin kept this ground plan for his 1537 catechism, and for 1539 and 1541 editions of the *Institutio,* but the plan of the final 1559 edition is somewhat different.

The 1539 *Institutes*

Within a year the first edition was exhausted, and Calvin was asked to produce a revision of it. He managed to complete this only in 1538 after he had been turned out of Geneva. The second edition was published by Wendelin Rihel in Strasbourg in 1539. It was simply called *Institutio Christianae Religionis,* after which appeared a curious little note reading "at length truly corresponding to its title." This puzzles Professor Battles, but further convinces me of the truth of Benoît's conjecture that most of the earlier title was publisher's blurb, not Calvin.

The book had grown from six to seventeen chapters of about the same length as previously. The format was larger—folio 13 by 8 inches. There were 346 pages and wide margins for the student's notes. In copies to be circulated in France Calvin's name had been turned into an anagram Alcuinus. Despite his busy program in Geneva, Calvin had been reading hard, particularly in the Fathers. His dismissal from Geneva gave him more leisure (if that is ever an appropriate word for one as industrious as Calvin) than he was ever to have again, and he used it for writing. The second edition shaped much subsequent development of the *Institutio.* Peter Barth speaks of it being "distinguished from all the others by a peculiar liveliness and freshness in the management of the thought. . . . It proceeds upon the fundamental theological lines which were to be followed in all subsequent editions of the Institutes."

At Strasbourg, Calvin, like his friend Bucer, had been engaged in controversy with the Anabaptists, and much appears in the 1539 edition to counteract their heresies. He had been reading widely (Augustine, Origen) and in some places that may surprise us (Plato, Aristotle, Cicero, Seneca). The 1539 edition abounds with allusions to Plato, though he is rarely mentioned by name. Here is the continuing influence of Calvin's humanism, and I believe it may have been partly the same influences which led him to add two new chapters on the knowledge of God and the knowledge of man to the front of his book. Calvin was about to answer the letter Cardinal Sadoleto had sent to the people of Geneva trying to inveigle them back into the Roman fold. Now Jacopo Sadoleto was one of the Roman scholars who had been influenced by humanism, and he had written (not in the letter just mentioned but elsewhere) that all the Church's problems could be solved by *scientia,* the knowledge which would come out of a great conclave of scholars sitting down together. He had once put forward proposals on these lines, and had received some support from Melanchthon. This sort of *scientia* idea was common among humanists both Roman and Protestant, and it may have been partly to counteract this trend and show where true *scientia* was to be found that Calvin added his two chapters.

Among other additions, he expanded his section on the Trinity considerably, added a completely new chapter on the relations between the two testaments to combat certain Anabaptist misunderstandings. He wrote a section defending infant baptism and another against millenarianism, both aimed at the Anabaptists. The brief 1536 statements on justification and repentance are expanded into chapters in 1539. The influence of Bucer is to be seen in 1539. Calvin follows Bucer and Augustine in his expositions of providence and predestination, whereas as recently as 1535 Melanchthon had played the latter down. Again, in 1536 the main emphasis in the section on faith had been on trust and hope as in Luther, but while these did not disappear, the influence of Bucer and Calvin's Reformed humanism added an intellectual aspect to his discussion of faith, which is not found in Luther according to Benoît.

In short, Calvin is not only expanding but beginning to organize his material more, and he gives his reasons in the short but vitally important 1539 preface, which is unfortunately left out of the new Library of Christian Classics edition of the *Institutio.* "My object in this work was to prepare and train students of theology for the study of the sacred volume, so that they might both have an easy introduction to it, and be able to proceed in it, with unfaltering step. I have endeavoured to give such a summary of religion in all its parts. I have digested it into such an order as may make it easier for anyone who is rightly acquainted with it to discover both what he ought principally to look for in Scripture, and also to what head he ought to refer whatever is contained in it. Having thus paved the way, I shall not feel it necessary in any subsequent commentaries on Scripture to enter into long discussions of doctrine, or dilate on commonplaces. I will therefore always compress them. In this way the pious reader will be saved much trouble and weariness so long as he comes furnished with a knowledge of the present work as an essential prerequisite."

This passage is important for several reasons.

1. It shows that Calvin's intended readership, in his Latin editions at any rate, was students of the Bible and of theology.

2. It shows the relationships between the *Institutio* and the commentaries, which is important both for any general study of Calvin and to correct certain current misrepresentations of Calvin which are almost always built up mainly, if not exclusively, from his commentaries. We must interpret Calvin as Calvin intended us!

3. It shows pastoral wisdom in guiding people to Bible study and in helping them use commentaries. (Read Calvin's preface to his *Commentary on Romans* for more on this.) Bucer's commentaries, excellent though they are in many ways, are full of longwinded digressions. Luther's are, if anything, worse. No wonder Calvin's have stood the test of time better. They are shorter. They keep to the point. They avoid the interminable topical digressions which mar so many otherwise excellent Reformation commentaries.

After the 1539 *Institutio* Calvin turned to a French translation. Some have sought to maintain that the first French translation appeared in 1536, but there is no direct evidence for this, and the isolated fragments of 1536 which appear in 1539 translation are best explained as Calvin's own notes rather than parts of a lost edition. The translation, published in Geneva in 1541, was the first original theological work to appear in what we may call modern French. It is probably not too much to say that Calvin's French helped to mold the French language in the same way as Tyndale's New Testament shaped classical English. One effect of this today is that Calvin is studied for his contribution to the French language by some who would not otherwise trouble to read his theology.

The French edition was for those ordinary French Christians who could not read Latin, for Calvin, like all the other Reformers, was a patriot. He never forgot the needs of his fellow Frenchmen. Indeed with all his international contacts and with his Academy at Geneva, later to become the theological center of Protestant Europe, it is remarkable that he spent so much time translating into French. Perhaps in these days of international and intercontinental denominational groupings, we do well to ponder the biblical concept of the nation. Was Calvin just a child of his time, or was he onto something modern Christians, and especially modern ecumenists, have forgotten?

Benoît in one of his contributions to *Studies in John Calvin* gives an interesting survey of the changes Calvin made in his French editions. They show that such a mighty intellect as that of Calvin was not unaware of the problems of comprehension for ordinary Frenchmen. Once again the true pastor's concern not to go over the heads of his people. Let me cite a few examples from Benoît. Calvin removes, translates, or paraphrases the Greek words. He gets rid of references to Aristotle. He repeats himself much more, and adds explanations superfluous to scholarly readers. He explains, for example, that Caligula was a Roman Emperor and that Socrates was an ecclesiastical historian.

Calvin uses strong expressions in popular French, but in Latin just plain *illi*. He makes use of popular proverbs and vivid untranslatable expressions. The whole text is more familiar and easy to read. Listen once again to Calvin explaining his purpose in the French preface.

> First I wrote in Latin that it might be of use to all students, whatever their nationality. Afterwards, wishing to communicate any fruit it might contain to my fellow Frenchmen, I translated it into our language. . . . It will be a kind of key opening up to all the children of God a right and ready access to the understanding of the sacred volume. And so, if the Lord gives me means and opportunity in future to write some commentaries, I shall be as brief as possible, and avoid long digressions, since I have already set out at length all the articles pertaining to Christianity.
>
> Since we are bound to acknowledge that all truth and sound doctrine come from God, I shall venture to declare boldly what I think of this work, recognizing it to be God's work rather than mine. . . . I exhort all who reverence the word of the Lord to read it and remember it carefully, if they want first a summary of Christian doctrine, and sec-

ond an introduction to the profitable reading of the Old and New Testaments. When they have done this, they will know from their experience that I have not sought to impose on them with words. If anyone cannot grasp it all, he must not give up in despair but press on, trusting that one passage will illuminate another. Above all, I recommend that recourse be had to Scripture in considering the proofs I adduce from it.

Various other editions, and usually translations, followed till the definitive 1559 edition. Each added a little here and there but the main changes came in 1559, by which time the volume had grown to four books and eighty chapters. The 1559 edition saw the introduction of paragraph numbering—1217 of them in all. Two indexes were also added: first, of topics treated, and, second, of Bible passages and works cited.

The 1559 *Institutes*

In his 1559 preface Calvin says of previous editions, "Though I have not regretted the labour spent, I was never satisfied until the work had been arranged in order now set forth." The title of the book speaks for itself: *Institute of Christian Religion, Now First Arranged in Four Books and Divided by Definite Headings in a Very Convenient Way: Also Enlarged by So Much Added Matter That It Can Almost Be Regarded as a New Work.* In 1559 Calvin entirely recast his arrangement. Up till then he had still formally followed the catechism pattern. Now he abandons that for a loose following of the pattern of the Apostles' Creed. He makes certain theologically significant changes in structure, though as Beza, his first biographer observed, he never changed his basic theology.

1. He divides up his treatment of predestination and providence which had previously formed one section in the Creed chapter. Now providence is moved to book 1 under the doctrine of God, and predestination moved to book 3 where it is discussed under salvation.

2. The section on the Church, its powers, organization, etc.,
    is moved to book 4 away from the heading of faith.
3. The chapter on the Christian life which had previously
    been the final one in the volume is now moved to book
    3 where it is treated as the work of the Spirit in us.

The age of the Reformation saw the great discovery, or rather rediscovery, of justification by faith alone. It was therefore natural that its greatest works should be soteriologically orientated. Certainly this is true of Calvin's *Institutio.* It is primarily about salvation because the Bible is primarily about salvation. There have, of course, been many books written about salvation before and since, but in the history of soteriological studies Calvin will always hold a unique place, for he was the first to relate the whole work of the Trinity so closely to salvation. He was the first to work out the theology of salvation in terms of the threefold office of Christ—prophet, priest, and king. He was the first to give the Spirit His proper place in salvation.

The *Institutio* is a theology of the gospel, and in some ways I think it has affinities with Paul's Epistle to the Romans and Calvin's commentary on that book, for it was with this book that Calvin started his commentaries, and deliberately. It was to this book that he referred in the 1539 preface. Book 1 opens with the age old question—How can a man know God? Calvin replies through nature to a limited extent, but savingly only through his revelation in the Bible. Then he proceeds to God the Creator, and man a helpless sinner after the fall. That has opened up the way for the center of book 2, Christ the mediator, God's answer. Book 3 follows the third section of the Creed on the Spirit. The Spirit applies salvation in repentance and faith. Then follows the central exposition of justification, and after it what results from justification and what the justified sinner is to do in living the Christian life. Then in book 4 he turns to the sacraments, for the ministry of word and sacrament are God's appointed ways of strengthening faith. Finally there follows the duty of Christian citizenship.

Calvin was not the first Reformer to produce a systematic study of biblical theology. Melanchthon's *Loci,* first published in 1521, had done it, and so had Zwingli's *De Vera et Falsa Religione* in 1525. But Calvin's *Institutio* is by common consent the greatest of Reformation theologies, and some of us might want to go further and say of all times. I have deliberately refrained from trying to put down Calvin's theology. One can do that with lesser men, but with great seminal thinkers like Calvin, and such men as Augustine before him, it would be a rash and unwise venture. Certainly it is one which I should not dare to attempt in one paper. I have read a good many books on Calvin's theology, but I have no hesitation in adding that I have always returned to the *Institutio* with a feeling of relief. Like all great books, it is its own best interpreter.

When we consider the development from the *libellus* of 1536 following the lines of Luther's Catechism, through the first major revision in 1539 when there was a slight shift from Luther to Bucer emphasis, through the various semi-popularized French translations and subsequent smaller Latin revisions to the *magnum opus* of 1559 with its very considerable expansion and structural recasting, when we consider all this, we can see what probably was the printer's gloss on the title did in fact turn out to be a prophecy, for *The Whole Sum of Piety and Whatever It Is Necessary to Know in the Doctrine of Salvation* is an accurate description of the definitive edition of the *Institutio*.

First, it was a magisterial study of biblical theology, centering as does the Bible on the gospel theme of salvation.

Second, it was an introduction to Bible study, and to the charge of critics that Calvin stuffed the Bible into a straightjacket of his own fashioning, we may reply by pointing to that 1545 French preface where Calvin explicitly urges his reader to check what he says from the Bible texts given. If he had distorted the Bible, it was as he said on his deathbed "not wittingly," and Calvin would be the first to urge emendation if any distortion be proved.

Third, it was a magnificent *apologia* for the Reformation. It refuted the Roman claims and equally the Anabaptist claims. We are today rather more inclined to notice the former than the latter, but perhaps the first two chapters of book 4 and several similar passages are timely for us today when many are exercised on when to separate from churches which teach or tolerate various degrees of doctrinal error. The constant repetition of the Preface to the French king showed that the book was a perpetually cogent defense of French Protestantism.

And fourth, it was a *summa pietatis,* a handbook to show ordinary people how to live. Calvin would not have known the difference between intellectual and pastoral theology. His approach was too biblical to allow such a distinction, and that is why ordinary Christians as well as experts can benefit from the pastoral wisdom of the *Institutio.*

Professor Battles is correct in saying this of Calvin's *Institutio:* "The secret of his mental energy lies in his piety; its product is his theology, which is his piety described at length." To understand this we must remember the real meaning of *pietas,* and not think of its debased modern usage for something sentimental and ostentatious. But four centuries earlier Philip Melanchthon had summarized Calvin's achievement with praiseworthy humility, because Melanchthon himself was something of a scholar, when he described Calvin in two words, *ille theologus,* or in English *the theologian.*[1]

9

JOHN CALVIN'S GENEVA

W. J. Grier

Geneva at the beginning of the sixteenth century was a city of some thirteen thousand people. Its situation near the best Alpine passes made it an important trading center. Prof. H. D. Foster of Yale has given a picture of the city and its people:

> The Genevans, in fact, were not a simple, but a complex, cosmopolitan people. There was, at this crossing of the routes of trade, a mingling of French, German and Italian stock and characteristics; a large body of clergy of very dubious morality and force; and a still larger body of burghers, rather sounder and far more energetic and extremely independent, but keenly devoted to pleasure. It had the faults and follies of a medieval city and of a wealthy center in all times and lands; and also the progressive power of an ambitious, self-governing, and cosmopolitan community.

At their worst, the early Genevans were noisy and riotous and revolutionary; fond of processions and "mummeries" (not always respectable or safe), of gambling, immorality and loose songs and dances; possibly not over-scrupulous at a commercial or political bargain; and very self-assertive and obstinate. At their best, they were grave, shrewd, business-like statesmen, working slowly but surely, with keen knowledge of politics and human nature; with able leaders ready to devote time and money to public progress; and with a pretty intelligent, though less judicious, following.

In diplomacy they were as deft, as keen at a bargain and as quick to take advantage of the weakness of competitors, as they were shrewd and adroit in business. They were thrifty, but knew how to spend well; quick-witted, and gifted in the art of party nicknames. Finally, they were passionately devoted to liberty, energetic, and capable of prolonged self-sacrifice to attain and retain what they were convinced were their rights. On the borders of Switzerland, France, Germany and Italy, they belonged in temper to none of these lands; out of their Savoyard traits, their wars, reforms and new-comers, in time they created a distinct type, the Genevese.[1]

Williston Walker says that "no city in Christendom had had a more eventful or stormier history than Geneva during the generation and especially during the decade preceding Calvin's coming." Indeed through the fifteenth century and into the third decade of the sixteenth, there were three parties contending for the control: (1) the bishop of Geneva, (2) the House of Savoy, and (3) the citizens of Geneva. The bishop was in theory the sovereign of the city under the overlordship of the Emperor. The Duke of Savoy had certain rights in the city and tried to gain control of both bishop and townsmen.

As early as 1387 the townsmen secured from the bishop the sanction of certain rights, known as "The Franchises." The chief of these was to gather in general assembly (or council) to choose magistrates. Four syndics or magistrates were to be chosen annually and a treasurer to be elected for three years, and the judgment of cases involving the laity was taken from the bishop's court and given to the magistrates. There speedily grew up the Little Council, composed of the four syndics with the syndics of the preceding year plus counsellors elected by the syndics in office. At first this Council varied in number, but it came to be fixed at twenty-five. It was charged with the administration of the rights of the citizens.

From 1457 there was a second Council of fifty members at first, later of sixty, to discuss and debate matters not easily dealt with in the General Council. From 1459 onward the members of this Council were named by the Little Council.

From 1527 there was a new Council called the Two Hundred, elected (from 1530 onward) by the Little Council. This Council tended to take over little by little the work of the Sixty.

In the early part of the fifteenth century the citizens had the support of the Bishop in withstanding the encroachments of the Dukes of Savoy, but toward the middle of the century the House of Savoy, as Bonivard tells us, began to "poke its nose into the bishopric of Geneva." In 1444 Amadeus VIII of Savoy, elected counter-pope by the Council of Basel, took upon himself the bishopric of Geneva, and the House of Savoy seems to have held a controlling influence on the bishopric right into the third decade of the sixteenth century. Geneva now began to look to the confederate cities of Switzerland for help against Savoy, and in 1477 signed a treaty with Berne and Friburg, establishing political, military, and commercial relations between them.

Within the city from the beginning of the sixteenth century there was a struggle between the partisans of Savoy and those favoring the alliance with the confederate cities. On the side of Savoy there were the clergy and many of the richest citizens and families who had certain ties with the ducal house. On the other side there were the merchants and business men who had contact with the neighboring cities and the bulk of the common people who wished to be free from feudal and ecclesiastical bondage.

In 1520, before ever the Reformation touched the city, the people rose against the bishop (John, known as the "Bastard of

Savoy") who had pardoned one of his rich partisans in the city. The Duke with his soldiers seemed to have gained control of the city in 1525, but in 1526 the partisans of Savoy were defeated and a treaty was signed with Berne and Friburg. In 1527 the bishop left the city, never to return except for a few days in the summer of 1533. And the vice-dominus or agent of Savoy was expelled in 1528.

The First Preachers of the Reformation

In 1529 the Emperor Charles V addressed a strong warning to the citizens of Geneva, stating that he had heard that some preachers had proclaimed Luther's ideas among them and that this was tolerated by them. He ordered them to seize these ministers and punish them severely. William Farel visited the city in 1532 and 1533. He had to flee, but his pupil Peter Viret replaced him. Farel returned a little later and drew up a liturgy (in 1533) and a catechism or summary of faith (in 1534).

At this time, owing to the attacks and threats of Savoy, the city took the step of destroying the suburbs and erecting new walls where the suburbs had been. Apparently there was also at this time an attempt to poison the preachers—an attempt which was almost successful in the case of Viret.

By the summer of 1536 the city was coming increasingly under the control of those sympathizing with the Reformers, though a Reformed observer claimed that scarcely one-third of its inhabitants could be counted against the bishop and the Duke. Farel pressed for a public debate, to make clear to every eye the weakness of the case of their opponents. This was held between May 30 and June 24, 1535. Two Roman friars were the defenders of the Roman cause, but Farel carried the day on all points. The five points he defended make clear that Reformed doctrine was preached in Geneva before Calvin came.

On June 13, 1535, the bishop, who had fled, fulminated against the city, charging the people with listening to false preachers, renouncing the holy sacraments of Mother Church, and casting down the cross and images of our Lady. On August 10, 1535, the Council of Two Hundred decreed that the celebration of Mass cease till further notice. Most of the Roman clergy and monks fled the city. Those who wished to stay could do so on condition of attending upon the preaching of the Word of God. One contributory cause to this victory was the low morals of the Roman clergy. Prof. Foster says that "on this point there is substantial agreement between Catholic and Protestant historians."

In February 1536, the Council of Two Hundred forbade blasphemy, oaths, and card playing, and regulated the sale of intoxicants. In June 1536 presence at the sermon was required under penalty of a fine. It is clear that there were disciplinary laws in Geneva before Calvin's coming.

On May 21, 1536, urged on by Farel, the Little Council and the Two Hundred called a meeting of the general assembly of the citizens in the Cathedral, and there it was voted, without dissent, to live by the Word of God and abandon idolatry. They also agreed to maintain a school to which all would be obliged to send their children and where the children of the poor would be taught free of charge.

The Reformed cause was not by any means triumphant. The Genevese desired to be rid of papal abuses, but they were far from desiring with equal ardor to adhere to the new evangelical community formed in the city. There was a party which supported the Reformation, merely from patriotic and political motives—out of opposition to bishop and duke.

In 1532 when Farel first arrived, he could say: "they have little sympathy for the gospel, but are still very cold, carnal, worldly, knowing almost nothing, except taking the sacrament and speaking evil of the priests." Calvin at the end of his life bore testimony: "When I first came to this Church, there was practically nothing. . . . There was preaching, and that is all . . . all was in confusion. . . ."

This is an accurate picture. If the city was not to fall into anarchy or come under the domination of Berne (which sought by all means to seize possession of the power formerly enjoyed by the bishop), it was necessary to accomplish a work ecclesiastical, moral, social, and political.

Calvin's Early Reform Efforts

In January 1537, after the arrival of Calvin, the Little Council received from the ministers and adopted a document entitled "Articles concerning the organization of the Church and of Worship at Geneva." This set of Articles was designed as a constitution for the Church, securing its existence and status. It is likely that Calvin was the principal author—possibly it was by Farel's hand, but it expressed Calvin's thoughts. It begins: "Most honoured lords, it is certain that a Church cannot be called well-ordered and regulated unless in it the Holy Supper of our Lord is often celebrated and attended—and this with such good discipline that none dare to present himself at it save holily and with singular reverence. And for this reason the discipline of excommunication, by which those who are unwilling to govern themselves lovingly, and in obedience to the Holy Word of God, may be corrected, is necessary to maintain the Church in its integrity."

It is evident that behind these Articles there was a tremendous concern for that which is holy. Three leading points should be noted:

1. To enforce discipline the ministers requested that there be appointed "certain persons of good life and repute among all the faithful" to keep an eye upon the life and conduct of the citizens. These were to report notable offences to one of the ministers and join with him in fraternal admonition to the offender and as a last resort proceed to excommunication.

2. They urged in these Articles that all the inhabitants make confession and give account of their faith.

3. They urged that measures be taken to train the young in religious truth. It may be noted here that Calvin drew up a Catechism to help in this matter.

While the Little Council and the Two Hundred authorized, with slight reservations, these Articles with their far-reaching program, they showed little zeal to put them into effect. It was a common thing then for city governments to adopt rules to regulate the behavior of the citizens and then fail to enforce them. "The novel element" in the Articles of 1537, says John T. McNeill, "was the association of the restraint of private extravagance and immorality with fitness for admission to the communion."

Opposition to the Reformers and their projects arose from various quarters: (1) those in sympathy with the old religion, (2) those seeking to be rid of the restraints of the old religion but desirous only of living according to their own pleasure, and (3) those to whom the demands of God were acceptable only in the measure in which they fitted in with their politics. These last were "nationalists" whose views were a mixture of religious faith and love for their city, the second element taking precedence of the first. At first they had favored the Reformation, but as soon as the Reformation began to claim supreme place (without at the same time serving the cause of patriotism), they turned against it. So old leaders of the cause of Reform like Jean Philippe and Pierre Vandel ranged themselves against Reform. They called the Reformers "strangers." They admired the arrangements at Berne where the Church was under the control of the State and did not claim the spiritual authority claimed in the Church of Geneva.

Calvin and Farel realized that a considerable section of the citizens was sympathetic to the old religion and stood in need of instruction. So Calvin issued his *Instruction in Faith*—a fine summary of the main teaching of the *Institutes*—and a brief Confession of Faith (presented to the magistrates in November 1536) to which all the citizens of Geneva were to be solemnly pledged. He and Farel pressed the Little Council in March, April, and May 1537 to get the citizens to express their assent, but many were unresponsive.

Berne demanded that the rites in Geneva be made uniform with her own. In Geneva under Farel's leadership the use of baptismal fonts in the Churches and of unleavened bread in the Lord's Supper and the keeping of such days as Christmas had been abandoned. Berne now demanded that the rites and practices followed in Geneva be made uniform with her own. On January 4, 1538, the Council of Two Hundred forbade the ministers to exclude anyone from communion, and a little later, without consulting the ministers, they adopted the Bernese ceremonies. Calvin and his colleagues in the ministry could not admit the right of the civil power to take church measures without consulting them. The result was that on February 23, 1538, he and Farel were bidden to depart within three days.

When Calvin resumed his work in Geneva on September 13, 1541, after the few years in Strasbourg, the party then in power was "weary of civil disorders, convinced of the ill-estate of the Church, and of the insufficiency of the ministers" (Williston Walker) who had taken the place of Calvin and his colleagues. They were therefore ready to give some support to Calvin's program. On the very day of his return he asked the Little Council to adopt the principles of ecclesiastical discipline which he had instituted before his exile. Three days after this request the Little Council voted that the Ordinances to restore order in the Church and city ought to be submitted to it for approbation, then to the Two Hundred, then to the General Council. The Little Council made modifications, the Two Hundred made further modifications, and then the General Council approved of the new Constitution—without the modifications being made known to the ministers!

In these Ordinances Calvin sought to safeguard at any price the spiritual independence of the Church from the encroachment of the secular power and to put into operation an effective discipline. The Ordinances showed no essential alteration from the Articles of 1537, but were more elaborate and precise. The Councils by their alterations sought to preserve their control in Church affairs, which they often showed themselves jealous to maintain. These Ordinances of 1541 remained the moral and legal code of the city for more than three centuries (with some changes in 1561 relating particularly to marriage and excommunication).

This Constitution mentions four classes of office bearers: pastors, teachers, elders, and deacons. It laid down rules on the administration of the sacrament, on marriage, burial, visits to the sick and to prisoners, and the education of youth.

Examination of candidates for the ministry was to be in the hands of the pastors, to make sure candidates were suitable in doctrine and in life. The candidates entered upon office by the election of the ministers and the approval of the government. The Little Council changed the wording at this point to strengthen its control in the choice of ministers.

On Sundays there was to be preaching in St. Peter's at 5 a.m. in summer and 6 a.m. in winter, in each of the three city churches at 9 a.m., and again in the afternoon in two of the three. At noon instruction was given to the children in all three. Services were held in each of the three on Monday, Wednesday, and Friday in the mornings. Before Calvin's death a daily sermon had been instituted in all three churches in the city.

A most important provision of the Ordinances was that which required the ministers to meet weekly for discussion of the Scriptures. The exegetical exercises at these occasions were open to the public. This weekly meeting was on Fridays and was known as the Congregation. Every three months the ministers were required to meet for criticism of one another. If the ministers themselves proved unable to settle any contention which arose in their ranks, recourse should be had to the aid of the elders, and then to the magistrates. The meeting of the Venerable Company of ministers came to have a very important influence in Geneva—much greater than that actually laid down in the Ordinances.

No part of the Ordinances was more important than that concerning the office of elder. Here there was a great advance upon the Articles of 1537. The elders were to watch over the life of each individual, to admonish affectionately those who erred, and where necessary to make report to "the body which shall be appointed to make fraternal corrections." From the first meeting of the Consistory on December 6, 1541, a new system of supervision of the life and morals of the people was introduced. People of all ages were under its inspection. Such matters as examination in religious knowledge fell within its orbit. Disciplinary measures were taken for absence from sermons, criticism of the ministers, use of charms, family quarrels, cases of drunkenness, gambling, dancing, profanity, wife-beating, and adultery. Disciplinary procedure was taken for having fortunes told by gypsies, for making a noise during sermon, for saying the pope was a good man, against a woman of seventy about to marry a youth of twenty-five, and against a barber for tonsuring a priest. This list will give some idea of the extraordinary minuteness and variety of cases reported for correction.

Calvin had not secured all that he wished in this effort for sound discipline. "It is not perfect," he said, "but passable, considering the difficulties of the time." He did, however, provide for the exercise of church discipline up to the point of excommunication. But that right was not fully recognized until 1554, and many a battle had to be fought before this triumph was secured.

Calvin's Years of Struggle

In 1546 there were serious troubles for the Reformed cause in Geneva, arising specially from the Libertines, a faction which included in its ranks Genevans of easy morals. The struggle with them continued for a number of years. In 1551 it assumed fresh forms with fresh opponents—men who opposed Calvin's doctrine and even accused him of heresy. Jerome Bolsec, for example, assailed Calvin's teaching about predestination and charged that he was no true interpreter of Scripture.

In the summer of 1553 Calvin's position was almost desperate. His disciplinary measures had met with resistance; the influx of refugees, who of course were his admirers, aroused jealousy and opposition. In the elections in February of that year his opponents were triumphant, his chief antagonist being elected first magistrate. Access to the General Council was refused to the ministers and the right of the consistory to excommunicate was once more challenged.

It was at this point that Servetus came to Geneva. He had written against the Trinity. More than a hundred times he called the Trinity a "monstrous three-headed Cerberus," or dog of hell. To Protestants and Roman Catholics alike he was an extreme heretic. At Vienne he was imprisoned by the Roman Church but escaped. He was sentenced in his absence to be burned alive. John T. McNeill said recently: "Had Servetus not escaped from prison in Vienne but suffered death there under the Inquisition that condemned him, his burning would have been little noticed."[2]

When he escaped from Vienne, he came to Geneva. He ventured to attend Church, was recognized, accused by Calvin, arrested, and imprisoned. The Councils of Geneva passed by the authority of Calvin and sent the case for advice to the Swiss Protestant cantons. The case against Servetus was drawn up by a notary who was an adversary of Calvin. Servetus in his turn accused Calvin of heresy and demanded his death. The day after the trial began, Berthelier, one of the leading Libertines, took up his cause. As E. M. Wilbur, the Unitarian historian, points out, the Libertines had no interest in Servetus save to embarrass Calvin. The Swiss Protestant cantons all expressed horror of Servetus's blasphemies and advocated his punishment. Berne urged death by fire. The burning took place on October 27, 1553, Calvin's appeal for a less cruel form of death passing unheeded. Calvin shared the opinion of his time on this matter of the punishment of heretics. After the death of Servetus he wrote on this point, urging that slight errors be borne with, that graver errors be dealt with moderately, and that the extreme penalty be reserved for blasphemous errors touching the foundation of religion. Neither he nor any of his fellow Reformers saw that their views on this point contradicted the principle of liberty of conscience.

The Triumph of Reform

The Libertines gained nothing from their support of Servetus. In fact, their leaders were discredited, and it became clearer than ever that there was a bond between sound doctrine and the maintenance of order. The influx of refugees too contributed greatly to the victory of the Reformed cause. By 1554 no less than 1,376 of them had obtained the right of residence. In the decade from 1549 to 1559, over five thousand new inhabitants were admitted, among them noble men like the Marquis of Vico, Laurence of Normandy, and Theodore Beza.

In 1554 and 1555 the cause of the Reformation was triumphant in Geneva. On February 2, 1554, the Council of Two Hundred, at Calvin's prompting, swore with uplifted hands "to live according to the Reformation, forget all hatreds, and cultivate concord." Later he persuaded the Little Council to adopt (like the ministers) the custom of stated meetings for mutual correction. His position at Geneva was now assured. As McNeill puts it: "Geneva was at last Calvin's to command."

The establishment of the Academy in 1559 was one of Calvin's crowning attainments. To the true preaching of the Word and sound discipline was now added a sound education. "His [Calvin's] conception of a city obedient to the will of God in Church and State, served by an educated body of ministers, disciplined by ecclesiastical watch and strict supervision, and taught by excellent schools had at last been realized" (Williston Walker).

Conclusion

The success was due to the hand of God. The walls of God's Zion at Geneva were built in troublous times. The cause of the Reformation seemed again and again to hang by a tiny thread. Even at the end of 1553, when the triumph was not far distant, Calvin wrote to Viret: "I am broken unless God stretches forth His hand." In 1559, the year of the founding of the Academy and the issuing of the definitive edition of the *Institutes,* the threat from without was so serious that ministers, nobles, and workmen toiled feverishly to repair the fortifications. They could say: "If it had not been the Lord who was on our side, the proud waters had gone over our soul."

It was a triumph of the preaching of the Word. The Reformation began with the bold preaching of the Word by Farel and others. It was as a preacher of the Word that Calvin took up his task, and for twenty-five years he labored, often in great bodily weakness but in the Spirit's power. At the close of his ministry, Geneva was a city of the preaching of the Word more than any city on earth.

It showed the value and efficacy of sound discipline. For a sound discipline Calvin contended through most of his ministry, and when it was established, then victory was secure. So Geneva became, as Knox said, "the most perfect school of Christ since the days of the apostles." Knox went on: "Manners and religion to be so sincerely reformed I have not yet seen in any other place."

There was a social, as well as a spiritual and moral, revolution. Dr. Biéler emphasizes this tremendously in his *Economic and Social Thought of Calvin.*[3] There were measures for the care of the poor, the orphans, and the aged; and measures against overcharging and monopolies. The price of food was brought within the reach of all purses. Calvin said that if they neglected the poor, they ignored not only the poor but God whose representatives they were. The pastors of Geneva intervened to protect the weaker elements in the trades of the city, and so prevented the troubles and rebellions which broke out elsewhere. In 1560 there was the fuller organization of various trades with rules as to the conduct of masters and their relations to workers and apprentices, and hours of work were fixed and time of apprenticeship.

It was this application of the Word of God to every department of life which made out of unpromising material in Geneva what the Bishop of Ossory called "the wonderful miracle of the whole world."

Soli Deo gloria!

10

JOHN CALVIN AND GEORGE WHITEFIELD

D. Martyn Lloyd-Jones

Before I deal with the subject which has just been announced, I should like to read a few verses to you from the Book of Judges: "And Joshua the son of Nun, the servant of the Lord, died, being an hundred and ten years old. And they buried him in the border of his inheritance in Timnath-heres, in the mount of Ephraim, on the north side of the hill Gaash. And also all that generation were gathered unto their fathers: and there arose another generation after them, which knew not the Lord, nor yet the works which he had done for Israel" (Judges 2:8–10).

The title of my address needs a little explanation because as announced it sounds so pretentious. Those of us who have been in this Conference for the last two days will already have heard five addresses on John Calvin and different aspects of his work, so it looks at first sight as if I am claiming to be one who can not only deal with John Calvin but also throw in Whitefield into the bargain! I want to disabuse your minds of any such notion.

The second misconception into which you may have fallen I also want to dismiss. Some of you may think that, realizing that five men would already have spoken on John Calvin, I came to the conclusion that they would have said everything that could be said, so that little being left for me, I decided to talk about George Whitefield.

That, again, is entirely wrong. The subject of John Calvin and his work, and what he has left to us as a rich heritage, is so great and so vast that it would not have been at all difficult for me to continue the theme of the four hundreth anniversary of the death of John Calvin. The explanation of why I am going to speak on George Whitefield is much more interesting.

We had planned that the whole of the Conference this year should be devoted to the memory of John Calvin, and this meeting was to take that form like all the others. But I received a letter from Mr. Hilton Day, who was then the Minister of the Whitefield Memorial (Presbyterian) Church in Gloucester, pointing out how this year, being the two hundred and fiftieth anniversary of the birth of George Whitefield, they there felt that something must be done to celebrate this. So he invited me to go down to Gloucester on Wednesday evening, December 16, to speak on the subject of George Whitefield. Why did they choose December 16, which is today? Well, they chose it because Whitefield was born on December 16 two hundred and fifty years ago. I wrote back and said I was extremely sorry, that I could imagine no greater privilege than to speak on George Whitefield, and especially in Gloucester, but, alas, I was committed to this meeting in connection with this Conference. But they very kindly changed their date, and I had the great privilege on Tuesday, December 8, of speaking in the Whitefield Memorial Church in Gloucester on George Whitefield.

But it did not stop at that. All this immediately put into my mind the suggestion that we should devote this meeting tonight to commemorate George Whitefield and his great and glorious services in the eighteenth century, and Dr. Packer and others were very ready to agree with this suggestion. We felt that it would be very wrong, much as we revere the memory of Calvin, to allow this year, and this night of all nights in the year 1964, to pass without saying something about this great and mighty man George White-field. The difficulty was to discover how to put this on the pro-gram. The subject of all the other papers was to be John Calvin. Suddenly to introduce Whitefield would seem odd to people. So we decided on this compromise, and to announce it as "John Calvin and George Whitefield."

The connection is not quite as remote as some might imagine. There are many good reasons why these two men should be put together though they were two very different men in many ways. John Calvin was an extremely thin man, almost cadaverous. White-field on the other hand was rather stout and portly. John Calvin was what is called a typical introvert. Whitefield, I would say on the whole, was an extrovert. And there are many other differences. But the thing that connects them is the similarities. It is not some chance association based on dates that determines that these two men should be put together.

Here is one point which they have in common, if one may use such an expression—they were both Calvinists. We will leave it like that. What we mean is that they were both Paulinists. But it has become customary to use the term Calvinist. Anybody who knows anything about the eighteenth century will know that the Methodists of that century divided into two groups, into two camps, around the persons of George Whitefield and John Wes-ley. They did so largely in terms, at the beginning at any rate, of this difference in point of view theologically. George Whitefield was a follower of the teaching of Calvin. He was a truly Reformed man in his doctrine; whereas Wesley was Arminian. So this division came in. Now this clearly links Whitefield with Calvin. Whitefield remained more loyal to the Thirty-nine Articles of the Church of England than did John Wesley. Those Articles have a Calvinistic emphasis, and Whitefield adhered to that, whereas John Wesley departed from that and therefore was mainly responsible for the division. So Calvin and Whitefield had that in common.

But they had other things in common. We heard last night

from Dr. Packer about the zeal of John Calvin, and about the stupendous amount of work which he did. It was quite phenomenal: all those Commentaries and the Institutes and all the letters and the tracts and all the rest that he produced. How one man was able to do it all, and to preach so regularly in addition, is very amazing for us to contemplate. Exactly the same thing is true of Whitefield. There is no man who has labored with greater zeal in God's kingdom than George Whitefield. They are very similar in that respect also.

Another thing they have in common is that they both ended their earthly course around about the age of fifty-five. This is a remarkable thing. John Calvin died just short of fifty-five, and Whitefield died just short of fifty-six. These two men who did such stupendous work both died in their middle fifties.

Another thing they share in common—and I do want to emphasize this—is that they were both men who longed, perhaps more than any of their contemporaries, for unity among evangelicals. In this Conference we have considered that point in connection with Calvin. Calvin was tremendously concerned that all Reformed and Evangelical people should come together in unity. He bemoaned the divisions and the differences that had arisen, and he was prepared to do anything he could—he said he was ready to cross, if necessary, ten seas in order to attend a conference which would help to promote this unity among Reformed Evangelical people. Not unity with Rome, of course, but unity among Reformed Evangelical people.

The same thing is very true of George Whitefield. He had to stand on his principles, his doctrine, as against the two brothers Wesley, but at the same time he bemoaned the division, and he did almost everything a man could do in order to bring the parties together. And toward the end of his life they had come at any rate to the position in which they were preaching in one another's pulpits, and, by Whitefield's own request, John Wesley was the man who preached his funeral sermon. That is most interesting, that these two men, Calvin and Whitefield, have this again in common, this great concern about the unity of those who are united in the preaching of the Gospel of Salvation.

Lastly, they are similar in the matter of their tremendous influence upon their contemporaries and subsequent generations. I turn now to that. Somebody may ask, "Why are you commemorating the two hundred and fiftieth anniversary of the birth of George Whitefield?" There are many answers to that question. One is that he was, as our chairman has rightly pointed out, the greatest son of the City of Gloucester. Bishop John Hooper of the sixteenth century was Bishop of Gloucester, Robert Raikes was a Gloucester man, and Tyndale came from that shire. But I was glad to hear Dr. Packer saying that beyond any question the greatest of them all was George Whitefield.

But we are calling attention to him tonight, not for that reason, but because he is, beyond any question, the greatest English preacher who has ever lived. You notice my emphasis! I say the greatest "English" preacher. I am not saying the greatest preacher in the world. There was a contemporary of his two hundred years ago who, I am glad to note, even Bishop Ryle, himself an Englishman, has to grant and to admit was the equal of Whitefield. I am referring to a man called Daniel Rowlands who lived and ministered in Wales in that same eighteenth century. However, it is generally agreed that George Whitefield is beyond any question the greatest English preacher of all time. Let us be accurate. If you say that, and if you put Rowlands in with him, well then I think there are good grounds for saying that these two men were probably the greatest preachers since the days of the apostles. That is not an overstatement, as Ryle would agree.

Whitefield was not only the greatest English preacher of all time, we commemorate his memory because of his profound influence upon the course of history. Dr. Packer said that very thing last night of John Calvin. And it is, of course, true. It is equally true of Whitefield. His influence in England, his influence in Wales, his influence in Scotland, and his influence in America, in particular, is beyond calculation. If the historian Lecky is right in saying what is so often quoted—that it was undoubtedly the Evangelical Awakening that saved this country from a Revolution such as that which was experienced in France in 1789 and following—if that is true, well then George Whitefield more than anybody else is responsible for that fact. That, again, is why we believe it is right to call to mind the memory of this great man, this great preacher.

The Neglect of Whitefield

There is one remarkable fact about this man Whitefield to which I must turn for a moment, and that is the amazing neglect which he has suffered. It would be very interesting to discover what the result would be if I asked everyone present now to write an essay on George Whitefield. How much would you have to say? I venture to assert that he is the most neglected man in the whole of Church history. The ignorance concerning him is appalling. One is constantly discovering this in reading and in listening to people. It has become the habit to refer to the great Awakening and Revival of two hundred years ago as the "Wesleyan" Revival. It is spoken of always in terms of what John Wesley, in particular, did—even Charles has had to suffer. People seem to have the idea that all that happened in the eighteenth century was the sole result of the activity of John Wesley.

I came across an instance of this in a new book on Charles Wesley by Frederick C. Gill. It is called *Charles Wesley, the First Methodist*. In it there is a typical example of how Whitefield is depreciated. In dealing with the difference of opinion that arose about the doctrine of Election and Predestination and the parting that took place, he says about Charles Wesley, "It was with sorrow that he departed from the convert of his Oxford days."[1] In other words, Whitefield is referred to as a convert of Charles Wesley! Thus throughout the years Whitefield has been either forgotten or depreciated. I am glad to be able to say that the best and most distinguished Methodists are very ready to acknowledge this. The late Dr. J. Ernest Rattenbury was very ready to say that Methodism had never given its due place to the memory of George Whitefield. And Dr. Skevington Wood, a Methodist historian of today, is equally ready to say the same thing.

But the question is, Why has Whitefield been neglected like this? Most people know something about John Wesley—I do not think they know much even about him, but they know something—whereas Whitefield is an unknown man, and the great story concerning him is something that people never seem to have heard. Why is this? The explanation is most important; that is why I read those verses from the second chapter of the Book of Judges. You notice the point which is made: not only did Joshua die but "that generation was gathered unto their fathers"—the contemporaries of Joshua. And then we are told, "there arose another generation after them, which knew not the Lord, nor yet the works which he had done for Israel." That is a most interesting and significant statement. It always seems to me to cast great light upon our present position. When people do not know the Lord, they very soon become ignorant of Church history. Once you lose the knowledge of the Lord you lose an interest in His works.

That, I think, is what has happened during the last hundred years. Knowledge of the Lord always leads to, and stimulates, an interest in Church history. May I suggest in passing tonight that there is something wrong with an evangelicalism that is not interested in Church history? There is something surely wrong with an evangelicalism that seems to think that evangelical history began with the first visit to this country of D. L. Moody about 1873. There is a defect somewhere in our knowledge of the Lord; for once a man has a true knowledge of the Lord he has a lively interest in all the works of the Lord, in all the known and recorded events in the long history of the Christian Church. I think that this is something that should cause us to examine ourselves very seriously. These two things, according to the text, are indissolubly linked together: loss of knowledge of the Lord, loss of knowledge of His servants and His great works through them. Let us examine ourselves at our leisure in the light of that proposition.

But there is a second reason why people are so ignorant about Whitefield, and that is because of his humility. He was, like Calvin, a most humble man. He said, "Let the name of George Whitefield be forgotten and blotted out as long as the Name of the Lord Jesus Christ is known." Again may I throw out, especially for the members of the Conference, a theological question here? Is there something in the idea that those who tend to follow the teaching of John Calvin are less interested in advertising than those who follow the Arminian teaching espoused by John Wesley? I just put it to you. I just ask you to keep your eyes on the religious journals and papers and see whether there is not something in this suggestion. The teaching of John Calvin humbles man in the first instance; it glorifies God. It makes man feel that he is insignificant, that he is nobody; and however much a man may be privileged or enabled to do, he knows that it is God Who does it. That is the thing in which he is interested. Is that true, I wonder, of the other emphasis and teaching? The fact remains that we know so much less about George Whitefield than we do about John Wesley.

But the main explanation, I have no doubt, of the neglect of Whitefield is this, that he never founded or established a denomination. He may have felt a little toward the end of his life that he was wrong here. It is said that he said before the end that John Wesley was wiser than he had been, that he had "penned his sheep" whereas he had not. However, the fact is that he was not concerned to found or to leave behind him a religious denomination. He was content to preach the gospel, to fertilize every conceivable religious body. So he did not leave behind him a denomination. But John Wesley left a denomination behind him, and he left a denomination with a particular theological outlook, and great attention has been paid to his memory. Books have poured out on John Wesley without ceasing throughout the intervening years; but in the case of Whitefield there was no religious denomination to do so. That is, I think, the main explanation of why he has been so sadly neglected.

The Leader of the Awakening

But why should we take this trouble then to bring to memory again this man, and to put him before ourselves and the religious public? My answer is: because of the phenomenon of the eighteenth-century revival of religion, one of the most amazing episodes in the long history of the Christian Church. I am very ready to agree with those who say that this was probably the greatest manifestation of the power of the Holy Spirit since apostolic days. A very good case can be made out for saying that.

If you want to know what I mean you can look at it like this. Consider the state of this country before that Evangelical Awakening and Revival. It was deplorable. I must not go into it, I have not the time. There is a book which deals with it thoroughly. Note the title, *England before and after Wesley*. How significant it is! Of course it was written by a Wesleyan Methodist—Wesley only counts. But the facts that the author adduces are true. He was a good historian in that sense, but a bad theologian and lacking in understanding of what truly happened. But he was a very good collector of facts. Read that book by J. Wesley Bready and you will see that in almost every conceivable respect this country had sunk to one of the lowest depths that it had ever reached. The Church of England was dead; you know about the pluralities of livings, you know about the drunkenness and the fox-hunting—it has all been described so often. But the other denominations were not much better. They may have been a bit better on the moral side, but the Presbyterian Church of those days had fallen into the heresy of Arianism and eventually disappeared altogether. And the other Nonconformist bodies were in a state of lethargy, holding to a dead orthodoxy.[2]

Attempts had been made by certain people to stem this tide of degeneration. A man called Boyle established a Lectureship, Bishop Butler produced his *Analogy* in defense of the gospel, and various others wrote, but they were of no avail whatsoever. Then this great Revival came, and the whole face of England was entirely changed. The Church of England, in many respects, was revived, Nonconformity was revived, a new body came into being called Methodist Societies, and the repercussions in a wider area were really quite amazing and astonishing. The case has often been made out, and it can be proved it seems to me, that the Trade Union movement in this country rose indirectly out of that Revival. It was because men, who had formerly been ignorant and had been living a drunken besotted life, were changed and born again, that they began to realize their dignity as men and to demand education and better working conditions, and so on—that is where the

Trade Union movement came from. We know the connection between the abolition of slavery movement led mainly by William Wilberforce and this Revival. He was one of the results of this Revival, and indeed a case is made by some for saying that we would never have had the Reform Bill of 1832 were it not for this great Evangelical Awakening.

Now this is my point: those were some of the profound changes produced by the Evangelical Awakening. Very well; in all that, George Whitefield was the leader, he was the first. This is where the neglect of this man and the corresponding over-prominence of John Wesley is so scandalous. Do not misunderstand me. I am not just indulging in a kind of controversy. This is a matter of sheer justice, and of honesty, and of truth. This is where the neglect of Whitefield is so wrong, and so deplorable; because in all the following instances I am going to give, George Whitefield was the first.

He was actually the first to be converted. The author of the book I have just quoted refers to Whitefield as "Charles Wesley's convert in Oxford." The facts are these—that George Whitefield was converted in 1735, whereas Charles Wesley was converted only in 1738. Of course what the man means is that when Whitefield went to Oxford, Charles Wesley and some others had already started the Holy Club and Whitefield was invited to go to the meetings. But that was not his conversion, as I shall show. The first of them to be converted in England was George Whitefield in 1735, the same year in which Howel Harris and Daniel Rowlands were converted in Wales. So he is first even there.

But then he was the first of them to start preaching the true gospel in an awakening manner. Whitefield began to do this in 1736, and one of his greatest years was 1737; whereas we all know that the Wesley brothers only began to preach in an evangelical sense at all after the month of May 1738. So that Whitefield is ahead of them all along the line. In 1737 he was gathering great crowds here even in the city of London, and astonishing results were following.

Then everybody knows that one of the great characteristics of that revival was open-air preaching. These men preached to vast crowds in the open air, twenty thousand and more very often. Who was the first to preach in the open air? The answer is always the same—George Whitefield. George Whitefield was the first to preach in the open air, and he had very great difficulty in persuading both John and Charles Wesley to do the same. They were both much more conservative than Whitefield. He preceded them by several months in this respect and brought great pressure to bear upon them to persuade them to follow him. So you see he is the leader, the pioneer, the first in all these respects.

He was the first of them, also, to order societies—religious societies. He was also the first in works of charity. There is a very famous Methodist school called the Kingswood School, to which most Methodist ministers send their boys to be educated. It was started as a school for the poor children of miners and others. Who founded the Kingswood School? George Whitefield. It was always George Whitefield in the van, he was the leader. I trust that by now I have convinced you that my protest against this disgraceful neglect of this man is more than justified.

But in addition to all this he was the fructifier of the religious Revival in Wales. He was actually the first moderator of what is now known as the Welsh Presbyterian Church. It used to be known as the Welsh Calvinistic Methodist Church. Whitefield became the first moderator of this church in 1743. We must be accurate. I believe he became moderator for this reason. There were those two great men and great preachers in Wales—Daniel Rowlands and Howel Harris—and the problem was which of the two should be made first moderator. Well, Englishmen have many uses, but on this occasion one of them became very useful! They solved the problem by agreeing that neither of the two Welshmen should be made first moderator, and by putting the Englishman in the position. The two Welshmen were delighted to bow to him as moderator of this first Presbyterian Association in Wales.

He also had tremendous influence in Scotland. Anyone who has ever read about that Communion season at Cambuslang, which is now a part of Glasgow, will know exactly what I mean. His influence in America, again, is something that really baffles description. All the writers, including those who are concerned at the present time to reproduce the writings and the works of Jonathan Edwards, are all careful and honest enough to say that the influence of Whitefield in America about 1740 and onward was simply overwhelming. There was a second "great awakening," greater, even, than the first that had taken place in 1735.

These are some of the reasons why we are calling attention to this man. He visited America seven times. Some of us find it difficult to cross the Atlantic now, but imagine doing so two hundred years ago! And Whitefield crossed the Atlantic thirteen times. He died there on his last, his seventh visit, so he actually crossed the Atlantic thirteen times. He visited Scotland fourteen times. It is computed that he probably preached eighteen thousand sermons in the thirty-four years of his preaching life.

Whitefield the Man

That is why, I say, it is right that we should commemorate the memory of this man. This man was simply a phenomenon. There was no man who was better known in London two hundred years ago than this man George Whitefield. What are the facts about him? Let me give a brief summary in order to try to give some conception of the phenomenon known as George Whitefield. He was born, as I have reminded you, in Gloucester at The Bell Inn on December 16, 1714. Many of his ancestors had been clergymen in the Church of England, but his father was not. His father was the keeper of this Inn, The Bell Inn in Gloucester, and there he was brought up as a boy. His father died when he was very young, and he tells us in his journal that he fell into many sins, most of the sins that young men tend to fall into. But he was never really happy, he had a tender conscience always. He left school for a while but then he began to feel that this was wrong. During the time when he left school he was just serving, drawing drink in the ordinary way in that public-house, in Gloucester. But his conscience was still troubling him, and he went back to school, and eventually was able to gain an entrance into a college in Oxford. There, as I say, he came under the influence of this Holy Club that had been formed by Charles Wesley and some others and which later was joined by John Wesley.

Having finished his course in Oxford, he was ordained by Bishop Benson, the Bishop of Gloucester at that time, on June 20, 1736, at the age of twenty-one. Now Bishop Benson had made a rule that he would not ordain anybody under the age of twenty-three, but having heard what he had heard about this remarkable young man, and having met him for himself, he decided to break his own rule, and so ordained him though he was only twenty-one.

On June 27, a week after his ordination, he preached for the first time in Gloucester in the Church of St. Mary le Crypt, where he had been baptized as a child and where he had taken his first communion. Naturally this was an event which caused a great deal of interest, and perhaps some excitement. His mother was well known as the keeper of the Inn and so on, and all the relatives and friends and others came to the service, with the result that the church was full. Now this is the interesting thing; immediately in this first sermon he showed that he was a man apart, that there was something quite unusual about him. The effect upon the congregation was tremendous. It was said afterwards, and even reported to the Bishop, that fifteen people had been driven mad by this sermon. Bishop Benson was a very wise man and his reported comment was this: "All he wished and hoped was that the madness might not be forgotten before next Sunday." However, he was a wise man, and he realized that here there was a most unusual preacher. Whitefield's very first sermon marked him out as an entirely exceptional preacher at the age, remember, of twenty-one.

I must not weary you with all the details. He came first to London in the following August, of 1736. His first sermon in London was preached in Bishopsgate. The post he came to was to act as a locum to the chaplain in the Tower of London, but he was given opportunities of preaching elsewhere, and again the moment he began to preach he attracted attention, and he attracted crowds. People had never heard preaching like this. Instead of reading a most prosaic kind of essay which was supposed to do duty as a sermon, here was a man preaching with the whole of his being, with authority and power and conviction—and, immediately, every time he preached the churches were always full, were always packed.

Then after spending about two months here in London, he went down to do a locum for a friend of his in a curacy in Hampshire. There it was exactly the same. As the result of this, of course, he was offered many curacies, and various possibilities and prospects of success and advancement in the Church of England were placed before him. But under the influence of his friends John and Charles Wesley, who were out in Georgia trying to do a bit of missionary work, he felt a call to go to Georgia, and so he decided definitely that this was the one thing he must do. There was not a ship available immediately and there were various arrangements to be made, so he was enabled to go back to Gloucester to pay farewell to his mother and friends and relatives. He preached there, and again it was remarkable. In a sense this proved to be the real turning point in his life and career.

He had some relatives in the neighboring city of Bristol, and he wanted to bid farewell before he left for Georgia. So he went there. Whenever he heard that there was any kind of lecture or preaching in a church on a weekday, he always attended. So, in Bristol he went to a certain church, and there he was sitting in the congregation when the man who was due to preach recognized him and went down to him and asked him if he would preach instead. Whitefield says, "I happened to have notes of a sermon in my pocket so I agreed to preach." And he did so. That was the beginning, in a sense, of the real phenomenon of George Whitefield. The whole congregation was electrified. He preached in other churches, and they were also crowded. People came from everywhere, and in the churches they would bc holding on to the lamps, holding on to the loft, to the gallery—anything in order to be in the building to hear him.

Now this is astounding. He preached in Bristol for the first time in January 1737. Delays occurred, he was still not able to go to Georgia, so he was able to pay a return visit to Bristol in May 1737 and arrived there on May 23. Here is something that will help you to realize what a phenomenon this man was. Remember, he was only a young curate of twenty-two years of age, but this is what he says about his return visit to Bristol: "Multitudes came on foot to meet me, and many in coaches a mile without the City, and almost all saluted and blessed me as I went along the street."

Can you picture this? A young man of twenty-two! People walking out a mile, travelling in coaches in order to meet him. It was a kind of "royal procession" and all was entirely the result of his amazing and astonishing preaching. And it continued like that—back he went to Gloucester, then to Oxford, and then to London. It is said that between August and Christmas 1737 he preached one hundred times, and he preached on each occasion to crowded audiences. He became one of the most famous men in the whole of London, and the whole of the country. There was a very popular magazine in those days called *The Gentleman's Magazine,* and to get your name in it was quite an achievement. Well, in November 1737 there was a poem on George Whitefield in *The Gentleman's Magazine,* and he was still only twenty-two years of age. Nine sermons of his were published in 1737, and they had a very great sale indeed.

Then at long last he was able to go to America, and he spent most of 1738 in America. Now this year 1738, remember, is the year in which the two Wesley brothers were converted during the month of May. But Whitefield came back to this country at the end of 1738 for various reasons. Now this brings us to the great year 1739. Going back again to his old haunts—Gloucester, Bristol, and so on—he began to hear about the terrible condition of the miners living in that village of Kingswood then on the outskirts of Bristol. They were living a most depraved kind of life. Whitefield felt concerned about them. They never went near a place of worship, so he began to feel that he must go to them, and he went one day and preached to just about a hundred of them. But the effect again was so tremendous that from there on he began to preach to at least five thousand of them at a time. These men would come up from the pit, they had no time to wash or anything, they just stood and listened, and there he would preach to them. It is said that he was soon preaching to twenty thousand people, all of them standing in the open air and listening to him. And after that, as I have told you, he influenced the brothers Wesley to do the same thing.

But when Whitefield came back from America, he found that a great change had taken place here in London in the attitude of the clergy and ministers to him. He had left on the crest of a wave of popularity, but when he came back, he found that many doors were closed to him. Why?

There were many reasons for this. Some of his converts had been a bit unwise, and they had acted in a way that was not becoming to the gospel, and had antagonized their own clergy and ministers. Moreover, some of the clergy had never really liked his preaching on the absolute necessity of the New Birth. Above all, parts of the Journal which he had begun to keep had been published, and they felt that this was exhibitionism, and that he was saying things that he should not say. These things no doubt, plus a great deal of jealousy, meant that many churches were closed to him. So he was driven to the open air still more. He was refused to be allowed to preach in St. Mary's Church in Islington; just as he was about to enter the pulpit, they stopped him. But he then decided that he would quietly close that service. He then led the people out, and preached to them in the churchyard. All this aggravated the situation, and the attacks that were made upon him became really quite unbelievable. Attacks were made upon his moral character, and they were even offensive to his personal appearance. Whitefield had the misfortune of having what is called a squint in one eye, and so he was known by the crowd, the popular crowd in London, as "Doctor Squintum."

However it did not make any difference. The point was that he was this well-known preacher, and that is how his life went on. He would preach on Moorfields Common, he would preach in Marylebone Fields—just north of the present Marylebone Road. He would preach in what was then called May Fair, which we now call "Mayfair." He used to preach on Kennington Common. He used to preach on Blackheath. Indeed, in any place where there was a great open space Whitefield had but to get up and to preach and thousands crowded to listen to him. His average congregation was somewhere in the neighborhood of twenty thousand people at a time, and, remember, they all had to stand. But they stood willingly.

He just went on doing this for the rest of his life. He did this all over England, he did it in Wales as I have told you, he did it in Scotland, he did it in America. Thus this phenomenon continued. When it was heard that he was in the neighborhood and about to preach, shopkeepers shut their shops at once, for they must hear him; business men forgot their business, farmers put down their tools. He could get a congregation of thousands any time of day or night; he could get them and hold them in snow, sleet, frost, rain—it did not matter what the conditions were. In America in one very cold winter they used to stand by the thousand listening to this man preaching the Gospel, and they would travel endless distances in order to get this great opportunity and privilege.

I can sum up the rest of his life by just telling you this—that from that beginning in the open air in that way in 1739 he just went on and on doing this in all these countries until at last in the early morning of September 30, 1770, he breathed his last breath and went on to be with that Lord whom he had longed to see from his earliest days as a young preacher. His end is very characteristic of him. He was not well by now. The amazing thing is that he lived as long as he did. For this man used to preach five or six times a day. That was quite ordinary for him, and thus he put his body under a tremendous strain.

There he was; he had promised to preach in a place called Newbury Port in New England, on Sunday September 30, 1770, and he was travelling in that direction. He had to go through a place called Exeter, and when they heard he was there, they all came crowding out. He must preach to them, and at last they persuaded him to do so. At first he could scarcely speak at all. He was in such a weak physical condition that he really could not articulate. He began slowly, and gradually he began to revive. He ended by preaching to them for two hours. That was George Whitefield. He became filled with power and strength, and the congregation, as usual, were deeply affected.

Then he arrived at the place where he was to stay that Saturday night at Newbury Port, and at last he said he was going to bed. They handed him a candlestick with a candle, but the place was crowded with people. Wherever he went, people crowded around him, asking questions, wanting to have a word from him. This last picture of him is a most wonderful, idyllic picture. He was trying to break away from them, and began mounting the stairs holding the lighted candle in his hand. Then he turned around and spoke to them again, and gave them another exhortation. And he went on doing so until the candle had burnt right out in the socket and he had just got the candlestick in his hand.

At last he got into his bedroom and into his bed. He had a very severe attack of what we would now call cardiac asthma and he died. He just went on, as I say, to be with the Lord whom he loved so much. When you read his wonderful *Journals,* keep your eye when you do so on the way in which he longed to go to be with the Lord. It was not mere talk; he meant it; he was reprimanded sometimes for saying this, but it was his greatest desire, and at last it was granted. Well, there is the phenomenon that is covered by the name of George Whitefield, and that is why it is good that we remind ourselves of all this.

Here was a man who could preach in that way to all classes. He had a great following among the aristocracy here in London. The Countess of Huntingdon thought there was no man like him as a preacher, and she used to open the rooms in her great house and invite all the leading aristocracy of the age to listen to him; and they all delighted in listening to Whitefield. He was the greatest of these preachers to the aristocracy, but as I reminded you, he was also the greatest preacher to the miners, the greatest preacher to the crowd in Moorfields, Kennington Common, or wherever he happened to be. He could preach to children equally well in the orphanage. What an astounding and amazing man he was!

He was also supreme in the matter of collecting money. He founded an orphanage in Georgia, and it cost a great deal to keep it going. So it became a custom with him to preach a sermon, and at the end of the sermon to take up a collection. He used to get enormous collections of money, and with this money he would also help anybody who was in need, any poor person, anybody in difficulties. The whole of England was talking about him. It was always known when he was in London, and he could attract people of every class or stratum in society.

Explaining This Phenomenal Man

What is the explanation of this phenomenon? It is very difficult for us to conceive it, is it not? We are living in very poor days. What a century that eighteenth century was! Here is the phenomenon; what is the explanation? Let me attempt some kind of analysis.

Let us start with the man himself. The natural man was very interesting. As a boy he is said to have been alert and able and very lovable. But the most outstanding thing about him was his gift of oratory. He showed that when he was quite a boy. He would imitate preachers in the Inn. He was a born actor, and he had wonderful elocution. A man is born an orator. You cannot make orators. You are either an orator or you are not. And this man was a born orator. He could not help it. He was always good at declaiming portions of Shakespearian drama. In school he was generally given a part, or if an address was to be delivered to the notabilities of the City of Gloucester, he was the boy who was chosen because of his amazing elocution and the ease and the grace with which he did it all. He was a born orator, and like all orators, he was characterized by the great freedom and appropriateness of his gestures.

The pedantic John Wesley was not an orator, and he sometimes tended to be a bit critical of George Whitefield in this respect. I remember reading in Wesley's *Journal* of how once they both happened to be in Dublin at the same time and how John Wesley went to listen to Whitefield. In his account of the service, Wesley refers to his gestures, and says that it seemed to him that Whitefield was a little bit too much like a Frenchman in a box. He means that Whitefield tended to speak with his hands as much as with his lips and mouth. But that is oratory.

One of the greatest orators of all time was Demosthenes. Somebody asked Demosthenes one day, "What is the first great rule of oratory?" And Demosthenes answered, "The first great rule of oratory is—action; and the second great rule of oratory is—action; and the third great rule of oratory is—action." An orator is not just a man who moves his lips and his tongue, his whole body is involved. "Action!"

We are living in evil days; we know nothing about oratory. George Whitefield was a born orator. Have you heard what David Garrick is reported to have said? David Garrick was the leading actor in London in those times and whenever he had an opportunity he always went to listen to Whitefield. He was not so much interested in the gospel as in the speaking and in the gestures and so on. Garrick is reported to have said that he would give the whole world if he could only say "Oh!" as George Whitefield said it. And somebody else said that if he could only utter the word "Mesopotamia" like Whitefield he would be completely happy.

I have a still greater authority to quote. One of the great men of the mid-eighteenth century was Bolingbroke. He was an able, cultured man, a man of the world, a very wise man, and again one who was interested in oratory and in speaking. Bolingbroke said of Whitefield, whom he heard many times, that he had a greater "commanding eloquence than any man he had ever heard." He had heard all the greatest statesmen and political orators and other types of orator also. He put Whitefield's at the top of the list, as the greatest "commanding eloquence" that he had ever heard. In addition to all this, Whitefield had a warm, sympathetic outgoing nature. There is the natural man.

But that does not explain the phenomenon of George Whitefield. Turn now to the spiritual. Here is the explanation. May I put it in a crude and almost ridiculous manner. God knows what He is doing, and when He chose this man George Whitefield, to whom He had given these natural gifts, He knew what He was doing. George Whitefield underwent a remarkable conversion. It was a long, painful process. There were many steps in it. As I have reminded you, his conscience troubled him as a boy, as a young man, and when he went to Oxford he would not join in the various parties to which he was invited. He would not do so; he was too serious. Then he went to the Holy Club meetings, and they made him still more serious. They did their good works, they had their fast days, and they visited the prisons. . . . But none of it really helped him.

Then he read a book, a famous book written by a Scotsman of the name of Henry Scougal who had lived toward the end of the seventeenth century. The title of the book was *The Life of God in the Soul of Man*. This had a profound effect upon him. It convinced him that he needed to be born again, that to be a Christian means not that you live a good life, or do this or that, but that you have the life of God in your soul. He realized that he had not got it; and this drove him to the depth of despair. He went through agonies. He used to lie prostrate on the ground in prayer, he would go out and pray in the open air; there was nothing he would not do. He went through this terrible process of conviction of sin; but eventually God graciously smiled upon him.

In other words the conversion of George Whitefield was not a question of "making a decision." It was not sudden. No, he went through this tremendous agony of conviction, and then the light broke upon him. In addition to this he was given what he called "the sealing of the Spirit" upon the fact that God had forgiven his sins. The Spirit sealed it. "There is no question but that this man received a "baptism of the Spirit." That is what explains the extraordinary character of his preaching from the very beginning.

But let us remember this. Though that is the beginning, he continued throughout his life to be characterized by a most amazing piety. The prayer life of this man puts us all to shame, and has often made me feel that I know nothing about these matters at all. I have already referred to his humility and saintliness. Nothing shows that more clearly than the way in which he was terrified at the thought of preaching. Though he had been trained for the ministry, and the time had come for him to be ordained, he was terrified of preaching. He felt it was such a sacred task; and who was he to enter into a pulpit and to preach? He felt he would run a thousand miles away in order not to preach. Such was his view of it all, and such was his view of himself and his own unworthiness, that it took a great deal to persuade George Whitefield to enter a pulpit and to preach.

Brethren, is there not a lesson there for some of us? He also hated press notices, and was always annoyed when he received them. He was, in other words, an extraordinarily humble and saintly man. John Wesley pays him the tribute of saying that there was only one man whom he thought he had ever known who was the equal of Whitefield in saintliness—and conceivably he thought this other man was a little higher, he was not sure—and that man was John Fletcher of Madeley. But for John Wesley to say that at the end of Whitefield's life, and in view of all that had happened between them, is a tremendous tribute to Whitefield's saintliness and godliness.

I have already emphasized his zeal. I want also to emphasize his brotherly spirit and the element of catholicity that characterized him. I reminded you at the beginning that he, like Calvin, was very concerned about true evangelical unity. There was nothing small about this man; there was nothing narrow about him. He had his strong views. He was ready to differ with his great friends John and Charles Wesley on doctrinal matters and to resist them. But that did not make him rigid and narrow; it did not make a small party man of him. No! I can prove this. In Scotland, for instance, the two brothers Erskine, Ralph and Ebenezer, who had gone out in the first Secession—and who had very good grounds for doing so—tried to persuade Whitefield to preach only for them in Scotland. But he would not do it. He said, if there are men in the Church of Scotland who believe the gospel, and who are ready to open their doors to my preaching of the gospel, I will do so. He would not be tied down by the Erskines. And he preached for Church of Scotland ministers, as I have reminded you, in Glasgow, in Cambuslang, Edinburgh, and various other places. Now this was all the result of the Spirit of God in him— the love and the brotherliness, the large-heartedness, the desire that all who really have an evangelical gospel to preach should be one and should be working together.

Whitefield's Message

There then is the man. Let me say just a word about his message. He described it as "honest," he described it as "plain." He was always direct. What did he preach about? One of his great themes was Original Sin. No man could expose the condition of the natural unregenerate heart more powerfully than George Whitefield.

Then another great theme was regeneration. He says himself that his sermon on "the nature and necessity of the new birth in Christ" began the awakening in London, Bristol, Gloucester, and Gloucestershire. He was himself convinced that it was his famous sermon on this theme that really led to the Great Awakening. It was his leading theme.

Another theme that was prominent in his preaching was this. He believed in the direct, immediate, inward impressions of the Holy Spirit upon a man. Now Jonathan Edwards took him to task about this. There is a very interesting story in the Memoirs of Jonathan Edwards of how Edwards and others once talked to Whitefield about this. Edwards says, "I tried to deal with him on this question of the emphasis that he places on inward impressions." Whitefield placed great emphasis upon the direct leadings of the Spirit. He believed the Spirit was speaking to him directly, and he acted upon it. Edwards was a much abler man and a much greater genius in an intellectual sense. Edwards was unhappy about this; and it is most interesting, and almost amusing, to notice how Edwards records that it was quite clear that Whitefield was really not listening to what he, Edwards, was saying. However, that was something which Whitefield did preach and did emphasize a great deal.

Then the next great theme, of course, was justification by faith. Some may wonder why I put regeneration before justification by faith. I did so for this reason—that Whitefield preached regeneration before he preached justification by faith. It is most interesting to observe that he underwent a change in this respect. At first his preaching was almost entirely on the corruption of the natural unregenerate heart and the need for the new birth. This was undoubtedly the effect of Scougal's teaching. In the nine sermons of his that were published in 1737 there is no mention of justification by faith. In his *Journals,* with reference to the theme of justification by faith, he states significantly, "though I was not so clear in it as afterwards."[3] He admitted himself that he was not as clear on justification by faith in 1737 as he should have been. Later in his *Journals,* you will find that the two men who had to put him right on that particular aspect of truth were John and Charles Wesley.[4] They preached justification by faith from the very beginning; Whitefield did not. And they helped him to come to a better balance in this respect. We must be honest. I have said that Whitefield was not a party man; and I must not be a party man. All honor to John and Charles Wesley for helping Whitefield to see the importance and the place of justification by faith in the preacher's message.

I have already reminded you of the Calvinistic emphasis in his preaching. He was clear and unequivocal on this.

Another thing that characterized his preaching, especially at the beginning, was his strictures on unconverted preachers. Jonathan Edwards ventured to pull him up on that also; but Whitefield did not listen to him. Whitefield used to denounce an unconverted ministry, and he would do so even when large numbers of ministers were listening to him. Another way in which he put that was to say that, to him, for a man to preach what he called an "unfelt Christ" was a most terrible thing—to preach about Christ without feeling the Christ within. He would denounce without measure men who were guilty of that.

Whitefield's Preaching

I have said something about the man, I have said something about the message, I end with what was the most characteristic thing of all about this man, namely, his preaching. Do you recognize that distinction and division? I ask the question for this reason. There is nothing that has so often discouraged me, if I may make a personal reference as a preacher, as the failure of people to differentiate between the message and the preaching. There is a tremendous difference between uttering truths and preaching. You may have a correct and an orthodox message, but it does not follow that you are preaching it. The thing that puts Whitefield in a class apart with Rowlands is the preaching.

What do I mean? I mean the way in which the message is presented and conveyed. There were other men at that time, as there have been since, who preached the same message, but it was not the preaching of George Whitefield. How can one describe his preaching? You can only describe it as apostolic and seraphic. I like the remark of an American preacher who heard him a lot and who was responsible for publishing some of his sermons. Commenting upon his style of preaching, he said, "A noble negligence ran through his style." What does he mean? He means that Whitefield did not sit down and write wonderful literary masterpieces of sermons, with every sentence perfectly balanced, and always finished, and polished and so on. No, he did not do that. He had not got the time to write sermons. He was an extemporary preacher, and there was what this man calls "a noble negligence" in his preaching. He broke the rules of grammar now and again, he did not remember to finish his sentences always, but to those who know anything about preaching that is nothing. "Noble negligence!"—oh that we had a little more of it, and a little less of the polished essays that pass for sermons in this our degenerate age!

But the thing that characterized the preaching was the zeal, the fire, the passion, the flame. He was a most convicting and alarming preacher. You remember what was said about the first sermon in Gloucester. The effect he continued to produce was like that. He could so expose the darkness and the sinfulness of the natural human heart that men were terrified and amazed and in agonies of soul as they listened to him. But that would be followed by a pathos, a love, and a melting quality that were irresistible.

That is preaching! I like Whitefield's own comment about this matter of preaching. He was asked one day for a copy of the sermon he had preached in order that it might be published, and this was his reply. He said, "I have no objection, if you will print the lightning, thunder and rainbow with it." You cannot put preaching into cold print; it is impossible. You can put the contents of the sermon, but you cannot put the preaching; you cannot put the "lightning," you cannot put the "thunder"—the roar of the thunder, the flash of the lightning—you cannot capture the "rainbow." All that is in the spoken word, in the action, in everything about the preacher. You cannot put that in print. That is why people when they have read the sermons of Whitefield often say, "I cannot understand this. How could the man who produced sermons like this be such a phenomenon, such a wonderful preacher?" If you have ever said that, you are just displaying your ignorance of what is meant by preaching. You cannot put preaching on paper. I hold the view that that has been one of our great troubles since about the middle of the last century or even before. The printing of sermons, the printing of everything that is spoken, can have a devastating effect on preaching as such. Men have their eye upon the people who are going to read it rather than on those to whom they are preaching at the time. Concern about reputation and what the literary and pedantic critics will say, alas, comes in. Let us then remember the words of Whitefield on that matter.

The effect of such preaching of course was simply overwhelming. He tells us himself about what he observed in the past of the poor colliers at Kingswood. These poor men had just come up out of the mines and their faces were quite black with the coal dust as they stood listening to Whitefield. He says, "As I was preaching to them I suddenly began to observe white furrows in their black faces." What was it? Oh, the tears were streaming down their faces and making furrows in the coal dust and grime. That is preaching! These poor men who knew nothing about doctrine, who knew nothing about anything but sin, who were just living in drunkenness and even in debauchery, listening to this amazing preaching of the Word of God were weeping copious tears. Or take the way in which it is described by the author of the great hymn which begins with the words:

> Great God of wonders, all Thy ways
> Are matchless, godlike, and divine.

Samuel Davies himself was an astonishing preacher and a great intellect also. He had been in a revival in America in that same century. He was made principal of a college. Samuel Davies and Gilbert Tennant were sent over to this country to collect money for that college. They arrived after a terrible voyage, during which they thought they were going to be shipwrecked many times over. They at last arrived in London on a Saturday morning, and the first question they asked was—"Is Mr. Whitefield in town?" To their delight they were told that he was, and that he was due to preach the next morning, I think it was, in Moorfields. So they made certain that they would be there in very good time to listen to him. Samuel Davies writes the account of the service and this is what he says. He says, "It became clear to me quite soon in the service that Mr. Whitefield must have had an exceptionally busy week; obviously he had not had time to prepare his sermon properly." He adds, "From the standpoint of construction and ordering of thought it was very deficient and defective; it was a poor sermon. But," said Samuel Davies, "the unction that attended it was such that I would gladly risk the rigours of shipwreck in the Atlantic many times over in order to be there just to come under its gracious influence." That is preaching, my friends. Poor sermon, but tremendous preaching.

What do we know about this? Why do we talk about preaching as "giving an address" or "saying a word"? Preaching! That is the thing that produced that tremendous revival under God. You can read the accounts of what Jonathan Edwards and Mrs. Edwards felt under Whitefield's preaching. Let me tell you what the great Lord Chesterfield said. Chesterfield was a humanist, a typical eighteenth-century man, a "man about town" who wrote a famous book of advice to his son. He used to delight in listening to Whitefield, and he, like others, came under the power of the preaching.

You remember the famous story: Whitefield, one afternoon, was using an illustration to show the perilous danger of the sinner's position, how the sinner was walking in the direction of Hell without realizing it, and he introduced this picture. He compared the sinner to a blind man being led along by a dog. He had a staff in his hand, and he was being led along by the dog. The dog unfortunately broke loose and ran away, and left the man to grope along with his stick as best he could on his own. Unconsciously, said Whitefield, the poor man wanders to the edge of a precipice, his staff drops from his hand down the abyss, too far to send back even an echo. The blind man reaches forward, cautiously, to recover it; for a moment he poises on vacancy and . . . At that moment Lord Chesterfield sprang to his feet shouting, "Good God! Stop him!" and sprang forward involuntarily to try to stop the blind man from falling over the abyss. That is not only oratory, that is also preaching; and it can affect even a man like Lord Chesterfield in that extraordinary manner.

But the story I like best of all is the story about Benjamin Franklin listening to George Whitefield. Now here was another genius. Benjamin Franklin is famous as a scientist, famous as a man of letters, as one of the leaders in the American Revolution, as the first ambassador sent by the United States, as it became, to represent them in France. He often came here to London. This able, cultured man called himself a Quaker; he was nothing at all from the Christian standpoint. Now Benjamin Franklin used to live in Philadelphia, and at the time of Whitefield's visits he was a printer. He was an astute business man, and he used to print Whitefield's sermons and sell them. He never missed an opportunity of listening to Whitefield, and this is what he says concerning one of those occasions.

I have reminded you that Whitefield invariably at the end of a sermon took up a collection for his orphanage in Georgia, and Franklin knew this very well. He had seen it happen many times, and he had often put something into the collection; but he was getting a little tired of doing this. He thought that Whitefield was taking too much of his money. So he says that on this particular occasion as he went to listen to him, he had solemnly decided that he would not give anything at all in the collection at the end. He says, "I had got in my pocket gold, silver and copper; but I decided I would give nothing at all, I had given so often." But this is what he goes on to say, "As the preacher proceeded I began to soften, and concluded to give the copper. Another stroke of his oratory determined me to give the silver. And he finished so admirably that I emptied my pocket wholly into the collector's dish—gold and all." Now that is preaching. This is beyond oratory, this is inspired oratory—oratory inspired by the Holy Ghost, conveying the message of the Word of God and its glorious gospel.

Whitefield's Lessons for Us

Can I in a few headings indicate what I regard as some of the lessons that George Whitefield has to teach us today? I wish I had time to develop them. The first lesson he teaches us is this: that the position is never hopeless—never. Things could not have been worse than they were in the period leading up to 1736–37— absolutely hopeless, apparently. It was just at that point that God placed His hand on this unknown boy from The Bell Inn, Gloucester—George Whitefield. The sovereignty of God! Do not waste too much of your time in worrying about the future of the Christian Church. Do not listen too much to the mere analysts at the present time who simply describe the position confronting us. It is never hopeless. This was one of the most surprising things that God has ever done.

Second, let us, I hope, once and for ever put an end to that lie which says that Calvinism and an interest in evangelism are not compatible. (I do not like these labels, but as they are used I must use them.) Here is the greatest evangelist England has ever produced, and he was a Calvinist. Charles Haddon Spurgeon, the greatest evangelist of the last century, confesses that he had modelled himself as far as he had modelled himself on anybody—on George Whitefield. And he was a Calvinist. The objection which some of us have to certain aspects of modern evangelism has nothing to do with Calvinism at all. I am certain that John Wesley would object to the things that we object to in modern evangelistic methods quite as much as we do. The objection is not based on Calvinism. That doctrine which emphasizes the glory of God and the total depravity of man and God's eternal plan and purpose of redemption in the Lord Jesus Christ has always urged and driven its true adherents to evangelism. Whitefield alone is enough to establish that; but he is but an outstanding shining star in a great galaxy.

The third lesson, is the absolute necessity of an orthodox faith. This man preached the gospel as it had been preached by the Apostles, the Reformers, the Puritans. He lived in the Puritans and their writings. He sometimes even preached their sermons when hard-pressed! Wesley says more than once that he found Whitefield clearly preaching Matthew Henry. But there it is. It was the same message, and there it was ready-made in Matthew Henry! But what I am emphasizing is the absolute necessity of orthodoxy, of a belief of the Truth—the Truth that we were reminded of so excellently in Dr. Packer's address.

But—and, to me, this is the thing that Whitefield tells us more than anything else—orthodoxy is not enough. There were orthodox men in his time, but they were comparatively useless. You can have a dead orthodoxy. Orthodoxy is essential, but orthodoxy alone has never produced a Revival, and it never will. I say as I end that my main justification for speaking on Calvin and Whitefield is this, that in a sense John Calvin always needs George Whitefield.

What I mean is this. The danger of those who follow the teachings of Calvin, and do so rightly, is that they tend to become intellectualists, or they tend to sink into what I would describe as an "ossified orthodoxy." And that is of no value, my friends. You need the power of the Spirit upon it. To state the Truth is not enough; it must be stated "in demonstration of the Spirit and of power." And that is what this mighty man so gloriously illustrates. He was orthodox, but the thing that produced the phenomenon was the power of the Spirit upon him. He says that he felt something even at his ordination, as if he had received a commission from the Spirit Himself. He was always conscious of this—wave after wave of the Spirit would come upon him. No man ever knew more of the love of Christ than this man. It sometimes overwhelmed him, almost crushing him physically. He would be bathed in tears because of it.

This power of the Spirit is essential. We must be orthodox, but God forbid us to rest even on orthodoxy. We must seek the power of the Spirit that was given to George Whitefield. That will give us a sorrow for souls and a concern for souls, and give us the zeal, and enable us to preach with power and conviction to all classes and kinds of men.

Another thing—and this is very important today—he was a great believer in the value of religious societies. There were a number of religious societies in Whitefield's early days which had been started in the previous century, and he was greatly helped by them. His first sermon on that Sunday, June 27, 1736, in Gloucester was actually on "the value of religious society." I say that for the encouragement of little groups of evangelical people, for whom I thank God, and whom I know in different parts of this country today, who are meeting together, some of them every week, some of them every month, to study the Scriptures and to pray and to talk together about the things of God. Whitefield believed in the inestimable value of religious societies.

But, first, and I must end with this in the light of what I have been saying and for every other reason, Whitefield I believe is calling us back to preaching. I hope that I am not going to be misunderstood, but nothing can substitute preaching. I am a great believer in reading; I get much of my greatest enjoyment in reading. But reading is no substitute for preaching; and to read a sermon and to listen to it being preached are not the same thing. Thank God the Spirit can use a written sermon, but it does not compare with a preached sermon. There is a real danger today that people may think that reading alone will do or, perhaps listening to a wireless or a television sermonette. No, you need the freedom of the Spirit; you need "the lightning and the thunder and the rainbow." You cannot get them in books, and you do not get them on your controlled, time-limited programs provided by these modern agencies. No, when the Spirit comes the programs will be forgotten, time will be forgotten, everything will be forgotten except God in His glory, and my soul, and this blessed Savior.

What does Whitefield teach us about the theme of preaching? The theme was, "By grace ye are saved through faith; and that not of yourselves: it is the gift of God." That was the glorious message of the eighteenth-century preaching.

May God call us back to preaching! Not a mere mechanical statement of correct beliefs, but let us pray God so to grant us His Spirit that though we may never become, and never shall become it is certain, preachers in the sense that George Whitefield was— well, that at any rate we may be able to preach "in demonstration of the Spirit and of power." We are not meant to be imitators, but let us listen to this man as he calls upon us so to a living realization of this Truth, and so to be filled with the Living Spirit of God that with all we are we may tell forth the riches and the glories of

His grace. We all, I am certain, thank God for the memory of such a man. May He grant unto us grace to examine ourselves, to examine our ministry, and may He create within us all a longing and a desire to see the manifestation of the right hand of God again in this country in a mighty Revival of religion.

Notes

Foreword

1. Iain Murray, *D. Martyn Lloyd-Jones,* vol. 2, *The Fight of Faith, 1939-1981* (Edinburgh: Banner of Truth, 1990), p. 352.

Chapter 1, The Puritan Approach to Worship

1. Horton Davies, *The Worship of the English Puritans* (London: Dacre, 1948), p. 48.

2. George Swinnock, *Works* (1868), 1:31.

3. John Owen, *The Works of John Owen,* ed. T. Russell, 28 vols. (London, 1826), 16:125ff.

4. Ibid., 16:150-51,

5. Ibid., 16:152.

6. Stephen Charnock, *The Complete Works of Stephen Charnock,* 5 vols., Nichol's Series of Standard Divines, ed. J. Nichol (Edinburgh: Nichol, 1864-65), 1:298.

7. Ibid., 1:299.

8. Ibid., 1:307.

9. Ibid., 1:308.

10. Ibid., 1:315.

11. Owen, *Works,* 13:414.

12. Charnock, *Works,* 1:319.

13. Ibid.

14. Owen, *Works,* 13:423, 425.

15. Ibid., 13:425.

16. William Bradshaw, *English Puritanisme: Containening the Maine Opinions of the Rigidest Sort of Those That Are Called Puritanes in the Realme of England* (1605), p. 17.

17. Thomas Goodwin, *The Works of T. G.*, Nichol's Series of Standard Divines, ed. J. Nichol, vol. 11 (Edinburgh: Nichol, 1862), p. 364.

18. Thomas Adams, *The Works of T. Adams*, 3 vols., Nichol's Series of Standard Divines, ed. J. Nichol (Edinburgh: Nichol, 1861-62), 1:103.

19. David Clarkson, *The Practical Works of David Clarkson*, 3 vols., Nichol's Series of Standard Divines, ed. J. Nichol (Edinburgh: Nichol, 1864-65), 3:190ff.

20. Ibid., 3:194.

21. Swinnock, *Works*, 1:234.

22. Ibid., 1:229-30.

Chapter 2, Scripture and "Things Indifferent"

1. William Tyndale, *Expositions and Notes on Sundry Portions of the Holy Scriptures, Together with the Practice of Prelates . . .* (London: Parker Society, 1849), pp. 77-78.

2. *Conversations between the Church of England and the Methodist Church* (1963), p. 16.

3. John Owen, *The Works of John Owen*, ed. W. H. Goold, 24 vols. (London, 1850-55), 13:479-80.

4. Henry Barrow, *The Writings of Henry Barrow, 1587-1590*, ed. Leland H. Carlson, vol. 3 (London: Allen & Unwin, 1962), p. 320.

5. John Whitgift, *The Works of J. Whitgift . . .* , ed. J. Ayre, 3 vols. (Cambridge: Parker Society, 1851-53), 1:38, 41.

6. Richard Hooker, *The Works of . . . R. H., . . .* , ed. J. Keble, 3 vols., 5th ed. (Oxford, 1865), 1:334.

7. Whitgift, *Works*, 1:188. Cartwright's *First Reply* to Whitgift is printed with Whitgift's response. The Puritan leader's voluminous *Second Reply* has never been reprinted since the sixteenth century; some brief extracts from it are given in Whitgift, *Works*.

8. Samuel Rutherford, *The Divine Right of Church-Government and Excommunication: or, A Peaceable Dispute for the Perfection of the Holy Scripture in Point of Ceremonies and Church-Government . . .* (London, 1646), pp. 19-20.

9. Ibid., p. 505.

10. John Robinson, *The Works of John Robinson, Pastor of the Pilgrim Fathers*, 3 vols. (London, 1851), 2:476-78.

11. Whitgift, *Works*, 1:187.

12. Cartwright, in Whitgift, *Works*, 2:89.

13. Tyndale, *Expositions*, p. 257.

14. Rutherford, *The Divine Right*, p. 641.

15. The Uniformity Act, in Henry Gee and W. J. Hardy, eds., *Documents Illustrative of English Church History* (London: Macmillan, 1896), pp. 600-619.

16. Jasper Ridley, *Thomas Cranmer* (Oxford: Clarendon, 1962), p. 181.

17. Given in Edward Stillingfleet, *Irenicum: A Weapon-Salve for the Churches Wounds . . .* (London: Mortlock, 1681), quoted by A. H. Drysdale, *History of the Presbyterians in England: Their Rise, Decline, and Revival* (London: Presbyterian Church of England, 1889), pp. 32-33.

18. John Foxe, *The Acts and Monuments of J. Foxe*, 4th ed., ed. J. Pratt, 8 vols. (London: Religious Tract Society, 1877), 5:591.

19. Ibid., 5:576.

20. William Tyndale, *Doctrinal Treatises and Introductions to Different Portions of the Holy Scriptures*, ed. H. Walter (Cambridge: Parker Society, 1848), p. 273.

21. Vestments had a religious meaning, and kneeling to receive the sacrament had come in during the Middle Ages in connection with the teaching of transubstantiation, which gave worshippers to believe that Christ was corporeally present in the bread and the wine at the altar.

22. John Hooper's manuscript will be published for the first time in English in Iain Murray, ed., *The Reformation of the Church: A Collection of Reformed and Puritan Documents on Church Issues* (London: Banner of Truth, forthcoming [1965]).

23. This reply to Hooper will be found as an appendix in John Bradford, *Letters and Treatises*, pp. 375-95.

24. Printed by Peter Lorimer in *John Knox and the Church of England: His Work in Her Pulpit and His Influence upon Her Liturgy, Articles, and Parties . . .* (London, 1875), p. 104.

25. Whitgift, *Works*, 1:27.

26. Ibid., 2:108.

27. See Owen, *Works*, 13:463-64, 469, 481.

28. John Knox, *John Knox's History of the Reformation in Scotland*, ed. William Croft Dickinson (London: Thomas Nelson, 1949), 1:89.

29. Rutherford, *The Divine Right*, p. 63.

30. George Gillespie, *A Dispute against the English Popish Ceremonies*, in George Gillespie, *The Works of G. G. . . . Now First Collected*, The Presbyterian's Armoury, vols. 1-2 (Edinburgh, 1843-46), cf. 1:130-31. A helpful commentary on Gillespie's conditions will be found in James Bannerman, *The Church of Christ: A Treatise on the Nature, Powers, Ordinances, Discipline, and Government of the Christian Church*, ed. D. D. Bannerman, 2 vols. (Edinburgh: T. & T. Clark, 1868), 1:355-57.

31. Gillespie, *A Dispute*, in Gillespie, *Works*, 1:194-97.

32. Besides major works like Gillespie's, a number of shorter pieces on the subject appeared, such as the anonymous *Treatise of the Nature and Use of Things Indifferent* (Dr. Williams Library 12.55.3) and Daniel Cawdrey's consideration of *The XXIV Cases Concerning Things Indifferent in Religious Worship* (1663).

33. Cartwright had shortly before listed general rules governing the use of *adiaphora*, substantially the same as Gillespie's, cited above. They must (1) not

offend any, especially the Church of God; (2) be done in order and comeliness; be done (3) for edifying and (4) to the glory of God.

34. Cartwright, in Whitgift, *Works,* 1:196.

35. *Jus divinum regiminis ecclesiastici; or, The Divine Right of Church-Government, Asserted and Evidenced by the Holy Scriptures* . . . (London, 1646), pp. 48-49. This defense of Presbyterian church government was written by "Sundry Ministers of Christ within the City of London."

36. Puritans used the word *discipline* in a wider sense than our modern usage, so that it covered government and order.

37. Rutherford, *The Divine Right,* p. 7.

38. Owen, *Works,* 15:39-40.

39. Rutherford, *The Divine Right,* pp. 16-17.

40. Owen, *Works,* 15:41-42.

41. Bannerman, *The Church of Christ,* 1:367.

42. Quoted in Rutherford, *The Divine Right,* p. 77.

43. Foxe, *The Acts and Monuments,* 6:615.

44. Whitgift, *Works,* 3:180.

45. Hooker, *Works,* 3:205-6, 212-13.

46. William Cunningham, *Historical Theology: A Review of the Principal Doctrinal Discussions in the Christian Church since the Apostolic Age,* ed. James Buchanan and James Bannerman, 2 vols. (Edinburgh: T. & T. Clark, 1863), 1:72.

47. Lorimer, *John Knox,* p. 115.

48. Rutherford, *The Divine Right,* p. 30.

49. Daniel Gerdes, *Serinium antiquarium* [Antiquity Chest]: *Sive miscellanea Groningana nova, ad historiam reformationis ecclesiasticam praecipue spectantia,* 8 vols. (Groningen, 1749-65), 1.1.656-70. This important letter has not yet been printed in English.

50. Owen, *Works,* 13:463.

Chapter 3, Charles Haddon Spurgeon: Preacher

1. C. H. Spurgeon, *C. H. Spurgeon Autobiography,* vol. 1, *The Early Years,* ed. Susannah Spurgeon and Joseph Harrald (London: Banner of Truth, 1962), pp. 204-5.

2. *The Evening Star,* 5 November 1856.

Chapter 6, John Calvin the Man

1. Frederic van der Meer, *Atlas of Western Civilization,* trans. T. A. Birrell (Princeton: D. Van Nostrand, 1954), p. 149.

2. Williston Walker, *History of the Christian Church* (Edinburgh: T. & T. Clark, 1919), p. 401.

3. J. S. Whale, *The Protestant Tradition: An Essay in Interpretation* (Cambridge: Cambridge University, 1955), p. 120.

4. Ibid., p. 121.

5. Ibid., p. 123.

6. Ibid., p. 126.

7. Ibid., p. 132.

8. Ibid., p. 140.

9. Ibid., p. 142.

10. Ibid., p. 143.

11. J. T. McNeill, *The History and Character of Calvinism* (New York: Oxford University, 1954), p. 98.

12. Jean Cadier, *The Man God Mastered: A Brief Biography of John Calvin,* trans. O. R. Johnston (London: Inter-Varsity, 1960), p. 22.

13. McNeill, *History and Character,* pp. 99-100.

14. See Jean-Daniel Benoit, *Calvin, Director D'ames* (Strasbourg: Oberlin, 1947), pp. 48-49, where Benoit reads a harsher tone into Calvin's remarks than seems necessary.

15. John Calvin, *Institutes of the Christian Religon,* ed. John T. McNeill, trans. Ford Lewis Battles, 2 vols., Library of Christian Classics (Philadelphia: Westminster, 1960), 3.4.1.

16. Ibid.

17. McNeill, *History and Character,* p. 115.

18. Calvin, *Institutes,* 3.2.33.

19. Ibid., 3.2.7.

20. McNeill, *History and Character,* p. 131.

21. Cadier, *The Man God Mastered,* pp. 74-75.

22. McNeill, *History and Character,* p. 185.

23. John Calvin to William Farel, 8 October 1539.

24. Cadier, *The Man God Mastered,* pp. 66-67.

25. McNeill, *History and Character,* p. 229.

26. Calvin, *Institutes,* 1.5.1.

27. Ibid., 1.6.2.

28. Ibid., 2.6.1.

29. Ibid., 3.10.2.

30. John Calvin, *Commentaries on the First Book of Moses, Called Genesis,* trans. John King, 2 vols. (Edinburgh: Calvin Translation Society, 1847-50), on Gen. 4:20.

31. Calvin, *Institutes,* 1.11.12.

32. McNeill, *History and Character,* p. 233.

33. Benoit, *Calvin,* pp. 271-72.

34. B. B. Warfield, *Calvin and Calvinism* (New York: Oxford University, 1931), pp. 11-13.

35. John A. T. Robinson, *Honest to God* (Philadelphia: Westminster, 1963).

36. Benoit, *Calvin,* p. 13.

37. Ibid., p. 51.

38. Ibid., p. 53.

39. Ibid., p. 55.

40. Ibid., p. 275.

41. Cadier, *The Man God Mastered,* pp. 174-75.

Chapter 7, John Calvin: A Servant of the Word

1. J. T. Hoogstra, ed., *John Calvin, Contemporary Prophet: A Symposium* (Grand Rapids: Baker, 1959).

2. For a fuller survey of the disputed passages, see John Murray, *Calvin on Scripture and Divine Sovereignty* (Philadelphia, 1960), pp. 20-31.

3. Rupert E. Davies, *The Problem of Authority in the Continental Reformers: A Study in Luther, Zwingli, and Calvin* (London: Epworth, 1946), p. 116.

4. Benjamin Breckinridge Warfield, *Calvin and Augustine,* ed. Samuel G. Craig (Philadelphia: Presbyterian and Reformed, 1956), p. 491.

Chapter 8, The Growth of John Calvin's *Institutes*

1. In preparing this paper, I am happy to acknowledge the debt I owe to all who contributed to G. E. Duffield, ed., *John Calvin,* Courtenay Studies in Reformation Theology (Abingdon: Sutton Courtenay, forthcoming [1966]).

Chapter 9, John Calvin's Geneva

1. H. D. Foster, "Geneva before Calvin (1387-1536): The Antecedents of a Puritan State," *American Historical Review* 8 (Jan. 1903): 239 (n.2).

2. John T. McNeill, "Calvin the Man," *Christianity Today,* 22 May 1964, p. 5 [779].

3. Andre Biéler, *La Pensee economique et sociale de Calvin,* Publications de la Faculte des Sciences Economiques et Sociales de l' Universite de Geneve (Geneva, 1959).

Chapter 10, John Calvin and George Whitefield

1. Frederick C. Gill, *Charles Wesley, the First Methodist* (New York: Abingdon, 1964).

2. J. Wesley Bready, *England before and after Wesley: The Evangelical Revival and Social Reform* (London: Hodder and Stoughton, 1938).

3. George Whitefield, *George Whitefield's Journals . . .* (London: Banner of Truth, 1960), p. 81.

4. Ibid., pp. 193-94.